HERBS
AND
SPICES

Seventeenth-century Europe delighted in lively seasoning. The love of herbs is echoed in this engraving, "Herb Gardener at Work," by Adamus Lonicerus, from the *Kreuterbuch*, published in Frankfurt in 1679.

WAVERLEY ROOT
ROY GENDERS · NIKA S. HAZELTON
PAULA WOLFERT

HERBS
AND
SPICES

A GUIDE TO
CULINARY SEASONING

EDITED BY
WAVERLEY ROOT

Alfred van der Marck Editions

NEW YORK

Library of Congress Cataloging in Publication Data

Main entry under title:
Herbs and spices.
  1.Cookery (Herbs) 2.Herbs. 3.Spices.
4.Herb gardening. I.Root, Waverley Lewis,
1903 –
TX 819.H4H46 651.6′57 84–40450

ISBN 0-912383-08-9

Published by ALFRED VAN DER MARCK EDITIONS

Editor: David Baker
Managing Editor: Fancine Peeters
Original Design: Robert Tobler
Designers: Phillippe Maag
        Ernst Hodel
Graphic Artist: Franz Coray
Picture Procuration: Ruth Rüedi
Production Manager: Franz Gisler

Printed and bound by: Milanostampa - Farigliano (CN) Italy

TABLE OF CONTENTS

INTRODUCTION 7
    WAVERLEY ROOT

REFERENCE SECTION I
MATCHING HERBS AND SPICES
TO TASTE 13
    PAULA WOLFERT

PLANT LEXICON 26
    ROY GENDERS

REFERENCE SECTION II
GROWING AND PROCESSING 59
    ROY GENDERS

THE ART OF SEASONING 72
    NIKA S. HAZELTON

REFERENCE SECTION III
COOKING WITH HERBS 85
    PAULA WOLFERT

SEASONING AROUND
THE WORLD 101
    WAVERLEY ROOT

GLOSSARY   129
PICTURE CREDITS   130
INDEX   131

Introduction

WAVERLEY ROOT

Seasoning was invented by Neolithic Man, possibly the most astute creature in human history. When, for the first time, he deliberately added salt to his food to improve its taste, he launched the second gastronomic revolution. The first, of course, was cooking; to a certain extent it had opened the way for the second. When meat was first roasted, on a spit over an open fire, the juices which escaped from it took some of the flavor with it (we do not know how soon it occurred to prehistoric cooks to encase meat in a coating of clay and throw it into the fire, thus sealing in the juices and the taste). Loss of flavor in cooking was intensified when Neolithic Man, again the inventor, devised earthenware vessels sufficiently resistant to heat so that they could be placed over a fire. Boiling became common (it had, however, existed earlier when heated stones dropped into a hollow in a rock filled with water brought it to the boiling point). Boiling leached even more flavor from foods than roasting. The most important factor in making the second gastronomic revolution inevitable, however, was another sort of revolution, a revolution in the very nature of human society. Once more it was the work of Neolithic Man: he invented agriculture.

When the first wandering tribes planted seeds from plants they had found growing wild and had perforce to stay in the same place until the seeds grew and ripened, they exchanged a nomadic for a sedentary existence. They also changed the character of their diet. Before the advent of agriculture, game had played a much more important role in their nutrition than vegetables, and game came self-seasoned. (So did the saltwater fish which prehistoric man took when he lived near a coast.) Herbivorous animals added flavor to their flesh by regular visits to salt licks; carnivorous animals acquired it by eating the herbivores; man got it by eating both. As the proportion of vegetables to game increased, food became less interesting. Vegetables were apt to be less tasty than animals. True, some roots were spicy or sweet, some plants were peppery; but many others were dull and uninspiring. Besides, the most important vegetable foods were cereals. Some of their grains, crunched whole, possessed a certain nuttiness; but by the time they had been reduced to flour, they needed some sort of a fillip to become palatable.

We may presume, of course, that during the pre-agricultural period tastiness was not a particularly pertinent factor. Man ate to survive rather than to derive pleasure from what he was eating. But if at first he did not perceive a difference between his new diet and the old in terms of taste, there was another element which forced it upon his attention. When he began to eat more vegetable foods and fewer animal foods, he found himself also eating less salt. The presence of salt, it has been remarked, is felt only in its absence.

Neolithic Man may not have felt its absence at first in the form of a diminution of flavor; but he would have felt it instinctively, as animals do, in a diminution of health. Salt, the primordial seasoner, the only important food which comes from the mineral kingdom, is essential to well-being; so salt was added to vegetables to replace the salt which had been lost with meat. Prehistoric man could hardly have failed to notice that in adding salt, he had also added flavor. An aesthetic factor had been applied to eating, nutrition had become gastronomy, and the human race was launched upon the adventure of the pursuit of flavor. Man began to build up what would become a richly variegated treasury of tastes, some subtle, some strong, some caressing, some overwhelming. He drew his seasoners from the inexhaustible resources of the vegetable kingdom in the form of herbs, spices, and condiments.

The twin sources of Egyptian fertility—the heat of the sun and the waters of the Nile—are symbolized in the upper panel of this depiction of the Garden of Ialu, the Egyptian paradise. Aton, the sun god, identified by his circle-crowned cross, is flanked by two baboons, sacred to Toth, god of learning—including the art of agriculture, the subject of the two central panels. At the bottom we see ancient Egyptian plants, which included many herbs and spices—more widely used for embalming than for food.

What is a Herb?

"Anything that grew out of the mould / Was an excellent herb to our fathers of old," wrote Kipling, who was not exaggerating the area of meaning once covered by the word "herb." In early English usage "herb" was more or less synonymous with "vegetable." Later the name was restricted to vegetables, or parts of vegetables, which grew aboveground: a turnip was a vegetable but its leafy top was an herb. Molière did not tell us whether he was thinking of aboveground or underground growth when he wrote in *Les Femmes Savantes* of a woman *"épluchant ses herbes,"* peeling her herbs, but it is evident that in his time French, like English, covered more ground than it does today.

What does "herb" mean now?

For the botanist, an herb is a plant with a fleshy, not a woody, stem, which, after the plant has bloomed and set its seed, dies down to the ground, whether it is minded to rise again the following year or not. This definition is not perfect, but nobody yet has formulated one which is; all definitions leave out some plants which we perceive, unmistakably, as herbs, and let in others which, just as unmistakably, are not. Sage, thyme, and rosemary, indisputably herbs, do not conform strictly to the botanical definition, for all three have more or less woody stems, though they do not form true bark. The botanical definition would rule out laurel, an evergreen woody-trunked tree or shrub which gives us bay leaves, one of our commonest herbs, but would let in the banana, which it would occur to no one to call an herb. And where does one classify the undisciplined castor oil plant, which has a fleshy stem in temperate zones and a woody one in the tropics?

For the pharmacist, an herb is a plant whose properties permit using it as a medicine (or an anti-medicine, for a poisonous plant may be an herb, like the hemlock which removed Socrates from this world). Most of the herbs we think of today as seasoners were employed as medicines before they were used in food. They served for centuries as the principal medicaments of man; kept in pharmacies in dried form so that they might be available all year round, they gave the English language the word "drug," from the Anglo-Saxon *drigan,* to dry. They were gathered wild by specialists in wortcraft, a skill requiring much knowledge, since so many plants possess beneficial properties that Emerson once defined a weed as "a plant whose virtues have not yet been dis-

Most herbs and spices entered the Western world as medicines before they were used for seasoning. They were stored in porcelain jars that were lined up in long rows on the shelves of medieval pharmacies, like this one pictured in the *Hortus Sanitatis* (Strasbourg, ca. 1497).

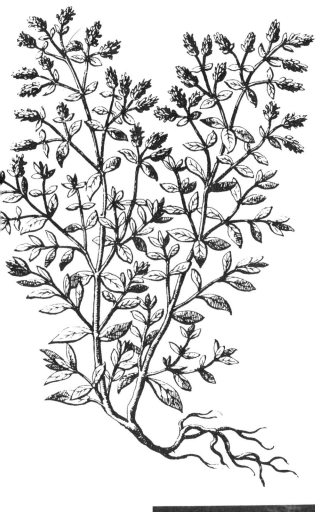

Origanum vulgare, or oregano, was preferred to its milder cousin, sweet marjoram, when this woodcut was made centuries ago, for those were times which liked strong flavors. Naples, which likes strong flavors too, uses it today to season pizza. Greece likes the even stronger *Origanum dubium,* of which the flowers instead of the leaves flavor Hellenic cooking.

covered." Today the most used herbs have been transferred to cultivation; some of them have become so thoroughly dependent on man that they could not survive if he abandoned them.

For the sorcerer—and there are many sorcerers still practicing today if you look for them in the right places—an herb is a plant capable of producing magical effects, usually operative only if the occult rules of the game have been properly observed. In Christian times and places, one such condition is often that the appropriate plant must be picked on St. John's Eve or Day, which bestow particular potency on philters. In other times and places the rules were different; in Babylon, for instance, magic-working herbs were plucked by moonlight, when they were steeped in the power of the moon god, Sin.

And for the cook, an herb is primarily a plant which adds flavor to food—a seasoner. It adds flavor to drinks too, such as herbal teas and wines, but these are beyond the scope of this work; let us note only, for the record,

Many seasoners are versatile in their uses, as for instance fennel. The seeds, often ground for Indian curries, are a spice. The flowers *(right)* serve as an herb in French pickles, and so do the leaves *(center right),* cooked with fish or raw in salads. The bulbs *(far right)* are eaten as a vegetable in Italy. And what name can we give to dried fennel twigs, when sea bass is cooked over them to pick up their delicate aroma?

that in medieval times it was customary both to precede and follow a meal with an herbal drink; and their modern descendants have in their names, in French at least, preserved for us a reminder of the properties which accounted for this practice—the herb-flavored vermouth taken before a repast is an *apéritif,* an arouser of the appetite; the herb-flavored liqueur taken after it is a *digestif.*

For the cook an herb is also a challenge and an oppor-

Cinnamon (also cassia)   Clove (also capers)

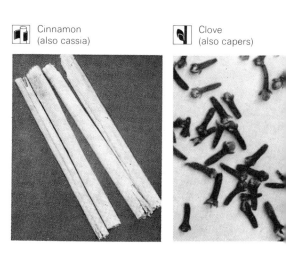

tunity—a challenge to his creative ability, which is enabled through seasoners to manifest refinement or imagination, an opportunity to rise above the routine, the humdrum, and the commonplace by using them, in the art which appeals to the sense of taste, as a painter uses highlights in the art which appeals to the sense of sight or a musician uses grace notes in the art which appeals to the sense of hearing.

All of us have instinctive feelings about the nature of herbs which transcend the restrictions of formal definitions. One of them is that herbs are green and leafy, like parsley, cress, or chervil. When we use other parts of herbs than their leaves, we deny them the name of herb. Mustard, nasturtium, and coriander are herbs when we use their leaves; when we use their seeds, we class them with spices. Coriander, indeed, even changes its name completely when it changes its function: we call the seeds coriander, but the leaves Chinese parsley.

In the case of fennel, the leaves are herbs, the seeds are spices, and the roots are vegetables.

We feel also that herbs, more than other seasoners, are mild, modest, gentle, and caressing (though there are exceptions). The cook uses herbs when he wants to woo us or seduce us, when the effect he seeks is delicate, refined, or subtle; but when he wants to shock or startle us, when he seeks the spectacular or the sensational, he turns to spices.

What is a Spice?

Nobody knows. Or at least, nobody yet has been able to put into words a definition which can encompass all, or even most, spices, and exclude all, or even most, non-spices. In another sense, everybody knows; it is a matter of feeling. If you are asked whether cinnamon or nutmeg or clove are herbs or spices, you will answer unhesitatingly that they are spices. But if you can put into words a description of the peculiarities of spices which will enable anyone unfamiliar with them to identify them unmistakably, you will prove yourself more skillful than any lexicographer so far.

For herbs one has at least a botanical description, even though it has exceptions, a grouping which exists in nature. But spices form no botanically describable family. Of herbs we can say that they are characterized by the fact that usually the parts eaten for all of them are the same, their leaves, but we have no such help in isolating spices. They may come from the bark (cinnamon), the buds (cloves), the flowers (saffron), the fruits (allspice), the roots (ginger), the seeds (caraway), or even from secretions (balm, a gum).

Faced with this confusion, the dictionary makers have had recourse to subterfuge. Webster's unabridged dictionary defines a spice as "any of various aromatic vegetable products... used in cookery to season food." It supplements this information by giving as examples a number of indisputable spices; but if you substitute examples chosen among herbs, the definition would serve just as well for them. *The Grand Larousse Encyclopédique* proposes similarly fuzzy distinctions: a spice is "an aromatic substance used for seasoning"; a herb "a vegetable substance used in function of the suave and aromatic odor which it gives off"; a condiment "a substance added to foods to season them." The definitions are virtually interchangeable.

In desperation, food writers have attempted to describe spices in terms of extraneous circumstances which apply to most of them—for instance, the sort of climate in which they flourish. "True spices," wrote Rosemary Hemphill in *Spices and Savour*, "are aromatic plants usually indigenous to hot countries." It is a fact that the seasoners we tend to think of as spices are as a rule stronger and more pungent than those we tend to think

Saffron
(also dill)

Allspice
(also chilies)

Ginger
(also licorice)

Caraway
(also mustard)

of as herbs; and it seems to be the further fact that the heat of spices may be attributed to the heat of the sun which beats down upon them in torrid climates. The fragrance of spices is often lodged in their essential oils; and, as books on medicinal herbs can tell you, all plants producing essential oils need strong sunshine to do so. The sunshine which has transferred its heat to most of our common spices is that of tropical Asia. It may well be that our present difficulty in defining them is in part a difficulty of language, itself rooted in an accident of geography. Tropical Asia was *terra incognita* to Mediterranean peoples at the time when they were developing the vocabulary which the Occidental civilization is obliged to use today in talking about seasoners.

The Venerable Bede (A.D. 672/3–735), the great English monk, scholar, and theologian, left a detailed list of the spices stocked in his monastery at the time of his death. Spices had by then become so rare in Britain that his supply was handed down as a precious legacy, and each of his seventeen seasoners was inventoried in the monastery records.

They did not even suspect the existence of these exotic flavorers; it is hardly surprising that they failed to evolve a concept which would take them all in, or a word to express such a concept.

Our word "spice" comes from the Low Latin *species,* whose origin precedes the period when the spices of the East reached the West. Language was slow to perceive that a new category of *species* had made its appearance, and required a new word to describe it. As late as the time of Gregory of Tours (538–594), *species* was still a word so imprecise that it covered such diverse products as wheat, oil, and wine, among others. If it was desired to single out seasoners, it was necessary to say "aromatic species," and this could stand for herbs as well as spices. Gradually, however, "spice" came to mean especially the hot seasoners which came from the Far East. This geographical basis—an explanation for the character of spices rather than a description of them—was resorted to by the *Encyclopédie* of 1755, which specified that "spice" did not apply to native plants (i.e., native to the Occident) but only to Oriental drugs and aromatic substances. Like Webster's today, it had to clarify its meaning by citing specific examples.

Nearly two and a half centuries later, we are still without a satisfactory definition of what is essential to spicehood. We must identify spices one by one, as we come upon them, by the extent to which each one appeals to instinct or to reason as belonging to this category. A spice, in short, is a seasoner which seems to those familiar to it to be a spice. This seems to be the best that we can do.

11

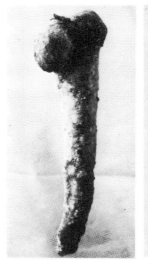

Roots and bulbs contribute a considerable number of condiments to the modern pantry. Important among them are the sharp peppery horseradish and the sweet onion. The versatile onion family (genus *Allium*) also gives us chives, shallots, scallions, rocambole, leeks, and garlic.

What is a Condiment?

If we are on unsound ground in attempting to define spices, when we attempt to define condiments we are on quicksand. Webster's dictionary does the best it can. A condiment, it tells us, is "something usually pungent, acid, salty, or spicy, added to or served with food to enhance its flavor." Something! The vaguest of words!

The difficulty about defining condiments is that condiments do not exist. They do not exist, that is, in nature. Herbs can be grouped into a single category on the basis of a botanical distinction; it exists in nature. Spices can be described, one by one, in terms of their characteristics, whereupon we perceive that there do exist among them certain common factors (heat, pungency) which permit us to fit them also into a single category; those characteristics exist in nature. The substances used as condiments by man possess no common elements in nature. "Condiment" does not describe a thing, it describes the use to which men put many different things—or "something." Any food can become a condiment when it is used to season other foods; but no food is a condiment in itself. All natural substances used as condiments have other independent roles to play. One might expect to find exceptions, foods used for seasoning and only for seasoning, among, for example, what the Middle Ages, mixing up culinary nomenclature a little more, called disdainfully "the strong spices of the poor" (which were nevertheless not neglected by the rich), the members of the onion-garlic family. The onion does indeed play an extremely important role as a seasoner, but it is not confined to that role: consider the sweet excellence of creamed onions. You might think that garlic has no function except that of lending flavor to other foods, though not if you are familiar with southwestern France, one of whose specialities is *tourin*, a thin garlic soup, which, believe it or not, is subtle, delicate, and restrained in flavor.

Some vegetables are used oftener as condiments than for their own sake, horseradish for instance, but even horseradish is also eaten alone, as an appetite-provoking prelude to a repast, like ordinary radishes, raw, dipped before each bite into a little heap of salt on the plate. Other vegetables are, on the contrary, usually eaten for their own merits, but are sometimes drafted to add flavor to other foods, carrots or celery for instance.

Vegetable oils, used on salads or in cooking, are condiments, and so are vinegar and mayonnaise, but these are products fabricated by man, which fall outside the scope of this work. We will not concern ourselves with the bewildering variety of artificial condiments which man has devised to enliven his food, such as New England cranberry sauce with turkey, Pennsylvania Dutch sweet and sour relishes, Louisiana tabasco, American ketchup, English Worcestershire sauce, European four spices, Chinese five powders, Indian curries and chutneys, southeastern Asia's all-purpose *nuoc mam*, Ethiopia's berberé pepper (misnamed, for it is not one spice but a combination of fourteen or more), or Morocco's *ras el hanout*, which is a mixture of thirty. Much less will we allow ourselves to be diverted into the far-flung reaches of this subject. We are at a far cry from herbs and spices when we meet kirsch poured over slices of pineapple as a condiment; or chorizo sausage adding its spiciness to Spanish *paella*; or anchovy fillets on a breaded veal chop or in a *salade niçoise*; or bits of chopped meat in sauces, salads, or omelets; or grated cheese sprinkled on pasta or in minestrone.

They may be, by virtue of their function, genuine condiments; but we will restrict ourselves here primarily to the seasoning plants provided by Nature, altered as little as possible by the mischievous manipulations of man.

Matching Herbs and Spices to Taste

PAULA WOLFERT

Reference Section I

In the chart found on the following pages, the 100 herbs and spices chosen by the authors are listed alphabetically, with appropriate foods and dishes provided for each. The food items under each seasoner are arranged by category: Soups, Sauces and gravies, Salads, Fish, Eggs and cheese, Meats, Poultry and game, Vegetables, Sweets and baking. Many seasoners have a variety of uses in several of these categories; other herbs or spices are more limited in range.

Cross-references to other parts of the book are included. A number accompanies each herb or spice; it refers to the exact location of the seasoner in the Plant Lexicon (pp. 26—57), where the 100 herb and spice plants are illustrated and described (under their Latin botanical names). An asterisk before the name of a dish refers the reader to a complete recipe in Reference Section III (pp. 85—99).

Cooking with herbs and spices is a longstanding tradition in most parts of the world. In olden times, even as now, the cook complemented his own homegrown seasoners with more exotic varieties raised under a hotter sun and shipped to local markets. This woodcut from Hieronymus Bock's *Kräutterbuch* printed in Strasbourg in 1577 shows a late medieval German market scene, with women selecting vegetables and spices.

The matching of an herb or spice to a specific food is, basically, a matter of taste. When all is said and done, each cook must depend on his own judgment; each will experiment on his own with herbs and spices, as with so many other elements of cooking. And yet guidelines are useful. The cook, especially the relative newcomer to the realm of seasoners, will find that suggestions and recommendations can save him a good deal of time, wasted ingredients, and heartburn.

The herb and spice chart on the following pages, then, is offered as a series of recommendations rather than hard and fast rules. An effort has been made to pass on to readers the fruits of past experience—the experience of the author herself, Paula Wolfert, as well as the wisdom of past masters she has consulted and the national cuisines that she has studied all over the world.

This reference section aims to help the reader in the selection, and indeed in the identification, of seasoners. Before anyone can decide whether to purchase and cook with a particular herb or spice, or to cultivate it

in his garden, it is logical to ask how it is going to taste, what kind of food it is likely to be used with. Once that information is obtained from Reference Section I, it is possible to follow up a particular seasoner in other sections of the book, where one will find other types of information.

A note on the choice of herbs and spices presented in this book. The number 100, while somewhat arbitrary, is also easily large enough to encompass all the basic seasoners. Most cooks, even the finest, manage a wide variety of dishes with far fewer than 100 seasoners. Thus it is unlikely that the authors of this book, in their selection of these 100 seasoners, will have to atone for any sins of omission. In the choice of the less familiar items, however, controversy is more difficult to avoid. Our authors have braved this risk, in the interests of variety, character, and originality. The result is a list of seasoners that, while covering all the requisites, also offers material for experimentation, a judiciously exotic touch, and, it is hoped, the element of surprise. –*Ed.*

REF. NO.	HERB OR SPICE	SOUPS	SAUCES AND GRAVIES	SALADS	FISH
72	ALLSPICE	Beef broth, tomato, split-pea	Tomato, barbecue, chili raisin sauce (for ham and pork), vinegar-pepper sauce (for oysters), brown gravy, catsup	Aspics, fruit cocktail, pickled carrots	Court-bouillon, shrimp marinade, stuffings, *gumbo
81	ALMOND	*Creamed, white gaspacho	Catalan sauce "Romesco," Greek skordalia with garlic, Toulousian aillade	Green bean, orange (with lettuce and dates), pimiento	Sautéed trout, soft-shell crabs, sole, stuffing
11	ANGELICA				Peeled stems baked
73	ANISE	Snail, Dutch milk soup, Hispanic soups	Vinaigrette	Melon, fresh leaves in salad, fresh fruit salad	Court-bouillon
40	ASAFETIDA		Curries, vegetarian dishes		
57	BALM	Chicken, cream		Fruit salads, vegetable salads	Eel or other oily fish
18	BAMBOO SHOOTS	Oriental		Oriental	Curried shrimp, abalon
	BASIL, see Sweet Basil				
51	BAY LEAF	Stock, beef, vegetable, chicken, fish	Tomato, creole, spaghetti, barbecue, Spanish	Cold rice and pasta, salads, aspics	Court-bouillon, fish stews, *gumbos, poach fish
59	BERGAMOT			Flowers fresh in salads	
77	BLACK PEPPER	Beef, chicken, fish, vegetables, stocks	Salad dressings, brown gravy, cream, barbecue, mignonnette	Meat, chicken, fish, and vegetable salads	All, broiled, baked and fried; croquettes, stuffi oysters; coating for fri fish
20	BORAGE	Eel soup, fish stews	Court-bouillon	Tomato salad, greens, nasturtium salad, cucumber	
74	BURNET			Greens, fish	
93	CACAO		Molé sauce, sweet-and-sour sauces for game		
23	CAPER		Sauce verte, piquant sauces (for fish, boiled meats, poultry), tartare, remoulade, *olive, mayonnaise, hollandaise, white wine, tomato sauce, beef gravy	Mediterranean-style salads, tomato	Tuna, anchovy, broiled fish, grilled trout

* An asterisk before the name refers to recipes in the section "Cooking with Herbs and Spices," pp. 85 ff.

EGGS AND CHEESE	MEATS	POULTRY AND GAME	VEGETABLES	SWEET AND BAKING
piced cheese, ckled eggs	Sausages, corned beef, lamb tarts, stuffings, tongue, Swedish meatballs, pot roast, *chili con carne, beef, lamb, veal, pork	Marinades (for game), stuffings	Tomatoes, spinach, carrots, beets, red cabbage	Mincemeat, fruit pies, spice cakes, plum cakes, pumpkin pie
	Lamb stews	Rabbit, stuffings, chicken with chick peas	Green beans	Tourtes, cakes, pies, custards, peaches, apricots, prunes
				Custards, creams, stewed fruit, jams, Scandinavian pies
esh cheese		Moroccan chicken with baby onions	Beets, carrots	*Moroccan bread, Languedoc cookies, candies, spice cake, German Christmas cookies, Swedish apple sauce, Italian cakes
	Meatballs		Beans, lentils, potatoes and cumin, mushrooms and cumin	
crambled eggs, esh cheese	Lamb stews, veal, pork	Chicken, stuffings for turkey	Mushrooms	Custards, jams and jellies, summer drinks
ggroll	Pork stir-fry, beef stir-fry	Steamed chicken	Mushrooms, cabbage, Buddha's delight	
	Beef stew, potted meats, tongue, lamb stews, veal ragouts, marinades, corned meats, *liver kebab, pork paté	Potted game, marinades, rabbit and wild bird stews, chicken stuffing	Carrots, potatoes, tomatoes, chestnuts	Rice pudding, custards
heese	Sausages, veal, pork	Stuffings		
eviled dips and spreads, rebits, all egg dishes	Beef, pork, lamb, veal, variety meats	All poultry and game	Tomatoes, carrots, broccoli, artichokes, creamed vegetables, peas-and-onions	*Cookies, mincemeat
melets	Pork stews		Sautéed in butter, green beans	Cakes, custards, ices, fruit dishes
heese			Tomatoes	Iced drinks
	*Chili con carne	Spanish partridge, Mexican turkey, rabbit and hare		Cakes, custards, pies, ice cream, sauce
ard-boiled with chovy	Boiled lamb, beef stew, tongue, *liver	Chicken	Stuffed tomatoes or peppers, onions	

REF. NO.	HERB OR SPICE	SOUPS	SAUCES AND GRAVIES	SALADS	FISH
27	CARAWAY	North African soups (use young leaves in soup)	Tunisian hot pepper sauce	Cucumbers in vinegar, coleslaw, *zucchini, potato	
37	CARDAMOM	Scandinavian fruit soup, pea soup	Curry basting sauce for duck, *spiced mixture for coffee	Orange, Waldorf, fruit	Boiled fish
13	CELERY SEEDS	Stocks, split-pea	Boiled salad dressing, tomato sauce	Potato, coleslaw	Court-bouillon, stuffings, shrimp
13	CELERY LEAVES	Stocks, meat, fish, poultry, potages, scotch broth	Meat, fish, and poultry sauces	Assorted green, tomato	Court-bouillon, marina stuffings
12	CHERVIL	Cream, cold tomato (with lemon and sorrel), green fish, stock	Salad dressing, tartare, butter, sauce verte, remoulade, white wine, cream	Greens, potato, beet, tomato, coleslaw, chicken, fruit	Boiled fish, court-bouillon, stews, mousses
25	CHILI (CAYENNE)	Cream, bisques, pepper-pot, fish, beef, chicken, vegetables	Creole, cheese, curry, barbecue, tomato, cock-tail, salad dressings, rouille for fish soups, catsup	Oriental chicken, orange-olive, rice, carrot, *tomatoes and green peppers	Any fish (broiled, boile poached, creamed, or fried), shellfish, devile seafood, Mexican and Indian dishes
6	CHIVES	Cream soups, oyster bisque, vichyssoise, cold lemon soup	*Butter sauce, sauce verte, mustard-tarragon sauce, gribiche, tartare, green goddess, sour cream	Shellfish, mixed greens, crab, chicken, tomato, meat, potato, fruit	Poached sole, marinad stuffing, creamed fish
29	CINNAMON	Moroccan Harira, Iranian soups	Chocolate sauce, curries, barbecue sauce, Catalan sauce	Orange-radish, *orange-carrot, fresh fruit	Catalan snails
30	CITRON		Latin American, Mexican, and Catalan sauces	Brazilian salad	
39	CLOVE	Green fish, Swedish pea, Russian crab, bean, beef broth, game	Cream, marinades, chili, curry, fruit, barbecue, catsup, tomato	Fruit salad	Crabcakes, court-bouil pickled shrimp, baked
32	CORIANDER SEED	*Fish, Scandinavian game soup, lentil, pea, chick pea	Curry		Crab, court-bouillon, Portuguese fish stew
32	CORIANDER LEAVES	Oriental soups, beef broth	Moroccan, Mexican	Avocado, egg salad	
53	CRESS	Cream soup, Oriental soups	Green sauce, white butter sauce, mayonnaise, vinaigrette	Chicken salad	
76	CUBEB		In Moroccan mixed spice Ras el Hanout		

16

...GS AND ...EESE	MEATS	POULTRY AND GAME	VEGETABLES	SWEET AND BAKING
...nster, deviled eggs, ...tage cheese, ...s and spreads	Pork, lamb and liver meatballs, goulash		Noodles, sauerkraut, potatoes, cabbage turnips, dumplings	Rye bread, cakes, cookies, salt sticks
	Swedish meatballs, ham, Norwegian meatloaf, hamburgers	Curried chicken, duck	Sweet potato, squash, stuffed cabbage, peas, rice	Apple pie, pumpkin pie, Norwegian waffles, pastries, buns, strawberry-rhubarb pie, gingerbread, cookies, spice bread, Danish pastry
...ese dips, omelets, ...ambled eggs	Corned beef tongue, meatloaf		Braised lettuce, tomatoes, noodles, potatoes, eggplant	Breads, salt sticks, rolls
...s and spreads, ...ttage cheese, ...ambled eggs	Boiled beef, meatloaf	Boiled chicken, stuffings	Lentils, *pureed celery rib, chestnuts	
...melet, *scrambled, ...ese dips and spreads, ...ufflés	Stews, stuffing, ground meat, veal, pork	Chicken, rabbit, venison, stuffings, fricassee	Peas, leeks, artichokes, green beans, potatoes, flans, tomatoes	
...viled eggs, scrambled, ...ese dips and spreads, ...ced cheese	Pork spareribs, *chili con carne, sausages, lamb ribs, spiced meats, marinades, Mexican and Indian entrees	Chicken, duck, rabbit, squab, game, marinades, Mexican, Indian, and Szechwan entrees	Potatoes, bell peppers, rice, corn, beans, eggplant, chick peas, tomatoes, onions	
...melet, scrambled eggs, ...viled eggs, dips and ...reads, cottage cheese	Lamb fricassee	Chicken fricassee, croquettes, rabbit	Creamed onions, artichoke ragout	
	Greek beef stew, meatloaf pâtés, ham, Portuguese pork	*Moroccan chicken stews		Crêpes and fritters, fruit compote, gingerbread, *cakes, cupcakes, ice cream, mincemeat, apple pie, rice pudding, custards
	Italian veal stew	Duck, rabbit		Marmalade, jams, cakes
...eviled eggs, dips and ...reads	Boiled beef, meatloaf, stuffings, corned beef, marinades, lamb stew, glazed ham, *chili con carne, pork stew	Curried chicken, duck pâté	Beets, sweet potatoes tomatoes, baked beans, pickled vegetables, onions, marinated mushrooms, choucroute	Fruit cake, mincemeat, applesauce, pumpkin pie, spice cake, *orange ice
	Meatballs, sausages, *roast lamb	Marinades for game	Marinated vegetables, mushrooms, artichokes, eggplant, *pureed celery	Gingerbread, cookies, pumpkin pie, apple pie
		Moroccan stews	Rice, lentils, falafal	
...ilton and pears, ...asted goat cheese			Stuffed vegetables provençale	

REF. NO.	HERB OR SPICE	SOUPS	SAUCES AND GRAVIES	SALADS	FISH
35	CUMIN		Curries, salad dressing, Mexican sauces	*Carrot, *green pepper and tomato, green olives	Baked whole fish, broiled fish
92	DANDELION			With crisp bacon	
10	DILL	*Russian fish soups, borscht, kidney soup	Sauce verte, sour cream, salad dressing, Scandinavian mustard, mayonnaise, hollandaise	Cucumber, chicken, fish, avocado, potato	Fresh salmon, smoke salmon, boiled crayfi poached fish, stuffin
10	DILL SEED	Fish soups, kidney soup	Salad dressings		Stuffings, court-bouillon, poached fis
86	ELDER, BLACK				
41	FENNEL SEEDS	*Fish soups, Bouillabaisse	Spaghetti, salad dressing	Potato salad, shell-fish salad	Salmon, mackerel, cc bouillon
41	FENNEL LEAVES		Butters, hollandaise, mayonnaise	Mixed greens	Court-bouillon, dried stalks (for grilled fish baked fish
95	FENUGREEK		Yemeni hot sauce, curries		
8	GALINGALE	Bali chicken soup	*Indonesian spice mixture for meat, poultry, and salads	"Gado-Gado"	
5	GARLIC	Provençal soups, fish, lentil, tomato, Vietnamese sour soup	Creole, Italian mayon-naise, Teriyaki, salad dressing, barbecue, curry, cream	"Chapon" cubed garlic bread, tomato, carrot	*Gumbos, fried fish, shrimps
100	GINGER	Chicken, Bali, stocks	Teriyaki, Moroccan sauces, fruit sauce for ham, curries, fresh tomato sauce	Shrimp avocado, bean sprout, fresh fruit, poached chicken	Indian fish cakes, Oriental dishes, stuff
28	GOOD-KING-HENRY	Lentil soup		Mixed green salad	Seafood, sausage
33	HAZELNUT	Vegetable soup		German salads	Filet of trout, cod à la biscayenne
42	HERB BENNET			Mixed green salad	
46	HOPS		Flemish dishes		
15	HORSERADISH		Cocktail, mustards, cream sauce, hollandaise, beet	Beet, seafood	Shellfish, smoked fish coulibiac
47	HYSSOP	Health, fish		Mixed greens, lentil, potato	Eel, stuffing

EGGS AND CHEESE	MEATS	POULTRY AND GAME	VEGETABLES	SWEET AND BAKING
Scrambled eggs, dips and spreads, hot cheese appetizers, deviled eggs	*Chili con carne, marinades for pork and veal, beef stew, kebabs, sausages, Bulgarian ham dish	Chicken stew	Curried: peas, eggplant, lentils, carrots, potatoes, cabbage	Eastern European bread
Scrambled eggs				
Stuffed eggs, cottage cheese	Scandinavian lamb stew, pork stew	Chicken fricassee	Boiled potatoes, beets, cucumbers, tomatoes, green beans	
Cream-cheese dips	Boiled beef		Sauerkraut, cabbage, turnips, green beans, coleslaw, marinades, beets	
			Sautéed leaves, Breton style	Fritters, jams and jellies, blossom pancakes, stewed fruits
	Marinade (for pork), meat loaf, lamb stew, Tuscan sausage	Rabbit stew	Marinated mushrooms, artichokes, and fresh fennel bulb	Bread
Cheese		Smoked duck	Cabbage, turnips, beans	
	Home-cured pastrami	Rabbit stew		North Africa bread, Greek honey and boiled seeds
		Curries, Indonesian chicken dishes		Confectionery
Fresh white soft cheese, mozzarella, curried eggs	Pâtés, beef, pork, lamb, veal, meatloaf, sausages, kebabs, marinades	*Chicken, rabbit, marinades	Eggplant, tomato, Spanish rice, spinach, beans, cabbage, potatoes	
Deviled egg, curried eggs	Sweet-and-sour pork, ham, pot roast, stuffing, steaks, marinades, sautéed calves liver	Oriental dishes, marinades, *Moroccan chicken, *chicken stew	Carrots, rice, onions	Gingerbread, spice bread, mincemeat, pumpkin pie, Christmas pudding, fresh fruit, a dash in chocolate cake
			Sautéed in butter	
		Stuffings	Green beans	*Cookies, cakes, buttercreams
				Cocoa substitute
Scrambled eggs with shoots		Stuffing	Young shoots (boiled or sautéed in butter or napped with fresh cream)	
	Roast beef, steak, smoked meats, boiled meats, smoked sausages	Boiled chicken	Beets	
	Stews, roast veal, roast pork			

REF. NO.	HERB OR SPICE	SOUPS	SAUCES AND GRAVIES	SALADS	FISH
50	JUNIPER	Lamb		Chicken	
52	LAVENDER	Vegetable (leaves)		Green (flowers)	
4	LEEK	Cream, stocks, fish, lentil, vichyssoise	Tomato, white wine, salad dressing	Mixed, composed	Poached, baked stews, court-bouillon, stuffing
55	LEMON VERBENA		Salad dressing		
44	LICORICE				Snail soup
54	LOVAGE (Use sparingly)	Beef broth		Mixed greens	
60	MACE		Spiced sauce for fruit	Fruit salad	
	MARJORAM, see Sweet Marjoram				
22	MARIGOLD	Beef broth, chowder, vegetable, Dutch soup		Mixed greens; buds are substitute for capers	
9	MELEGUETA PEPPER		Steak		
56	MELILOT			Mixed green (flowers)	
17	MUGWORT	Onion, vegetable		Green	Eel, carp
21	MUSTARD		Vinaigrette, hollandaise, barbecue, Lamaze, Robert, *tarragon, cheese	Coleslaw, avocado	Marinated salmon, deviled crab, mussels, stuffing
62	MYRTLE				
96	NASTURTIUM			Tossed salad; seeds as substitute for capers	
60	NUTMEG	Alsatian beer, cream	Béchamel, cream, fruit, wine	Chicken	Marinades, stuffings, croquettes
65	OLIVE	Pumpkin	*Spaghetti	Niçoise, chicken, potato	Baked filets, stuffings, casseroles
2	ONION	Fish, chicken, meat, vegetable	Brown gravy, barbecue, tomato, curry, soubise	Mixed, apple	Baked, marinades, cour bouillon
67	OREGANO	Minestrone, tomato, mushroom, vegetable	Italian salad dressing, spaghetti, mushroom, Spanish	Olives, seafood, *Greek, tomato, potato, *cucumber	Broiled fish steaks, marinade
24	PAPRIKA	Meat, chowder	Sour cream, mayonnaise, barbecue	Potato, egg, *cooked tomato and pepper	Broiled, poached, deviled crab, croquette

...GS AND ...EESE	MEATS	POULTRY AND GAME	VEGETABLES	SWEET AND BAKING
	Roast lamb, roast pork, pâtés and mousses, sautéed liver, kidneys	Marinades for game, chicken in beer, duck, rabbit stews, *roast squab	Cabbage, sauerkraut, choucroute	
	Stews (leaves)			Jellies (flowers)
...ches, flans	Lamb, veal, pork, boiled meats, marinades	Chicken, poached casseroles, marinades, rabbit, stuffing	Mixed vegetables, marinated vegetables, *potato cake	
...elets	Roast lamb		Asparagus, mushrooms	
				Confectionery, drinks
		Stewed rabbit (seeds)		
			Carrots	*Sweet and sour cherries, custards
			Rice	English country pudding
	Grilled steak			Bread
...osago	Marinades, sausage, stuffings	Hare stew		
	Veal stew, roast pork	Roast goose stuffing, duck, game		
...s and spreads	Cold meats, sausages, ham, lamb, pork chops meatloaf, beef steak	Roast chicken, stewed rabbit	Cabbage, sauerkraut, beets	
	Roasts, stuffing	Pâtés, game		Syrups, fruit compote, sauces
			Pickled in vinegar	Fruit cup
...iches, rarebits, ...ufflés	Meatloaf, liver pâté, lamb, veal, sausages	Marinades, stuffings, *Moroccan chicken stew	Broccoli, carrots, potatoes au gratin, cauliflower, Dutch style vegetables, spinach	*Cooked fruit, custards, pumpkin pie, eggnog, fruit pies, cakes, pancakes
...esh cheese, dips ...d spreads	Stews, *lamb steak	Chicken, stuffings, casseroles	Rice, stuffing, tomatoes, peppers, eggplant	
...gs à la tripe, omelet, ...iche	Meat stews, marinades, meatloaf, *meat pies	Chicken, duck, rabbit, goose, squab, game, marinades	Beans, eggplant, mushrooms, lentils, peppers, artichokes, marinated vegetables, fried rice, potatoes	
...ta, omelets	Meatloaf, canneloni, pork, lamb, beef, veal, *chili con carne	Chicken, rabbit, casseroles, stuffing	Potatoes, mushrooms, marinated vegetables, artichokes, peppers, beans, tomatoes, eggplant, zucchini	Pizza
...rambled eggs, deviled ...gs, rarebit	Goulash, beef, lamb, veal, spareribs, Mexican entrees	*Fried chicken	Stuffed cabbage, potatoes, cauliflower, rice	

REF. NO.	HERB OR SPICE	SOUPS	SAUCES AND GRAVIES	SALADS	FISH
70	PARSLEY	Game, fish, chicken, meat, vegetable soups, garnish	Salad dressings, tartare, herb butter, barbecue, spaghetti, brown gravy, garnish, *gremolata	Mixed greens, seafood, vegetable, potato, marinated vegetables, tomato, chicken, ham, garnish	Broiled, *fried, poach marinades, stuffings baked, casseroles, croquettes, court-bouillon, garnish or seasoning for all fish and shellfish
14	PEANUT		Indonesian kebab sauce, Indonesian salad dressing		Shrimp
58	PEPPERMINT	Cold yogurt-garlic soup, Senegalese	Paloise	Fruit, mixed greens, chicken, Waldorf, *Tunisian mixed	Garnish for shellfish
75	PINE NUT		*Pesto and primavera sauces for pasta		Catalan entrees
78	PISTACHIO			Mixed greens	
71	POKE			Mixed green	
68	POPPY		Fruit salad dressing	Fresh fruit	
79	PURSLANE	Cream		*Purslane-olive, winter salads	
7	ROCAMBOLE	Cream	Brown gravy		Court-bouillon, stuffin
38	ROCKET	Use sparingly in vegetable soups		Mixed greens	
82	ROSEMARY	Vegetable, chicken, turtle	Brown gravy, Spanish, cream		Broiled steaks
84	RUE			Use sparingly	
26	SAFFLOWER	Fish, corn	Curry, butter		Grilled steaks
34	SAFFRON	Fish, chicken, corn, Moroccan Harira	Curry, cream, butter		Boiled seafood, bouillabaisse
85	SAGE	Lentil, garlic, vegetable, beef broth, consommé, minestrone	Paprika-butter sauce for pasta		Grilled fresh tuna
80	SALAD BURNET			Fish, mixed greens, tomato slices	
87	SAVORY (Summer and Winter)	Fresh pea, Crimean fish, cream, chowders, vegetable, lentil	Barbecue, salad dressing	Cucumber, mixed greens	Broiled, stuffing, bake
3	SCALLION	Green bean, *Oriental	Salad dressing	Mixed greens	Baked, poached, *Chinese steamed

EGGS AND CHEESE	MEATS	POULTRY AND GAME	VEGETABLES	SWEET AND BAKING
...eam, cheese, herb ...iche, omelet, scrambled ...gs	Beef, lamb, pork, veal, meatloaf, variety meats, casseroles, *stews, marinades, stuffings, garnish	*Chicken, squab, game, duck, goose, rabbit, chicken livers, casseroles, stews, stuffings, garnish	Potatoes, carrots, noodles, tomatoes, eggplant, artichokes, turnips, parsnips, celery, mushrooms, rice, peas, cauliflower, lentils, asparagus, onions, leeks, marinated vegetables	
	Fried wonton	West African chicken stew	Chinese noodles	Candies, cookies, chocolate
...esh cheese	Lamb stew	Stuffing	Rhubarb, peas, carrots, potatoes, beans, zucchini and eggplant fritters	Chocolate, fruit salad, candy, sherbets
	Ground lamb tarts, sausages		Stuffed grape leaves, *stuffed tomatoes, spinach, rice	Mexican custard cookies
	Pâtés, mortadella, pork roll	Chicken ballotine, duck pâté	Rice	Greek and Italian sweets
			Garnish (leaves); eaten like asparagus (stalks)	
...ips and spreads			Noodles	Apple tart, strudel, Egyptian desserts, cakes, rolls, breads, coffee cake
...melet	Stews			
			Spinach, rice	
...eviled eggs, goat ...eese marinade	Roast lamb, pork, or veal, *beef rib steak	Grilled chicken or rabbit, roast duck, wild boar	Mushrooms, peas, potatoes	Italian chestnut pie
...heeses (use ...aringly)				
	Lamb curry	Chicken curry		
...crambled eggs	Lamb curry (also pork and beef)	Chicken curry, rabbit	Rice: *Paella, risotto	Swedish cakes, bread
...ream cheese	Ossobuco, *liver, German ham, Saltimbocca, roast pork	Stuffing, poultry liver spread	Fritters, tomatoes, onions, leeks, peas, eggplant	
				In cool drinks
...Deviled, goat cheese, ...narinade, omelets, ...flan	Pork, lamb, meat pies, smoked meats	Chicken livers, rabbit	Beans, lima, onions, string beans, peas, carrots, chick peas, oyster plant, lentils	
...crambled, dips and ...preads	Pork, lamb, veal, variety meats, beef stir-fry	Chicken, rabbit, chicken livers	Rice, potatoes, string beans, lentils, carrots, peas, *artichoke hearts	

REF. NO.	HERB OR SPICE	SOUPS	SAUCES AND GRAVIES	SALADS	FISH
69	SCENTED GERANIUM			Fruit	
31	SCURVY GRASS	Cream soup	Used like cress	In winter salads	
89	SESAME		Yogurt, cream	Garnish	Baked, poached, grill
1	SHALLOT	Billibi, bisques, game, sea urchin, mushroom, oyster	Bercy, bordelaise, *white butter sauce, salad dressing, butters	Mixed greens, tomato	Gratin, sautés, mous *potted salmon
83	SORREL	Cream, lentil, Germiny	Sauce verte, mayonnaise, hollandaise		Shellfish, *sausage, salmon, shad
43	SOYBEAN	Oriental soups	Soy sauce, Teriyaki	Bean sprout	Sweet-and-sour shrin
48	STAR ANISE				Oriental shrimp
88	STONECROP			Green (young shoots, leaves)	
45	SUNFLOWER			Garnish	
64	SWEET BASIL	Cream, vegetable, chowder, turtle, minestrone	Butter, *pesto, tomato, spaghetti, *cream	Chicken, mixed green, tomato	All kinds poached an creamed, broiled fish and shellfish
61	SWEET CICELY	Cream	Cream	Fruit, mixed	
66	SWEET MARJORAM	Lentil, Crimean fish, Italian Easter lamb	Tomato	Zucchini, cucumber, chicken, mixed greens	Baked halibut, cream clams, grilled tuna
90	TAMARIND	*Sour fish soup, chicken broth	Curry		Indian and Indonesian dishes
91	TANSY		Butter spread		
16	TARRAGON	Cream, consommé, vegetable	*Béarnaise, tartare, remoulade, mayonnaise, *mustard, salad dressing	Mixed, potato, chicken, tuna, shrimp, lobster, coleslaw, eggs	Broiled salmon, shell
94	THYME	Lettuce, chowder, vegetable, minestrone, scotch broth	Spaghetti, tomato, butter, barbecue, creole	*Cucumber, coleslaw, chicken, tomato, pimiento	*Gumbo, broiled, poached, baked
97	TRUFFLE	Consommé	Périgourdine, Bagna Cauda	Mixed greens, potato	Sole, lobster
36	TURMERIC	Senegalese	Curry, mayonnaise, chow chow	Céléri remoulade	Shellfish, pilaf
98	VANILLA	A drop in chicken soup		Fruit	
99	VIOLET			Garnish	
49	WALNUT	Yogurt-garlic	*Pesto, Turkish	Mixed greens, potato	Snails, trout
63	WATERCRESS	Cream	Butter, cream, mayonnaise, herb	Mixed greens	Poached, fish, *baked scallops
19	WINTER CRESS	Vegetable		Mixed greens	Substitute for watercr

EGGS AND CHEESE	MEATS	POULTRY AND GAME	VEGETABLES	SWEET AND BAKING
				Jelly, custard
			Stuffed	
	Lamb with prunes	Coating for *fried chicken	Tomato jam, chick peas, eggplant, noodles	Italian bread, Halvah
Deviled, scrambled eggs, quiche	Beef, veal, pork, pâté	Chicken livers, pâtés, mousse	Mushrooms, green beans	
Quiche, scrambled eggs		Stuffing		
Egg foo yung	Oriental stir-fry	Oriental stir-fry	Watercress, broccoli, Buddha's delight	
	Oriental pork, *beef, and spareribs			
Dips and spreads			Green beans	
Scrambled eggs, omelets, spreads, mozzarella	Lamb, pork, veal, liver	Chicken, duck, rabbit, squab	Tomatoes, potatoes, onions	
			Turnips, carrots	Fruit cups, apple pie
Omelets	Meatloaf, *lamb stew, shish kebab, roast pork, sausage, stuffing	Grilled chicken, stuffing, duck, rabbit	Zucchini, cucumber, carrots, marinated mushrooms	
	Lamb	Chicken	Mixed vegetable curry	
		Turkey stuffing		Pudding, cakes
Scrambled eggs, omelet, stuffed eggs, fresh cheese	Lamb, veal, pork, casserole, variety meats	Grilled chicken, pâtés, mousses, duck, squab, rabbit	Tomatoes, marinated: leeks, carrots, potatoes, mushrooms	
Omelet, deviled eggs, dips and spreads	Pork, lamb, veal, beef, meatloaf, stuffing, sausages, pâtés	Chicken, rabbit, duck, stuffing	Tomatoes, beans, potatoes, mushrooms, eggplant, zucchini	Figs in red wine, bread
Omelet, scrambled eggs, brie	Lamb, beef, pâté	Chicken, duck and goose livers, pâtés	Potatoes, pasta, risotto	
Deviled eggs	Indian curried lamb, pork, beef, lamb stew	Indian curried chicken, *Moroccan chicken	Rice, Paella	
				Custard, cake, rice pudding, cookies, pies
				Cakes, sherbet, jellies, garnish
Roquefort	Stews (lamb, veal, and beef), beef stir-fry	Chicken, coating for frying, stir-fry	Green beans, potatoes, zucchini, peas	Ice cream, *cakes, pies, soufflés
Scrambled	Hunan beef stir-fry	Chicken	Potatoes	

25

Plant Lexicon

INDEX AND KEY
TO THE PLANT LEXICON

Each of the 100 herbs and spices presented in this book is derived from a plant. The following section, the Plant Lexicon, constitutes an illustrated guide to the botanical properties of these plants. The reader will find here detailed information on the appearance, dimensions, location, and habits of the 100 herb and spice plants.

The heading of each text includes the following details: Latin name, English name, plant family, plant number, and references to the geographical distribution of the plant. The distribution is indicated in two lines. The first line gives the plant's original habitat or place of provenance; the second, in italics, indicates areas in which the plant has been introduced by man and grows either wild or cultivated.

Because English common names of herbs and spices are unstandardized and variable, the 100 herbs and spices of the lexicon have been arranged in alphabetical order according to their standard *Latin names* and each plant has been assigned a number from 1 to 100. To locate a plant in the Lexicon, it is necessary to know its Latin name, or else to obtain its *reference number* by looking up its English name in the list printed at right.

Allgood	28	Elder	86	Mugwort	17
Allspice	72	Estragon	16	Mustard	21
Almond	81	Fat hen	28	Myrrh	61
American cress	19	Felon herb	17	Myrtle	62
Angelica	11	Fennel	41	Nasturtium	96
Anise	73	Fenugreek	95	Nutmeg	60
Aniseed tree	48	Field poppy	68	Nut Pine	75
Asafetida	40	Filbert	33	Olive	65
Balm	57	Food of the gods	40	Onion	2
Bamboo	18	French sorrel	83	Oregano	67
Basil	64	Galanga	8	Oswego tea	59
Bay leaf	51	Galingale	8	Paprika	24
Bee balm	59	Garden cress	53	Parsley	70
Bergamot	59	Garlic	5	Peanut	14
Bird pepper	25	Ginger	100	Pepper	77
Black caraway	74	Golden-buttons	91	Peppermint	58
Black elder	86	Goober	14	Pigeon berry	71
Black mustard	21	Good-King-Henry	28	Pine (nut)	75
Black pepper	77	Goosefoot	28	Pinyon	75
Blowballs	92	Grains of paradise	9	Pistachio	78
Borage	20	Green almond	78	Poke	71
Burnet	74	Green pepper	24	Poke weed	71
Cacao	93	Groundnut	14	Poppy	68
Caper	23	Hazel	33	Porret	4
Caraway	27	Herb bennet	42	Pot marigold	22
Cardamom	37	Herb-of-grace	84	Purslane	79
Cayenne pepper	25	Hop	46	Red poppy	68
Celery	13	Horseradish	15	Rocambole	7
Chervil	12	Hyssop	47	Rocket	38
Chili	25	Indian cress	96	Rosemary	82
Chinese parsley	32	Juniper	50	Rue	84
Chives	6	King's clover	56	Rugula	38
Ciboule	3	Laurel	51	Safflower	26
Cinnamon	29	Lavender	52	Saffron	34
Citron	30	Leek	4	Sage	85
Cive	6	Lemon balm	57	Salad burnet	80
Clove	39	Lemon verbena	55	Sand leek	7
Cloveroot	42	Licorice	44	Savory	87
Cobnut	33	Lovage	54	Scallion	3
Cole	15	Mace	60	Scented-leaf	
Coriander	32	Madeira nut	40	geranium	69
Corn poppy	68	Malabar cardamom	37	Scurvy grass	31
Cress	53	Marigold	22	Sesame	89
Cubeb	76	Marjoram	66	Shallot	1
Cumin	35	Melegueta pepper	9	Skoke	71
Dandelion	92	Melilot	56	Soja bean	43
Dill	10	Mercury	28	Sorrel	83
Dragon plant	16	Mirasol	45	Soybean	43
Dyer's saffron	26	Monkey nut	14	Spearmint	58

Spoonwort	31
Star anise	48
Stonecrop	88
Summer savory	87
Sunflower	45
Sweet basil	64
Sweet bay	51
Sweet ciceley	61
Sweet fern	61
Sweet marjoram	66
Sweet pepper	24
Sweet violet	99
Sweetwood	44
Tabasco	25
Talewort	20
Tamarind	90
Tansy	91
Tarragon	16
Thyme	94
Truffle	97
Turmeric	36
Vanilla	98
Violet	99
Walnut	49
Watercress	63
Welsh onion	3
White mustard	21
Wild parsnip	11
Wild spinach	28
Winter cress	19
Winter rocket	19
Winter savory	87
Wood avens	42
Zedoary	36

An enlarged close-up of a tiny sprig of rosemary in blossom. It is one of the most aromatic flavoring plants because of the location of its essential oil immediately beneath the surface of the leaf's underside. Its well-known, distinctive flavor, though not universally loved, is often used in combination with roast lamb and other meats, as well as with poultry and several different vegetables.

ALLIUM ASCALONICUM

SHALLOT

Liliaceae

1 C Asia
Warm Temperate Zones

ALLIUM CEPA

ONION

Liliaceae

2 S Eur, C Asia
Warm Temperate Zones

ALLIUM FISTULOSUM

SCALLION, WELSH ONION

Liliaceae

3 N Eur, N Asia

A bulbous perennial, with a small rounded pear-shaped bulb 1 in. (about 3 cm) in circumference and tapering to a point, with fleshy hollow leaves which grow 16 in. (40 cm) long. There are two forms, one whose bulbs have a silver skin; others with a reddish-brown skin. The small onion-like bulbs form close together about the parent bulb. Propagation is by planting the bulbs on the surface of a well-nourished soil. This is done early in spring by pressing the bulbs into the soil which has been made firm on the surface. Plant in rows 6 in. (15 cm) apart and allow 10 in. (25 cm) between the rows. The tops of the bulbs (the necks) should stick out of the soil. Late in summer, the leaves should be bent over at the neck of the bulbs to encourage ripening. Early in autumn when the leaves turn yellow, lift the clumps and separate the bulbs. Dry them on trays in an airy room and use through winter, replanting leftovers.

A large bulbous plant which takes its name from the Latin *cepa*, a head, for the bunched florets are borne in heads at the end of a hollow 18 in. (45 cm) stem. The bulbs, which are covered with a light brown tunic or skin, can with good culture grow to enormous size, each weighing up to 2 pounds (1 kilo) or more. When grown in a warm climate, they are sweet and juicy; elsewhere they are strong smelling and when cut cause the eyes to water. The name onion is derived from union, single or one, denoting that the bulbs do not form offsets. Onions are raised from seed sown in gentle heat in a greenhouse or frame; or in a warm climate, in shallow drills outdoors early in spring. Plant out the seedlings into a rich soil in early summer. In cooler climates, sets are grown. These are tiny bulbs which have been retarded and stored under refrigeration. In spring they are pressed into the surface of the soil like shallots and will make rapid growth. Allow 6 in. (15 cm) between the bulbs and 10 in. (25 cm) between the rows. In autumn, when the foliage dies down, the bulbs are lifted, dried, and stored for winter use. Spring or salad onions which make only a small bulb are pulled "green" to use in summer salads and are of the White Lisbon variety.

A perennial of the extreme north of Europe and Asia, it takes its second name, Welsh onion, from its being grown in the coldest regions of that country. The plant resembles chives in that it forms no bulb in the accepted sense, its leaves being the part used to impart their mild onion flavor. Like chives, the plant forms dense fibrous roots and has thin hollow stems which grow 6 in. (15 cm) tall. They remain green all winter. Propagation is by division every 3 or 4 years (as for chives), and by seed sown in autumn or in spring in shallow drills 6 in. (15 cm) apart. The grass-like foliage is cut 1 in. (2.5 cm) above soil level, and thus the plants will continue to increase. The plants will be ready to use 3—4 months after sowing and will remain green all year no matter how severe the winter. Like chives, this is a suitable plant for edging. It may be grown in a window box or tub and grows well in ordinary soil.

ALLIUM PORRUM

LEEK, PORRET

Liliaceae

4 N Eur, N Asia

ALLIUM SATIVUM

GARLIC

Liliaceae

5 C Asia
Warm Temperate Zones

An annual or biennial of extreme hardiness, grown for the lower blanched portion of the stem which is the leaves. These arise tightly clasped together from a flat underground plate which forms the base of the leaves. Leeks require a rich soil and a long season to mature, and copious water. Seed is sown in autumn in a frame or greenhouse. Seedlings are planted out in spring in ground trenched to a depth of 10 in. (25 cm), with humus material placed at the base to retain summer moisture. To plant, make a hole 2 in. (5 cm) deep with a piece of cane and drop in the base of the plant. Do not firm or cover with soil. Plant 6 in. (15 cm) apart in a double row the same distance apart. After planting, water in. Well-grown leeks will grow 16—18 in. (40—45 cm) tall and 3 in. (7.5 cm) in circumference. As the plants make growth, draw up the soil at the base to blanch (whiten) the stems. No frost will harm them.

Garlic may well be the most pungent of the 325 species of the genus *Allium*. It is at least the strongest of those commonly used, sufficiently potent so that persons who have not recently eaten it are apt to avoid persons who have. Yet it can be tamed in cooking to an extent which brings out its basic sweetness and makes it inoffensive on the breath. Its great versatility—it can be a subtle whisper in a leg of lamb or an aggressive assault on the taste buds in a green salad—has made it one of the most frequently used seasoners throughout the world.

Garlic is a perennial with irregular shaped bulbs, around which grow small bulblets called cloves. The broad, flat, strap-like leaves taper to a point and arise from an elongated sheath which encloses the bulb. The flowers, whitish-mauve with paper-like bracts, are borne in capitate heads.

Rich in alkaline salts and sulfur compounds, garlic is a blood purifier and is used in the kitchen to impart its unique flavor to many savory foods. For the cloves to ripen well (as they do in the Near East), they require a light sandy soil and an open sunny position. It is one of the few plants to enjoy a loose soil which was well manured for a previous crop, or with a little decayed manure worked in before planting. This is done in autumn where winter frosts are not troublesome, or in spring. Propagation is by the cloves or bulblets, since seed is not produced in the cultivated plants. Plant in rows 2 in. (5 cm) deep and 6 in. (15 cm) apart, with 10 in. (25 cm) between the rows. Cloves planted in autumn will be ready to lift late the following summer; those planted in spring are lifted in autumn when the leaves turn yellow. A related species, bear's garlic or ramsons *(A. ursinum)*, is sometimes found growing in the humus-enriched soil of deciduous forests and river valleys. Its elliptical, lance-shaped basal leaves are used to impart bright color and a light garlic flavor to spring salads. A flowering stalk appears later, bearing an umbel of many snowy-white 6-petaled blooms. Small black seeds—rather than cloves—are produced for propagation.

ALLIUM SCHOENOPRASUM

CHIVE

Liliaceae

6 N Eur, Asia
Temperate Zones

ALLIUM SCORODOPRASUM

ROCAMBOLE, SAND LEEK

Liliaceae

7 N Eur, N + W Asia

ALPINIA OFFICINARUM

GALINGALE, GALANGA

Zingiberaceae

8 SE Asia

AMOMUM MELEGUETA

MELEGUETA PEPPER, GRAINS OF PARADISE

Zingiberaceae

9 Tropical W Af
Tropical Af, India, Guiana

It takes its name from the Danish *rockenbolle*, a wild onion. A perennial, it resembles garlic in that it forms cloves or small bulbs around the parent bulb. From the bulb, with its elongated tunic which protects the thin base of the flat-toothed strap-like leaves, arises the flower stem which grows 2 ft (60 cm) tall. The brilliant purple flowers like those of chives are borne May—August. The plant requires a light loose soil, like the garlic, and the cloves are planted in spring 6 in. (15 cm) apart in drills made 2 in. (5 cm) deep. Lift in autumn when the leaves turn yellow, shake off surplus soil, and separate cloves.

Widespread on cliffs and mountainous slopes. An evergreen perennial with round, hollow, rush-like leaves, tapering to a point and bearing, on 8 in. (20 cm) stems, small globular flowers of deep mauve-pink, with paper-like bracts. In bloom July—September, the plants form a clump of small bulbs, like spring onions, and are heavily rooted. They are readily propagated by division. This is done at almost any time of year except when the soil is frost-hard. Plant the offsets 6 in. (15 cm) apart, the bulbous part just below soil level. They require a soil containing humus, to retain moisture in dry weather when the plants will continue to increase through the year. The rush-like leaves are cut away just above the bulbous part and are chopped into small pieces. The plants make a neat edging to the herb garden and they may be planted to good effect in window boxes or tubs.

Native of the tropics, the plant takes its name from the Arabic *khalanjan*, mild ginger. It is grown for its thick tuberous roots which are used in confectionery and medicine as a substitute for ginger. From the roots the flower stem arises to a height of 3—4 ft (1 m) and is enclosed by the leaf sheaths. The leaves are about 12 in. (30 cm) long and are lanceolate but not stalked. They are of shining bright green. The flowers, borne in terminal spikes, are white with veins of dark red. When the plants are several years old, they are lifted and the roots dried in the sun. They are then cut into cylindrical pieces about 3 in. (7.5 cm) long and are about 1 in. (2 cm) thick, marked by rings which are the lower leaf scales. The roots are reddish-brown and have many uses. Arabs ground them to take as snuff and use them to flavor wine and beer. Hindus include them in perfumes and in the preparation of curries.

It is native to Liberia and the Gold Coast, that part of tropical western Africa known as the pepper coast, and it is a herbaceous perennial with a long slender rhizomatous root covered with sheathing leaf bracts. The flower stems arise to a height of 6 ft (2 m) and are enclosed by leaf-sheaths. The leaves are ca. 8 in. (20 cm) long with prominent veins; the handsome wax-like flowers are large and cylindrical. The fruit is a cylindrical yellow capsule, spotted with red, the thick fleshy pericarp enclosing a colorless pulp that contains the shining, hard, round, reddish-brown seeds which have an aromatic taste but no smell and are used as a condiment and to flavor spirits and liqueurs. The pungent principle contained in the seeds or grains is paradol. The name *melegueta* is from an Indian word meaning pepper. When the seed pods, which attain the size of large almonds, are harvested, the seeds are removed.

ANETHUM GRAVEOLENS

DILL

Umbelliferae

10 SE Eur, SW Asia
Temperate Zones

ANGELICA ARCHANGELICA

ANGELICA, WILD PARSNIP

Umbelliferae

11 N + E Eur, N Asia
N Am

ANTHRISCUS CEREFOLIUM

CHERVIL, SWEET CHERVIL

Umbelliferae

12 C Eur, C Asia
N Am

A hardy annual which takes its name from the Saxon *dilla,* to lull (because the water in which the seeds were immersed for several hours was rubbed on nursing women's breasts to lull children to sleep after feeding). It grows 2 ft (60 cm) tall with smooth stems and linear leaves which have sheathing footstalks. The small yellow flowers are borne June—July in a terminal umbel and are followed by oval seeds which are flatter than those of caraway and have a warm, aromatic taste. Seed is sown early spring in drills 10 in. (25 cm) apart, the plants being thinned to 8 in. (20 cm) in the rows. The fern-like leaves are used in summer to make sauces to serve with fish, and the seeds to make vinegar for pickling. The seeds ripen early in autumn, when the heads are removed and placed on trays in an airy room to complete their drying. An open, sunny position is always necessary for the seed to ripen in cooler climes. Dill is believed to be the aneth of antiquity, which imparted strength to gladiators, and in some countries today it is still called aneth. Dill is particularly appreciated in central and northern Europe, especially in Poland and in Scandinavia. One of its commonest uses is for pickling cucumbers.

One of the hardiest of plants, distributed as far north as Lapland and Iceland. A perennial, it is often given biennial treatment but it will not usually flower until its second year. To be long living, it should not be allowed to flower, though if seed is required for flavoring, the plants can be left to flower in July—August and the seed is harvested late in summer. Also, if one or two seed heads are left on, the plants will seed themselves each year. It has smooth unfurrowed stems which grow 6—7 ft (2 m) tall, with leaves 2 ft (60 cm) across, with decurrent segments and toothed margins. The greenish-white flowers appear in August in rayed umbels and are visited by bees and other insects for nectar. All parts have a musk-like scent, the roots being used to make vermouth, the seeds to flavor liqueurs. The stems impart a musky flavor to fruit pies. Set the plants 3—4 ft (1 m) apart at the back of a border.

A pubescent annual growing 16 in. (40 cm) tall, its hollow stems covered in silky hairs. The leaves are 3-pinnate, pubescent on the underside, and emit a sweet aniseed scent when pressed. If a sowing is made each month from early spring until late summer, there will be a continuous supply of young leaves. Like parsley, sow fresh seed or it will not germinate-well. Sow in shallow drills 8 in. (20 cm) apart and thin the seedlings to 6 in. (15 cm) in the rows. Begin using the leaves when the plants are 6 in. (15 cm) tall and the plants will become all the bushier. The white flowers are borne in sessile umbels early in summer.

31

APIUM GRAVEOLENS	ARACHIS HYPOGAEA	ARMORACIA RUSTICANA	ARTEMISIA DRACUNCULUS
CELERY	PEANUT	HORSERADISH	TARRAGON, DRAGON PLANT, ESTRAGON
Umbelliferae	Leguminosae	Cruciferae	Compositae
13 Eur, W Asia, N + S Af *Warm Temperate Zones*	**14** S Am *Tropical Zones*	**15** Eur, Asia *Temperate Zones*	**16** S + N Eur, N Asia *Warm Temperate Zones*

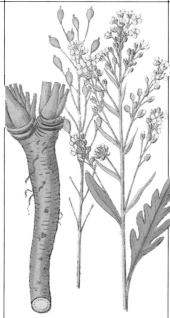

There are two forms of this hardy perennial. First is French tarragon, native of southern France and Spain, a plant with smooth dark green lance-shaped leaves which is not as hardy as the second variety. This second form is Russian tarragon, *A. redowskii,* which has rougher leaves of paler green. The French tarragon, of much more piquant flavor, is that most often grown for making vinegars, an essential ingredient of sauce tartare. The plants bear drooping white flowers in flat heads, but French tarragon does not set seed in northern parts. Tarragon is a corruption of the Latin *dracunculus,* a little dragon,

An annual or biennial all parts of which have an unusual pungent flavor. Wild celery is found by the wayside, usually in damp places. It grows 2 ft (60cm) tall with a grooved stem and lobed leaves, the lower stalked, the upper sessile. The small greenish-white flowers are borne in terminal umbels and are followed by light brown ovoid seeds. For garden culture, celery requires a long growing season and fresh seed is sown in gentle heat early in the year, the seedlings being transplanted and grown on in a frame until ready to plant out early in summer. It requires a rich soil and is best grown in trenches. Plant 10in. (25cm) apart in a double row and keep the plants watered in summer or the stems will be woody. Begin earthing up the stems toward the end of summer to blanch them. Plants can remain in the ground all winter, lifting as required. For seed, leave several plants to run to seed.

Native of tropical America but grown commercially in the tropics everywhere, it is one of the few plants *(Trifolium subterranean* is another) which bear fruit underground (geocarpy). The flower stems downward, forcing the seed pods to form beneath the soil where the fruits ripen. *Arachis* grows 16in. (40cm) tall, its leaves divided into 4-pinnate oval leaflets with short stalks and prominent ribs. As many as 20—30 fruits are formed below ground and are ripe by the end of summer. The nuts are enclosed in capsules 2in. (5cm) long, 2 to each, with one nut at each end of the capsule. After lifting, they are dried in the sun and the nuts are usually marketed in the capsules. The almost round nuts when fully grown have a circumference of about 1in. (2cm), and are covered in a thin brown tunic. They are highly nutritious, being 28 percent protein, and contain a valuable oil used as an alternative to olive oil.

A perennial growing 2 ft (60cm) tall with a stout cylindrical rootstock which may grow down to a depth of 2 ft (60cm). Once planted, it is difficult to eradicate, for the smallest piece of root broken off when lifting will grow again. A plant of extreme hardiness, it has large dark green root leaves with 12in. (30cm) footstalks and toothed margins, while the small white flowers are borne in loose terminal spikes. Horseradish sauce made from fresh root will bring tears to the eyes if consumed in too large amounts but helps the digestion of rich meats as an alternative to mustard. Grow it in an out-of-the-way corner, in a rich, deeply dug soil, planting the thongs or roots in autumn or winter, 18in. (45cm) apart; or sow seed in spring and plant out at the same distance late in summer. The plants should not be lifted until 3 years old, when the roots are of reasonable size. It will grow in semishade.

ARTEMISIA VULGARIS	BAMBUSA VULGARIS	BARBAREA VULGARIS
MUGWORT	BAMBOO	WINTER CRESS
Compositae	Gramineae	Cruciferae
17 Eur, Asia *Temperate Zones*	**18** SE Asia *Tropical Zones*	**19** Eur, Asia *N Am*

from its serpent-like roots. Both forms are perennial and grow 2 ft (60 cm) tall. Plant 20 in. (50 cm) apart in autumn or spring and in ordinary well-drained soil. The French tarragon requires a sunny, sheltered situation. The leaves are used fresh or are cut and dried in late summer and can be frozen in ice cubes, or after blanching in boiling water for a few seconds, placed in plastic bags in the deep freezer. They will keep fresh for one year. Tarragon vinegar can be made at home using fresh tarragon picked just before it flowers. The herb is placed in a bottle, which is then filled with white wine vinegar and stored.

An erect perennial growing 3–4 ft (1 m) tall with grooved stems and 1–2-pinnate dark green leaves, with the leaflets toothed and slightly downy on the underside. The small fluffy flowers are yellowish-brown or red and are borne in panicles or spikes during late summer. It is a common plant of the wayside. The leaves contain the bitter principle absinthe. The plant is hardy and grows well in ordinary soil. It is propagated from offsets removed in autumn and planted 2 ft (60 cm) apart; or from seed sown in spring.
A. abrotanum, southernwood or lad's love, makes a bushy plant 3–4 ft tall (1 m), its gray-green leaves being twice pinnately dissected. A perennial but which may lose its leaves in a cold winter, the leaves are lemon-scented and used in stuffings. The plant is native to southern Europe and was introduced early into America, being mentioned in John Gent's *New England's Rarities Discovered* (1672).

A shrubby grass of perennial habit with woody culms which may reach a height of .100 ft (30 m) under natural conditions. The cylindrical stems are bright green and hollow and are grooved with short internodes. The bright green leaves arise in a tuft from the root and are about 30 in. (75 cm) long, being sharply serrated on both edges, terminating to a point and with the leaf surface rough. The fruit is a nut. Under garden culture, the flower stems reach a height of 6–7 ft (2 m), terminating in a large silver inflorescence which will retain its beauty for years when dried. The young shoots are used in salads and are boiled and served with butter. The seeds (nuts) also have culinary uses. The plants require an open situation and a deep, moist soil. Otherwise they suffer from summer drought. Propagation is by division in autumn or spring. There is a form with handsome pink inflorescences, called *Bambusa roseum*.

A perennial with glossy, deep green leaves and angled, furrowed stems, the leaves on the upper part being undivided. The flowers are bright yellow, borne in terminal cymes. It is present throughout the Northern Hemisphere and is completely hardy. Where there is no running water, it may be grown as a substitute for watercress to which it is closely related. A bed made up in semishade and in a soil containing humus will be productive for several years and the plants may be used all year. Like watercress, it is rich in iron and sulfur. Seed is sown in spring in a frame or in shallow drills, and germination takes about 3 weeks if the soil is kept moist. When the seedlings are large enough to handle, move to a prepared bed and plant 8 in. (20 cm) apart. The first green will be ready to cut in late autumn. To keep the plants growing in cold weather, surround half the bed with 12 in. (30 cm) boards; cover in plastic.

BORAGO OFFICINALIS

BORAGE, TALEWORT

Boraginaceae

20	W Asia
	Eur, N Am

BRASSICA NIGRA, SINAPIS ALBA

BLACK MUSTARD, WHITE MUSTARD

Cruciferae

21	S Eur, N Af, W Asia
	Temperate Zones

An annual or biennial growing 20 in. (50 cm) tall, all parts being covered in bulbous hairs. The oval leaves are gray-green and the flowers which are borne in forked cymes June—August are brilliant blue with purple-black anthers which meet cone-like and dehisce slowly, allowing pollen to fall onto the cone which encloses style and stigmas. When a bee thrusts its proboscis between the stamens, the anthers are displaced and the cone opens to allow pollen to fall on to the stigmas. The flowers are included in salads and the leaves and stems in summer drinks, to which they impart a cucumber-like flavor and give the drinkers a sense of exhilaration. This is due to potassium salts present in the mucilage. Borage is best used freshly picked, since its leaves do not keep very well. For a continuous supply, make a sowing under glass (in a cold frame) in July and set out the plants in spring 20 in. (50 cm) apart. Make another sowing in spring where the plants are to mature. One or two plants should be let seed themselves each year. The plant is named from the Latin *borra*, hair, though the Greeks named it *euphrosynon*, meaning a ''sense of well-being.'' It is present on waste ground, growing in sandy soil.

Brassica nigra, black mustard, is an annual growing 3—4 ft (1 m) tall with a branching stem, the lower leaves pinnate with rounded terminal lobes, the upper leaves narrow and pointed. The flowers, borne June—August, are bright yellow, followed by quadrangular shortly beaked pods, the seeds providing the condiment mustard. A plant of cornfields and hedgerows, it has been grown commercially in many parts of Europe and Asia since the sixteenth century, to accompany meats to aid their digestion. The finest mustard is grown and made at Dijon in France, in recognition of which Philip the Bold granted armorial bearings to the town in 1382. Dijon mustard is made with tarragon vinegar, anchovies, and capers. It was not until the end of the eighteenth century that Mrs. Clements of Durham, England, invented the modern method of dressing mustard with flour. The green pods form along the upper half of the stem and remain upright, each pod containing 4—8 black seeds. Under field culture seed is sown in drills 12 in. (30 cm) apart in spring, and at the end of summer, the crop is cut and the seed threshed and dried.

White mustard is *Sinapis alba*, an erect annual growing 12 in. (30 cm) tall with pinnate leaves and yellow flowers followed by horizontal seed pods containing 4—5 round pale yellow seeds (hence its name to distinguish it from the black). It is grown ''green'' for salads, sowing the seed thickly in boxes of shallow soil or on wet flannel in a kitchen window. It is ready to cut in 3 weeks and is grown all the year.

Persons acquainted with the often fiery nature of commercial mustards may be surprised if someone offers them mustard seeds to chew. They have a nutty flavor, are pleasant to eat thus directly, and acquire heat only when processed.

CALENDULA OFFICINALIS

MARIGOLD, POT MARIGOLD

Compositae

<table><tr><td>22</td><td>S Eur, N Af, W Asia
Temperate Zones</td></tr></table>

CAPPARIS SPINOSA

CAPER

Capparidaceae

<table><tr><td>23</td><td>S Eur, W Asia
Warm Temperate Zones</td></tr></table>

CAPSICUM ANNUUM

PAPRIKA, SWEET PEPPER, GREEN PEPPER

Solanaceae

<table><tr><td>24</td><td>C + S Am
Torrid + Warm Temperate Zones</td></tr></table>

CAPSICUM FRUTESCENS

CHILI, CAYENNE PEPPER, TABASCO PEPPER

Solanaceae

<table><tr><td>25</td><td>C + S Am
Torrid + Warm Temperate Zones</td></tr></table>

A shrubby branched perennial arising from a large taproot and growing to 3—4 ft (1 m), with short-stemmed opposite dark green leaves terminating to a point and small purple-white flowers borne in the leaf axils. The fruit is a large rectangular fleshy berry, the seeds being enclosed in pulp, with the outer case thick and fleshy. Fruits may measure 3 by 2 in. (about 8 by 5 cm), each of 3 or 4 unequal lobes. They can be used green or ripe, when they will have turned bright red (like tomatoes of the same family and are rich in vitamin C. Hybrid varieties have recently been raised which are resistant to mosaic disease.

A pungent-smelling annual or biennial of easy culture, which grows well in any soil and in the colder regions of the world. Growing 12 in. (30 cm) tall, with a succulent stem and pale green oblong sessile leaves, the flowers are borne with freedom all summer and autumn and are about 2 in. (5 cm) across with orange or yellow ray florets and disk florets of black or brown. The flowers are dried (and are also used fresh) to include in soups and stews, to impart their pungency, hence its old name, pot marigold. The flower heads are cut when dry and spread out in an airy room to complete their drying; then the ray petals are pulled from the disk which is discarded. It readily transplants and seed is sown in pots or boxes in early spring and the seedlings set out 12 in. (30 cm) apart when large enough to handle. Or alternatively the seed can be sown where the plants are to bloom.

A shrubby perennial with slender stems spreading to 3—4 ft (1 m) in length. The alternate simple leaves are fleshy. They are oval with twin reflexed spines formed at the base of the leaves which replace the stipules. The large 4-petaled flowers are borne solitary and are about 2 in. (5 cm) across with the stamens protruding beyond the corolla. They bloom May—June and are followed by large berries 2 in. (5 cm) long containing the kidney-shaped seeds, but it is the unopened flower buds that are removed for pickling and used to flavor vinegars and sauces. They are known as capers and are harvested in early summer. The plant is present on rocks and cliffs around the Mediterranean. The variety *C. inermis* has large, dark green fleshy leaves with straight spines and more pendulous branches. It is present on old walls and mountainous slopes and also provides the capers of commerce.

Chili (Cayenne) can be either *C. frutescens* or *C. minimum*, each of which is a perennial plant of similar habit and botanical characteristics to the sweet pepper. It bears larger numbers of fruits, which are smaller and cylindrical, usually growing 2—6 in. (5—15 cm) long and tapering to a blunt point. Each contains 10—30 small seeds embedded in the pulp and protected by the outer flesh which turns from bright green to red or orange as the fruit ripens. The fruits are "hot" and spicy, hence the name "hot" pepper, and are used for making pickles and chutneys. The seed when dried and ground provides the cayenne pepper of commerce, the plants being grown in those parts of the New World close to the equator. In northern Europe the plants are treated as annual and are grown under glass, as they are less hardy than sweet peppers. Seed is sown early in March in a temperature of 65 °F (18 °C), the seedling replanted.

CARTHAMUS TINCTORIUS	CARUM CARVI	CHENOPODIUM BONUS-HENRICUS	CINNAMOMUM ZEYLANICUM
SAFFLOWER, DYER'S SAFFRON	CARAWAY	GOOD-KING-HENRY	CINNAMON
Compositae	Umbelliferae	Chenopodiaceae	Lauraceae
26 S Eur, C + S Asia, Af	**27** N Eur, Asia *N Am*	**28** Eur, W Asia *Temperate Zones*	**29** SE Asia *S Am*

Native of tropical Southeast Asia including Ceylon, Malaysia, and Indonesia, it is an evergreen tree which grows in sandy soil and requires a high rainfall for its cultivation. It will reach a height of 35ft (10m). The large leathery leaves are glossy and pale green above, white on the underside. The flowers are white and borne in panicles. They are followed by small, oval blue berries. The bark, smooth and ash-gray, is removed from the branches when the tree is about 6 years old. The younger branches yield the finest

The genus, with about 20 species, is native of the Canary Islands and the Mediterranean region as far as Central Asia. *C. tinctorius* is believed to have come from Eurasia. It is an annual growing about 30in. (75cm) tall with a branching stem and with spiny oval stem-clasping leaves. The rayed flowers have yellow outer petals and a central boss of red petals which, in the East, are used to dye silk red, hence its second popular name "dyer's saffron." The dried outer petals yield the safflower of curry powder when dry; it is also used as a substitute for saffron, or added to saffron as a less expensive adulterant. The flowers are mixed into bread and some other foods in Eastern Europe. The almost white fruits are rectangular and yield an essential oil used as a substitute for olive oil; safflower is among the salad oils lowest in cholesterol content. When ground, the seeds are used for flavoring food.

A glabrous biennial growing 2ft (60cm) tall with hollow stems and a parsnip-like root running deep into the ground. It has an aromatic smell like that of parsnip and the 2-pinnate leaves resemble those of parsley. During its first year, the plant forms a rosette of leaves and in its second year the flower stem arises, at the end of which are borne umbels of small white flowers. They are followed by the carpels (the fruit) which are oblong and boat-shaped with small ridges. When dry they divide and emit a powerful scent. The value of the seed depends on the amount of carvol present and the extent of its purity. Besides its use to flavor cakes and bread in most northern European countries, its seed gives a special flavor to the liqueur kummel. In northern climes it will ripen its seed only in a dry, hot summer. Seed is sown in shallow drills in July where the plants will mature.

A hardy perennial growing 2—3ft (60—90cm) tall with long stalked arrow-shaped leaves of dark green which are thick and fleshy and are as if frosted on the underside. The flowers are green, without petals and borne on leafless spikes in midsummer. It is a common plant of the wayside and seashore, for all members of the family are maritime plants. It is named after Henri IV of France who discovered its culinary properties. The young shoots are earthed up in spring and when 6—8in. (about 20cm) long are cut, peeled, and steamed to serve with melted butter. Later in the year, the leaves are used as a substitute for spinach. Seed is sown in spring in shallow drills and when large enough to move, the young plants are set out 12in. (30cm) apart in well-prepared soil. Established plants may be lifted and divided in spring in alternate years. The plant has had a great number of popular names.

bark. It is removed throughout the year by making an incision lengthwise on each side of the branch, so that the bark comes away as a hollow cylindrical section. It is tied into bundles, each weighing 2 pounds (1 kilo). The inner bark is the best. It is sold in the markets of the East for drying, then ground and shipped to all parts as cinnamon powder. It is one of the world's oldest commodities, having been imported into Egypt and Judea by the Phoenicians, the caravans meeting at Babylon on the Euphrates. Oil is obtained from the berries.

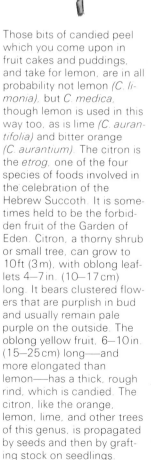

Those bits of candied peel which you come upon in fruit cakes and puddings, and take for lemon, are in all probability not lemon *(C. limonia)*, but *C. medica*, though lemon is used in this way too, as is lime *(C. aurantifolia)* and bitter orange *(C. aurantium)*. The citron is the *etrog*, one of the four species of foods involved in the celebration of the Hebrew Succoth. It is sometimes held to be the forbidden fruit of the Garden of Eden. Citron, a thorny shrub or small tree, can grow to 10ft (3m), with oblong leaflets 4–7in. (10–17cm) long. It bears clustered flowers that are purplish in bud and usually remain pale purple on the outside. The oblong yellow fruit, 6–10in. (15–25cm) long—and more elongated than lemon—has a thick, rough rind, which is candied. The citron, like the orange, lemon, lime, and other trees of this genus, is propagated by seeds and then by grafting stock on seedlings.

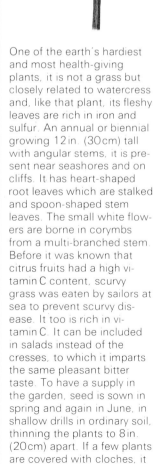

One of the earth's hardiest and most health-giving plants, it is not a grass but closely related to watercress and, like that plant, its fleshy leaves are rich in iron and sulfur. An annual or biennial growing 12in. (30cm) tall with angular stems, it is present near seashores and on cliffs. It has heart-shaped root leaves which are stalked and spoon-shaped stem leaves. The small white flowers are borne in corymbs from a multi-branched stem. Before it was known that citrus fruits had a high vitamin C content, scurvy grass was eaten by sailors at sea to prevent scurvy disease. It too is rich in vitamin C. It can be included in salads instead of the cresses, to which it imparts the same pleasant bitter taste. To have a supply in the garden, seed is sown in spring and again in June, in shallow drills in ordinary soil, thinning the plants to 8in. (20cm) apart. If a few plants are covered with cloches, it can be cut all the year.

An annual growing 8–12in. (20–30cm) tall with solid branching stems which are ridged and with 2-pinnate dark green leaves, the lower divided into deeply cut segments. The white or pale pink flowers are borne in 5–8-rayed umbels and are followed by pale yellow fruits of peppercorn size and shape with 2 oil ducts in each half. The whole plant and the unripe seed has the offensive smell of bugs, and takes its name from the Greek *koros*, a bug. But when the seed is fully ripe it assumes the sweet smell of orange, and the longer the seeds are kept, the stronger the orange smell becomes. The seed is included in most curry powders and imparts its delicious flavor to junket and blancmange. The leaves, known as Chinese parsley, are sometimes used as an herb. Seed is sown in spring in shallow drills, in an open sunny situation. Thin the plants to 6in. (15cm) apart and harvest the seed in early autumn.

CORYLUS AVELLANA

HAZEL, FILBERT

Betulaceae

33 C + S Eur, W Asia
Temperate Zones

CROCUS SATIVUS

SAFFRON

Iridaceae

34 S Eur, W Asia

CUMINUM CYMINUM

CUMIN

Umbelliferae

35 S Eur, W Asia, N Af

Small trees or shrubs growing 16 ft (5 m) tall with heart-shaped saw-edged leaves, broad at the base, pointed at the apex. The trees are present in open woodlands and a hazel coppice is a valuable part of the economy of the country-side. The stakes are used to make hurdles for sheep enclosures and for fencing and windbreaks; also for basket making, while the nuts (fruits) are an economic crop, gathered when ripe in autumn, when the husks and nuts have turned dark brown. The female flowers are borne on the old wood and rely on wind for their fertilization, which carries pollen from the drooping golden-yellow catkins which are the males. The flowers appear early in spring and rely on dry weather for their successful pollination and a heavy crop. For satisfactory pollination, plant 3 varieties together. Plant 12 ft (3—4 m) apart. It will take a tree 5 years to come into bearing, at about 5 ft (1.5 m) tall.

Believed to be the Karkom of the Song of Solomon, it takes its name from the Persian *karkum*, yellow, from the dried grains (powder) collected from the stigma. It is from *karkum* that the genus takes its name; and saffron is from the Arabic *sahafarn*, a thread, from the thread-like stigma. To the ancients, it was the most important of all plants, and in the time of Alexander the Great, merchants distributed it to all parts of Europe. A late-flowering crocus, it produces its narrow gray-green leaves in early summer and its purple-red chalice-like flowers in autumn. They open flat and do not close up again so that where grown commercially, a dry climate is essential. Also, to be free flowering, the corms must be baked in the sun during summer. The oval corms are planted 2 in. (5 cm) deep and 4 in. (10 cm) apart, in well-drained soil in June and the stigmas are removed in early autumn when dry. When they are then put under pressure by heavy boards, the stigmas will form a solid mass. The yield increases for 5 years; then the corms are lifted, divided, and replanted. It takes 70,000 blooms to produce 1 lb (½ kilo) of saffron grains (powder); yet a century ago, 50,000 lb (25,000 kilos) were imported each year into Britain from Spain.

An annual cultivated in Egypt, Syria, and Malta for its many uses in curry powders, pickles, and Indian chutneys to which it imparts a hot spicy taste. In Germany, it is put into bread and cakes and the Dutch use it to flavor cheese. It grows about 16 in. (40 cm) tall, with branching slender stems and fern-like leaves biternately dissected. The tiny flowers which appear in late summer, are white or blush-pink and are borne in 4—6-rayed umbles. They are followed by large elongated seeds, ½ in. (1 cm) long, light brown and straight, whereas caraway seeds are curved. The taste is more bitter than that of caraway but the flavor is aromatic and spicy. In northern Europe, it will ripen its seed in a sunny garden only in a hot dry summer. Sow in shallow drills early in spring and thin to 6 in. (15 cm) apart. Ordinary soil is suitable. Tithes were paid in aromatic seeds in Biblical times.

CURCUMA LONGA, CURCUMA ZEDOARIA

TURMERIC, ZEDOARY

Zingiberaceae

36 S Asia
Torrid Zones

ELETTARIA CARDAMOMUM

CARDAMOM

Zingiberaceae

37 SE Asia
India, Ceylon, Guatemala

ERUCA VESICARIA SUBSP. SATIVA

ROCKET, RUGULA

Cruciferae

38 S Eur, W Asia, N Af
Temperate Zones

EUGENIA CARYOPHYLLATA

CLOVE

Myrtaceae

39 SE Asia, Madagascar
Tropical Zones

Curcuma longa produces the turmeric used in curry powders, the best coming from Malabar and Java. A perennial with a multi-rhizomatous rootstock each of which is cylindrical and varies in size from 2 to 3 in. (5 to 7 cm), tapering at each end. When dried and ground the orange-colored powder has a "hot" aromatic peppery taste. In habit, the plant resembles ginger, the dark green erect leaves being enclosed in a sheath while the cylindrical flowers are borne in an erect spine and are deep yellow. It is propagated by small pieces of root planted 4 in. (10 cm) deep and 12 in. (30 cm) apart. *C. zedoaria*, zedoary, is also grown for its rhizomatous roots and has a more camphor-like odor. Its roots are also yellow and covered in rings, the marks of the old leaves. The flower stems consist of the leaf sheaths which are covered in down. The flower spike arises to a height of 16 in. (40 cm) and the flowers are scented.

Known in commerce as Malabar cardamom, it grows on the coast by spontaneous germination. This is done by felling a number of older trees and shaking up the soil. In a month, seedlings appear and produce a crop in 4 years. It forms a thick rhizome-like root from which arises a stem 6—7 ft (2 m) tall, enclosed by the spongy sheath of the leaves which grow 2 ft (60 cm) long and terminate in a point. The flowers and branches alternate. The plant needs an annual rainfall of more than 100 in. (250 cm) to flourish. The fruits, called Malabar "shorts" in the trade, are about 1 in. (2 cm) long, being smooth and pale yellow and containing 3 valves each of 16 small seeds.

This subspecies of *E. vesicaria* is cultivated as a flavorer for salads, its leaves being quite strong in taste. It is a half-hardy annual, which branches to a height of 2—3 ft (60—90 cm). The plant bears erect siliques at least 1 in. (2.5 cm) long. The flowers, white to cream colored, have purplish veins. The sepals are early-deciduous. Because of its pronounced flavor verging on pepperiness, the leaves are best if used when young and tender. Keep them well trimmed back to stimulate fresh growth. Running quickly to seed in summer, the plant is best used in spring or autumn. Sow in open ground in early spring; first leaves should be ready within 2 months. Rocket is used primarily in England, Greece, Turkey, and Italy; its strong peppery flavor is particularly appreciated in Rome, where rockets are the basis of the mixed salad which is the local favorite, *misticanza*.

Native to Indonesia (Moluccas) and introduced into Mauritius by the French in 1770, and later to Zanzibar where it flourishes in the yellow clay subsoil as nowhere else. Long before then, cloves were imported into Britain and northern Europe for flavoring food. Shakespeare mentions the custom of sticking cloves into dried oranges to hang from the waist, to be inhaled to counteract unpleasant smells. They became known as pomanders. It is an evergreen tree growing to a height of 60—65 ft (18—20 m) with smooth gray bark; its lance-shaped leaves covered with oil glands which release the aromatic clove smell when pressed. The crimson-purple flowers are borne in cymes at the ends of the branchlets, and it is the dried flower buds that yield the cloves of commerce. A tree begins to yield when 6 years old and continues for 100 years. The season lasts from August until November.

39

FERULA ASSAFOETIDA

ASAFETIDA, FOOD OF THE GODS

Umbelliferae

40 C Asia
Iran, Afghanistan, India

FOENICULUM VULGARE

FENNEL

Umbelliferae

41 S + E Eur, N Af, W Asia
Temperate Zones

GEUM URBANUM

HERB BENNET, CLOVE-ROOT, WOOD AVENS

Rosaceae

42 Eur, N Af, Asia
N Am, Aus

GLYCINE MAX, GLYCINE SOJA

SOYBEAN

Leguminosae

43 SE Asia
US, Brazil, SE Asia

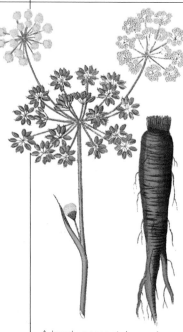

A hardy perennial growing up to 10ft (3m) tall and up to 4000ft (1200m) above sea level, with large cabbage-like heads which are edible. From the woody root of the plants when 3—4 years old, a milky resinous juice is obtained which coagulates upon exposure to air. Soil is pulled away to expose the roots and a deep incision is made in them. After 4—5 weeks, the hardened juice, now reddish-brown after exposure to air, is collected by scraping it from the roots. The soil is then replaced. The gum resin acts as a stimulant and with its garlic-like flavor has culinary uses. The Romans used it to rub onto the gridiron on which meat was to be cooked. It quickens the appetite and improves the digestion. John Evelyn tells that in ancient Greece it was so highly esteemed that it was dedicated to Apollo at Delphi, hence its name "food of the gods." The center "bud" or head also contains the aromatic juice.

An erect perennial growing 5—6ft (1.5m) tall, its 3—4 pinnate leaves divided into numerous narrow segments, with the whole plant taking on a bluish appearance. The small yellow flowers are borne in compound terminal umbels and are followed by narrow ovoid fruits with blunt ends and with 8 longitudinal ribs. The seed, believed to allay the pangs of hunger, was eaten by the poor and for the same reason was included in bread and cakes to which it imparted an aromatic flavor. From the fresh leaves is made a sauce to serve with fish. The Romans named it *Foeniculum* because of its hay-like smell when dried. The plant grows best in a chalk or limestone soil and seed is sown in summer where it is to mature, but it transplants easily. Plant 2—3ft (60—90cm) apart and in a sunny position or the seeds will not ripen. The plant is present on waste ground and cliff tops, usually in calcareous soil.

An erect hairy perennial growing 16—20in. (40—50cm) tall, its radical leaves pinnate; its cauline leaves ternate. It has reddish stems and bears golden-yellow scentless flowers about 2cm across. Self-fertilization of the flowers occurs in the absence of insects. It is present in open woodlands and by the wayside, preferring shade and moisture about its roots which are clove-scented and when dried were placed among clothes and vestments to impart an aromatic perfume. The clean and washed roots may be included in apple pies instead of cloves. Plants are raised from seed sown in pots or boxes in spring and set out 12in. (30cm) apart when large enough to handle. The water avens, *G. rivale*, is present in ditches and by streams and bears drooping flowers of reddish-orange nearly 1in. (2.5cm) across. In North America, the dark brown roots when dry are used as a substitute for cocoa and to make a beer.

Closely related to the dwarf or bush bean, it makes a low bush 16in. (40cm) tall with trifoliolate leaves with long stipules and pea-like flowers borne in the leaf axils. In some regions it grows erect to 6ft (2m) high. The white beans are borne 3—4 to a pod, which are formed in threes or fours. They are similar to broad beans, though shorter. Like all beans, they have a high protein content and are rich in Vitamin B; indeed soybeans are the richest protein vegetable food known. They also yield soya flour, which is sold in health food stores, and a valuable oil which has many seasoning uses (including value as a substitute for olive oil). Soybean can be cultivated under very diverse soil and moisture conditions, and for this reason as well as its high protein content, it has become an increasingly frequent crop, particularly as a food crop in overpopulated developing countries. Seeds cannot be sown until all risk of frost is past.

GLYCYRRHIZA GLABRA

LICORICE

Leguminosae

44 SE Eur, SW Asia
SW Eur, N Af, C Am

HELIANTHUS ANNUUS

SUNFLOWER

Compositae

45 Mexico, Peru
Temperate Zones

HUMULUS LUPULUS

HOP

Moraceae

46 Eur, Asia
Temperate Zones

Native of Mexico and Peru whose peoples adopted it as the emblem of the sun god (hence its name from *helios*, the sun) and carved it on the walls of Aztec temples. The Spaniards introduced it into Europe. An annual, it sends up its thick hairy stem to a height of 10 ft (3 m) and has large heart-shaped leaves. If seed is sown in spring, plants will grow about 3 ft (1 m) during each month of summer, the stem terminating in a flower 12 in. (30 cm) across and of brilliant gold, with the center "like some curious cloth wrought with a needle," this being in reference to the many tubular florets which form a cushion-like boss. It is grown commercially in southern Europe and Asia, its leaves for cattle food; its seed to make into cooking fats and margarines, for sunflower seed oil is low in cholesterol and is now recognized as a valuable health food. The oil is pale yellow and equal to olive oil for table use. The seeds yield 50 percent high-quality oil. With commercial plantations, seed is sown singly 10 in. (25 cm) apart in drills made 3 ft (90 cm) apart, but for garden culture, seed is sown under glass early in spring, one seed to a small pot, and the plants set out without root disturbance, early in summer. The stems need support as they will grow tall.

A plant of the Mediterranean and Near East, it is perennial, increasing by underground stolons or runners while the roots penetrate to a depth of 3—4 ft (1 m). It grows 4—5 ft (1.5 m) high with dark green leaves divided into pairs of narrow leaflets. From the leaf axils in midsummer arise the flower spikes, pea-like and purple-blue. Long pencil-like roots are required by the trade so it is given a deeply worked soil. It grows well in volcanic ash and in sandy soil. The roots are cut into 4 in. (10 cm) long, each with 2 "buds" or eyes, and they are planted early in spring 16 in. (40 cm) apart in the rows and just below the surface. The rows are made 3—4 ft (1 m) apart. The plants are undisturbed for 3—4 years; then they are lifted early in autumn. The soil is scooped away to enable the entire plant to be removed. They are washed and the juice extracted while fresh. The best licorice root is said to come from Spain.

A hardy perennial growing 16 ft (5 m) tall. The 3—5-lobed leaves, cordate at the base, are serrated and have a petiole as long as the blade. The flowers are greenish-yellow, the males borne in a catkin-like inflorescence, the females in the axils of the bracts to form a cylindrical spike, like a pine cone. The bracteoles bear glandular hairs which yield the gold dust lupulin, the chief ingredient in brewing beer. Plants are raised by sowing seed in a frame or in the open in shallow drills in spring. When large enough to move, plant them 3—4 ft (1 m) apart, in autumn; or propagate by root division in spring or autumn. A rich humus-laden soil is needed. Poles about 18 ft long (5 m) are placed close to the plants in spring and the plants will begin to yield heavily from their third year. The hop canes (strobiles) are picked late in summer when they turn dark brown. Commercially, they are dried in kilns before using.

HYSSOPUS OFFICINALIS

HYSSOP

Labiatae

47 S Eur, SW Asia
Temperate Zones

ILLICIUM VERUM

STAR ANISE, BADIAN

Magnoliaceae

48 SE Asia
Warm Temperate Zones

JUGLANS REGIA

WALNUT

Juglandaceae

49 SE Eur, SW Asia
Temperate Zones

JUNIPERUS COMMUNIS

JUNIPER

Cupressaceae

50 Eur, NW Af, Asia, N Am
Temperate Zones

It is a plant primarily of the Holy Land and was mentioned so often in the Bible that it was named *azob*, holy herb, from the Hebrew. An evergreen, it makes a dense bush 16 in. (40 cm) high and is hardy in all but the coldest regions but needs a sunny aspect and a light, well-drained soil. It has square stems and linear leaves and during summer bears pink, white, or purple flowers in racemes. They are attractive to bees. All parts of the plant are aromatic, but the tops of the stems contain the most flavor and perfume and this is the part used. In northern Europe it has become naturalized on old buildings. In the garden it is planted 2 ft (60 cm) apart and is propagated by seed or from cuttings removed with a "heel" in summer and rooted in sandy compost. Set out the plants the following spring. The flowers and leaves are used in soups and stews, to which they impart a sharp, aromatic taste. The leaves are also used in stuffings.

A genus of 6 trees or shrubs, native of China and Japan and the warmer parts of America. *I. verum* is evergreen with broad elliptic leaves which are poisonous; it grows 30 ft (9 m) tall. The tree bears spice-fragrant creamy-yellow red-tinted flowers in clusters, which gives the tree its name *Illicium*, meaning "allurement." They are followed by flat star-like fruits, with 8-rayed boat-shaped carpels arranged around a central disk, in appearance like a starfish. Since early times the seeds have been exported from the Chinese province of Kuang-si to use in cooking, for they are cinnamon-scented. *I. griffithii* is native of the Khansia Hills of Bengal, the seed pods having 15-rayed carpels. *I. floridanum* of the United States has lance-shaped leaves and bears purple-red flowers.

Deciduous nut-bearing trees, *J. regia* grow to 100 ft (30 m) with a trunk 9—10 ft (3 m) in circumference, covered in smooth gray bark and with dark green stalked leaves 16 in. (40 cm) long, divided into 7—11 opposite pairs. The male flowers are borne in long, drooping catkins; the female or pistillate flowers in small clusters at the end of the shoots. The walnut is not self-fertile and 2 trees must be planted together (though not too close) for reliable pollination. Walnuts take 10 years to bear fruit; of irregular shape, the nut is enclosed in a woody brown shell which is covered by an oval green husk divided longitudinally into 4 sections. The nuts will fall when ripe in autumn, when the shells are removed from the husks. The shells divide to expose a nut in each half. Plant trees not more than 3 years old, unless grown in pots, for older trees resent transplanting. Do not prune them or they will "bleed."

An evergreen tree growing 40 ft (10 m) high and of great hardiness and adaptability. It requires a chalk-laden soil to attain tree proportions, and in mountainous regions and in peaty moorland soil, grows dwarf and bushy. The small spiky awl-shaped leaves enable it to tolerate considerable warmth or intense cold, for there is a minimum of moisture loss through transpiration. All parts are fragrant. The tiny white flowers are followed by fleshy pea-like berries (fruits), really cones, and are first green, ripening to deep purple, which takes 2 years. They are used to impart their unique perfume to gin which takes its name from the plant. The tree has attractive red bark, which flakes off like that of yew, and the wood is also scented when burnt. In Scotland it is used to impart its flavor to smoked salmon. In *The Anatomy of Melancholy*, Robert Burton tells that it was used at Oxford on open fires, to sweeten the air of student's rooms.

LAURUS NOBILIS

BAY, SWEET BAY

Lauraceae

LAVANDULA SPICA

LAVENDER

Labiatae

LEPIDIUM SATIVUM

CRESS, GARDEN CRESS

Cruciferae

The Romans named it from *laudare*, to praise, for it was thought to be worthy of the highest honors and they crowned their victorious leaders and poets with chaplets made of the leaves. Its name bay is from the Anglo-Saxon meaning a crown or chaplet. An evergreen with glossy dark green lance-shaped leaves, it forms a multi-branched tree or shrub with smooth bark and grows about 20 ft (6 m) tall. The leaves emit a sweet balsamic scent when bruised and are an important part of the *bouquet garni*. The inconspicuous yellow flowers are followed by cherry-sized berries (fruits) which turn from green to black as they ripen.

Though adaptable to wide climatic variations, it is not fully hardy in colder regions where it should be grown in a tub of convenient size for moving indoors before winter, to be kept in a frost-free room or greenhouse. The plant is attractive when grown on a single stem and the head clipped into ball or square shapes. The plants are lifted outdoors in early summer when frost has vanished. In this way the fresh leaves are available all year. "Bitter and aromatic, with something of both vanilla and nutmeg" according to the description by Elizabeth David, the bay leaf imparts a fragrance more like that of a spice than an herb.

A shrubby perennial growing 2–4 ft (1 m) tall with opposite entire oblong leaves terminating to a point and downy on both sides which gives them a silver-gray appearance. The flowers, blue or violet, occasionally white or pink, are borne 6–10 in an erect spike early in summer. The flowers have a 2-lobed upper lip and a 3-lobed lower lip. *L. spica* is the Old English lavender and grows 4 ft (1 m) tall and the same across. The Grappenhall variety bears flowers of deepest lavender. *L. nana compacta* makes a dwarf hedge 12 in. (30 cm) tall and bears mauve flowers; and *alba*, a variety, bears white flowers. The twickle purple variety bears dark violet flowers and is of similar habit. These lavenders are hardy in northern Europe but *L. stoechas* is not and needs a warmer climate. The flowers have purple (instead of green) bracts which intensifies their color. Lavenders require an open, sunny situation and well-drained soil.

A quick-growing annual, native of Persia and the Near East, and cultivated all the year in most parts of the world to provide "green" for salads, especially in winter. It grows 16 in. (40 cm) tall with much-divided leaves, though for salads it is cut (as white mustard and rape) when only 3 in. (7.5 cm) tall. There is a plain-leaf variety which is of milder flavor and is more popular for salads and for garnishing. When allowed to develop, the plants bear white flowers. Seed is sown thickly outdoors in spring and summer or in a frame or a sunny window in winter. Sow in shallow boxes containing 1 in. (2.5 cm) of soil and do not cover the seeds. Or sow on flannel without soil. In a temperature of 48 °F (9 °C) cress will be ready to cut within 3 weeks of sowing. If grown with mustard, sow the cress 4–5 days earlier so that both will be ready together. (If sown on flannel, cress must be used quickly.)

LEVISTICUM OFFICINALE

LOVAGE

Umbelliferae

54 S Eur
Temperate Zones

LIPPIA CITRIODORA, ALOYSIA CITRIODORA

LEMON VERBENA

Verbenaceae

55 C + S Am
Warm Temperate Zones

MELILOTUS OFFICINALIS

MELILOT, SWEET CLOVER, KING'S CLOVER

Leguminosae

56 Eur, Asia
Temperate Zones

MELISSA OFFICINALIS

BALM, LEMON BALM

Labiatae

57 S Eur, SW Asia, N + W Af
Temperate Zones

An erect branched biennial growing 2—3 ft (60—90 cm) tall with pale green trifoliolate leaves and yellow pea-like flowers borne in one-sided racemes, the keel shorter than the wings and standard. In bloom throughout summer, the flowers are sweetly scented and the leaves and stems contain coumarin. As they dry they release the refreshing scent of new-mown hay. The flowers are followed by black one-sided hairy seed pods, containing black seeds which are also scented when dry. Seed is sown in late summer in shallow drills for the plants to bloom the following year. Thin to 16 in. (40 cm) apart.

A hairless perennial growing 3—4 ft (1 m) tall with hollow purple stems and bright green glossy leaves with broadly toothed leaflets, like those of celery and with a similar pungent smell. The yellow flowers are borne in umbels and are followed by yellow fruits, curved like those of caraway and with much of the celery flavor. The plant forms a taproot about 6 in. (15 cm) long which is also pungently scented. It grows on cliffs by the sea but under garden culture requires a rich moist soil. It is propagated from seed (which must be fresh) sown in shallow drills in spring, thinning the plants to 16 in. (40 cm) apart; or by division of the offsets in autumn. The fresh leaves are included in salads and the stems when blanched are used like celery in summer. The seeds are also used for flavoring and the plant has numerous medicinal virtues. It will die down in winter but comes into fresh growth in spring each year.

A shrubby deciduous perennial growing 6—7 ft (2 m) high and bearing its leaves in whorls of 3, the pale green narrow leaflets being 2 in. (5 cm) long and pointed. The pale lilac flowers are borne in slender spikes. In northern Europe the plant requires a warm wall to survive an average winter and even then may be cut down by frost. A light, sandy soil is necessary for its long life. Or the plants can be grown in tubs during summer and lifted indoors before winter. The crinkled leaves are harvested in late summer and after drying are rubbed down to impart their lemon flavor to stuffings. The powdered leaves may also be included in pot pourris and talcum powders. It is propagated by young shoots removed late in summer and rooted under glass. Plant out from small pots in spring. This plant is suitable to growing in a greenhouse, at a temperature of 55 °F (13 °C); the pots are then planted outside in summer.

A perennial plant of the Mediterranean countries but long naturalized in Britain and northern France, where it may have been brought by the Romans. It is present in hedgerows and open woodlands and grows 2 ft (60 cm) tall with hairy upright stems and stalked ovate leaves, deeply wrinkled and serrate, and of palest green. The flowers which appear late in summer are blush-white and borne in short-stalked axillary whorls from the upper part of the stem and leaf joints, with the calyx covered in long white hairs. All parts of the plant are deliciously lemon-scented when handled. The sweetness of balm was proverbial in olden times and all parts were used. The plant requires a cool, moist soil and is propagated from seed sown in summer in a frame, setting out the plants the following spring; or from cuttings removed in July and rooted in a sandy compost. The plant takes its name from the Latin for honey.

MENTHA PIPERITA

PEPPERMINT

Labiatae

 58 S Eur
Temperate Zones

MONARDA DIDYMA

BERGAMOT, OSWEGO TEA, BEE BALM

Labiatae

 59 E-N Am
Temperate Zones

MYRISTICA FRAGRANS

NUTMEG, MACE

Myristiceae

 60 SE Asia
Tropical + Warm Zones

Possibly a natural hybrid between *M. aquatica*, the water mint, and *M. spicata*, spearmint, peppermint grows 16 in. (40 cm) tall with opposite lanceolate leaves, serrated at the edges and purple flowers borne in a blunt terminal inflorescence. The stems are reddish-purple, and in dry weather the plant takes on a similar hue. It is widespread in ditches throughout Europe but not Scandinavia. Oil of peppermint is extracted from the plant. *M. spicata* (syn. *M. viridis*) is spearmint, the best for mint sauce. It is a hairless erect perennial growing 12 in. (30 cm) tall with brilliant green lanceolate leaves, unequally serrate, and lilac flowers borne in a spire-like inflorescence, hence its name should be spiremint. *M. aquatica* grows 3 ft (90 cm) tall, its ovate leaves downy on both sides and releasing a fruity scent when pressed. Its reddish flowers are borne in terminal whorls.

A hardy perennial growing 2–3 ft (60–90 cm) tall with square deeply grooved stems branching at the top and lance-shaped leaves with serrated edges, slightly hairy on both surfaces. The white, pink, or crimson flowers are borne in whorls at the end of the stems and have green bracts, the reflexed petals being long and narrow. They appear throughout summer. The plant takes its botanical name from that of Dr. Monardes of Seville, who published his herbal on the flora of America in 1569; and its popular name is from the scent of its foliage, which was likened to that of the bergamot orange of Spain. The plant was first collected at Oswego, near Lake Ontario, in 1744 by John Bartram, who sent seed to England. The plant requires a moist soil and increases by underground stems. It is propagated by division in winter; or from cuttings; also by seed.

It grows naturally in western New Guinea and in the Molucca and Banda Isles, the "Nutmeg" Isles of Indonesia, in volcanic ash and where it enjoys great humidity. It was introduced into Bourbon and Zanzibar and several West Indian islands, especially Jamaica. An evergreen tree growing to 30 ft (10 m) high with an undivided trunk, the large leaves are deep green and glossy and highly aromatic. The small, fragrant white flowers cluster in the axils of the leaves and are followed by golden-yellow pear-shaped fruits with a longitudinal groove on one side (like a peach) which when ripe burst open into 2 parts. The seed is enclosed by a red fleshy part known as the aril, which is the substance called mace. The seed has a thick outer shell which encloses the nutmeg which, because of the intense pressure of the aril, is deeply wrinkled. A mature female tree will bear about 2000 nuts and will bloom and ripen its fruit the whole year. It will be productive for at least 80 years. One male tree will fertilize 20 female trees. The leaves, on distillation, yield a colorless oil with a nutmeg-like odor. Oil of mace has a similar perfume.

MYRRHIS ODORATA	MYRTUS, COMMUNIS	NASTURTIUM OFFICINALE	OCIMUM BASILICUM
SWEET CICELY, SWEET FERN	MYRTLE, COMMON MYRTLE	WATERCRESS	SWEET BASIL
Umbelliferae	Myrtaceae	Cruciferae	Labiatae
61 Eur, Asia	**62** S Eur, N Af *Warm Temperate Zones*	**63** Temperate Zones	**64** Asia *Temperate Zones*

In the East it is sacred to the Hindu gods, Krishna and Vishnu, and is grown in pots in most homes, worshipped by the household. In the cooler west, it is also grown in small pots indoors for it is frost-tender. To accompany tomato dishes, it has no equal; it is grown in Italy in large quantities for this purpose. From the leaves, the French make a sauce to accompany fish, and in England the plant gave its unique sweet spicy smell to the once famous "Fetter Lane" (London) sausages. In northern Italy basil leaves, crushed or ground with fresh garlic, form the basis of *pesto* sauce.

Sweet basil is a much-

A hardy pubescent perennial growing 4–6 ft (1.5 m) tall, its stem hollowed and furrowed and with large downy pinnate leaves of palest green. The white flowers are borne in terminal umbels and are scented as are all parts of the plant, resembling myrrh. The leaves when included in salads, though spicy, taste as if they have been steeped in sugar, hence its popular names. The seeds reach 1 in. (2.5 cm) in length and have 5 prominent ribs. The unripe seeds are used in salads, and, when ripe and after being ground, to flavor cakes. From the leaves a sauce is made to accompany fish, and the candied roots are eaten as a sweetmeat. They have a warm aniseed taste. The plant requires a rich, well-drained soil and is best raised by sowing seed in spring where it is to grow, at the back of a border. In its second year, thin to 2 ft (60 cm) apart and begin using the leaves when young.

To the ancient Greeks and Romans, no plant was more highly prized, for the berries (fruits) have a pleasant aromatic taste and were used to flavor food as they are today. Pliny said that the best myrtles grew in Egypt and their gum exudations resembled myrrh, hence the plant's name. It forms a large bush 6–8 ft (2–2.5 m) tall with shining evergreen box-like leaves and in July bears pure white flowers of powerful scent in the axils of the leaves. They have protruding golden stamens. The leaves, too, are scented and retain their fragrance when dried. The essential oil is contained in pellucid dots (cells) embedded in the leaf. From the leaves and flowers is distilled a perfumed water, eau d'Ange. The fruits are yellow and large and are harvested at the end of summer. Like the flowers, they have a sweet, aromatic taste. The wood is also fragrant. There is a pretty small-leaf form called Jenny Reitenbach.

A hardy aquatic perennial growing about 8 in. (20 cm) tall with hollow stems and bright green pinnate leaves. The small white flowers which appear throughout summer are followed by cylindrical seed pods, and the plant increases by underground stems. It has been appreciated by man since earliest times. It is so rich in iron that the leaves and stems turn purple-brown if exposed to the air for too long before consuming. It is a blood purifier as well as having many culinary uses. It requires slow-running water to grow and the plants are set out 4 in. (10 cm) apart. They need 4 in (10 cm) of water over them. Use rooted offsets to make up a bed; early summer is the correct time to do so. The plants will then become established before winter. The beds will crop all year in a mild winter climate; otherwise cover the beds with polythene frames placed 12 in. (30 cm) above the plants to exclude frost.

OLIVE

OLEA EUROPAEA

OLIVE

Oleaceae

65 S Eur, N Af, SW Asia
S Af, W-N Am, Aus

ORIGANUM MAJORANA

**SWEET MARJORAM,
KNOTTED MARJORAM**

Labiatae

66 S Eur, W Asia, N Af
Warm Temperate Zones

ORIGANUM VULGARE

**OREGANO,
WILD MARJORAM**

Labiatae

67 Eur, C + N Asia
N Am

branched annual growing 16 in. (40 cm) tall with reddish-green ovate leaves obscurely toothed and bearing small white flowers in leafy clusters. The variety dark opal has bronze leaves. *O. minimum* is the bush basil which makes a small bushy plant 6 in. (15 cm) tall and if grown outdoors is used as an edging to the herb garden. Its taste is practically identical with that of the larger plant. Seed is sown under glass early in spring, the seedlings being moved to small pots in which they are grown or planted outside early in summer. Allow 10 in. (25 cm) between plants of sweet basil; 6 in. (15 cm) between bush basil.

A small evergreen tree growing about 20 ft (6 m) tall with twiggy branches clothed in lanceolate leaves about 2 in. (5 cm) long, pale green above, silver on the underside. The small creamy-white flowers appear in the leaf axils and are followed by olive-green drupes (the fruits) which change to reddish-purple as they ripen. The fruits contain a single seed. The flesh of the drupe contains the oil which is extracted by pressure of the ripe fruit. The trees begin to crop in their second year and continue to grow slowly for 200 or more years, the weight of crop increasing each year. The finest oil, greenish-yellow, known as "virginal oil," is that obtained from the first crushing of the fruits. Further crushings follow, to produce oil of inferior quality. The unripe fruits are also used. The trees have pale gray bark and the wood can be polished so that it is used in cabinet making.

A perennial which in northerly climes is treated as a biennial, seed being sown in boxes in April, for it is long in germinating and the plants are wintered under glass to be set out the following spring 8 in. (20 cm) apart in a sunny position. The plant grows about 16 in. (40 cm) tall with downy oblong ovate leaves. Early in summer it bears white or purple flowers in terminal spikes. In hot dry weather, the plants secrete an essential oil from the stems which leaves on them a deposit of crystalline matter with a camphor-like smell. The flowering tips of the young plants are the most fragrant and make an ideal seasoning for sausage meat and for stuffings. The plant also has valuable medicinal qualities. Pot marjoram is *Origanum onites*. It is a perennial undershrub, growing 12 in. (30 cm) tall, and is propagated by cuttings. Its ovate serrate leaves are unstalked; its white flowers borne in terminal clusters.

A hardy perennial growing 16—20 in. (40—50 cm) tall with square stems and broadly ovate, short-stalked opposite leaves, covered in down and with oil glands. The rosy-mauve flowers are borne in crowded terminal cymes. They have reddish bracts which are longer than the calyx and appear late in summer. It is present on hilly pastures (downland) growing in calcareous soils. Its name is from the Greek words *oros* and *ganos*, "joy of the mountain." There is a variety with variegated leaves and one with golden leaves. The flowering tops are used fresh or dry (oregano) for stuffings and seasonings while the leaves are included in salads. Bees visit the flowers of all the marjorams during summer. Plants are raised from seed or from cuttings, removed in summer, and rooted in sandy compost. When rooted, move to small pots and plant out the following spring. They require a well-drained calcareous soil.

PAPAVER RHOEAS

POPPY, CORN
POPPY, FIELD POPPY

Papaveraceae

68 C + S Eur, C Asia
Temperate Zones

PELARGONIUM CAPITATUM

SCENTED-LEAF GERANIUM

Geraniaceae

69 S Af
Warm Temperate Zones

PETROSELINUM CRISPUM

PARSLEY

Umbelliferae

70 C + S Eur, N Af, SW Asia
Temperate Zones

An annual of cornfields and waste ground, growing to 20 in. (50 cm) tall with branched hairy stems and 1–2-pinnately cut leaves, the ascending lobes having a bristle at the tips. The brilliant red flowers, about 3 in. (7.5 cm) across, are shaded with purple at the base and appear throughout summer. They are followed by large globular fruits (capsules) which open by means of small valves, to release the seeds. The small seeds are blackish-purple; dried, they are used in baking and for their oil. Seed is sown thinly in spring in shallow drills or in circles where the plants are to bloom, and the seed capsules are removed.

A branched woody subshrub with alternate bright green 3–5-lobed leaves, cordate at the base and toothed at the margins, the peduncles longer than the leaves and pink flowers veined with purple borne on short pedicels. The stems and leaves are covered in glandular hairs and when pressed release a rose-like perfume which provides a basis for rose geranium, an adulterant of the expensive attar of rose. There are numerous scented-leaf varieties. *P. clorinda* has leaves smelling of eucalyptus and bears large flowers of orange-pink; *P. tomentosum* is peppermint-scented and makes a delicious mint sauce. Its stems and leaves are densely covered in hairs as protection against strong sunlight and transpiration of moisture. These geraniums make admirable pot plants, being always in leaf and bloom and are attractive when used for summer bedding. They require a sunny situation and a light porous soil.

A biennial with perennial tendencies, it takes its botanical name from *petra*, a rock, for this is where it grows naturally but in the garden it requires a rich deep loam. It grows 10–12 in. (25–30 cm) tall with a long taproot and bright green 3-pinnate leaves which form a rosette. One variety of parsley is plain-leaved; it is the more flavorful. The curly-leaved is more favored for decorative garnishing. There are three other principal varieties which are seldom found on the market today. These crimped leaves retain their color and freshness for several days after cutting. If seed is sown in spring in

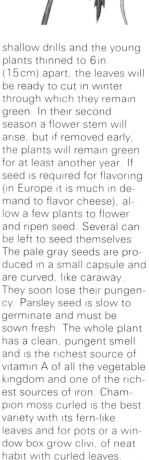

shallow drills and the young plants thinned to 6 in. (15 cm) apart, the leaves will be ready to cut in winter through which they remain green. In their second season a flower stem will arise, but if removed early, the plants will remain green for at least another year. If seed is required for flavoring (in Europe it is much in demand to flavor cheese), allow a few plants to flower and ripen seed. Several can be left to seed themselves. The pale gray seeds are produced in a small capsule and are curved, like caraway. They soon lose their pungency. Parsley seed is slow to germinate and must be sown fresh. The whole plant has a clean, pungent smell and is the richest source of vitamin A of all the vegetable kingdom and one of the richest sources of iron. Champion moss curled is the best variety with its fern-like leaves and for pots or a window box grow clivi, of neat habit with curled leaves.

PHYTOLACCA AMERICANA

POKE, POKE WEED

Phytolaccaceae

71 SE-N Am
Warm Temperate Zones

PIMENTA OFFICINALIS

ALLSPICE

Myrtaceae

72 S Am, West Indies
*Tropical Zones
of the New World*

PIMPINELLA ANISUM

ANISE, ANISEED

Umbelliferae

73 SW Asia, N Af
Warm Temperate Zones

PIMPINELLA SAXIFRAGA

BURNET, BURNET SAXI-FRAGE, BLACK CARAWAY

Umbelliferae

74 S Eur, C + W Asia
N Am

It should not be confused with the salad burnet which is of the Rosaceae order, though the burnet saxifrage has similar uses. It grows 20 in. (45 cm) tall, usually in dry chalky pastures, and is a branched perennial with solid ridged stems and leaves arising from the base which are divided into 5 or more pairs of toothed un-stalked 2-pinnate leaflets. The white flowers, in terminal umbels, appear in mid-summer and are followed by small, black shiny round fruits. The thick root grows to 8 in. (20 cm) in length. The leaves are mild and used in salads. Seed is sown in April and the young plants moved in autumn.

A hardy perennial growing to 10 ft (3 m) high with large fleshy poisonous roots and erect purple hollow stems branching at the top. The stems are removed in spring when 6 in. (15 cm) tall and cooked and served with melted butter. The stalked leaves are about 6 in. (15 cm) long with a prom-inent midrib and waved edges and appear first dark green, changing to purple late in summer. The flowers, which have 10 stamens and no corolla, are borne in ter-minal spikes on leafless stems and are followed by large purple fruits, like black-berries, made up of 10 unit-ed carpels and filled with red-dish-purple juice. They are eaten by poultry and pigeons but, like the roots, contain purgatives and may cause death if eaten in quantity. The plants, which should be set 3 ft (90 cm) apart, grow well in deep loam and in par-tial shade and are propagat-ed by root division in au-tumn.

Its warm, aromatic flavor and scent are due to .eugenol, also the principal ingredient of cloves, and it is to the New World as the clove tree is to the Old. Its odor, however, is more a mixture of clove, cinnamon, and nutmeg, hence its name allspice. An evergreen tree, it grows 35 ft (10 m) tall, its slender trunk covered in gray aromatic bark and with op-posite shortly stalked leaves like those of bay laurel. They are dark green with a prom-inent midrib and with glan-dular dots (cells) on the underside which release an aromatic perfume when pressed. The greenish-white flowers are produced in panicles at the ends of the branches, their fragrance being almost overpowering. The fruit is a shining suc-culent berry, first green, then ripening to dark purple and containing 2 flat pea-size seeds. They are gather-ed by hand and dried until the seeds rattle in the ber-ries.

An annual, only half-hardy in northern Europe and North America, where it is grown for flavoring liqueurs but re-quires long hours of sun-shine to ripen its seeds. The best anise comes from Egypt and the Near East. It grows 16—20 in. (40—50 cm) tall with finely serrated upper leaves and long stalked heart-shaped lower leaves. The flowers are white, borne in large rayed double um-bels. The fruit is small and round, with the peculiar sweet aniseed smell. This is due to the presence of anisic aldehyde and is also present in the leaves. The plant is mentioned in St. Matthew's Gospel, for it was included in the Mosaic Law concern-ing tithes. A single seed was enclosed in layers of hard sugar which took an hour or more to suck through. Seed is sown in spring in shallow drills where the plants are to mature, thinning to 10 in. (25 cm) apart. An open situ-ation is necessary.

A perennial climbing plant which will attain a height of about 20ft (6m) where growing in open forests; in commercial plantations, growth is restricted to about half that height. The plant has a woody stem and dark green ovate leaves with short footstalks. The small white flowers are bisexual and arranged in short spikes. They are followed by red globular berries which first form when the plants are 4 years old; they continue to crop for about 10 years. The red berries are removed when almost ripe and dried on mats in the sun. They are then ground down, the "hot" aromatic powder being dark brown. Malabar and Penang produce the best pepper, which was known to the Greeks of ancient Athens and highly prized as a condiment. White pepper is obtained from the same plant and is produced by immersing the berries in water for several weeks before drying. It is less pungent than black pepper. The natives make use of the old roots to extract a tonic drink as with the roots of *P. methysticum*, a species native to Polynesia known as kava bush.

Native of California where it is found at altitudes of up to 4000ft (1200m) and grows 90—100ft (30m) tall with a diameter of 3—4ft (1m). Widely branching, it has glaucous-blue twisted leaves 10in. (25cm) long and coffee-brown cones 6—8in. (15—20cm) long. The seeds (nuts) from the cones are sweet and juicy and since early times were prized by the native Indian peoples for their nutritional value. It is necessary to roast the cones over a low fire before they open and release the nuts. *P. sylvestris* is the European counterpart of *P. edulis*. Known as the Scots pine, it grows 80—90ft (almost 30m) tall with reddish-brown bark and twisted dark green leaves. The small stalked cones are borne in clusters and have square ridged scales. Completely hardy, the Scots pine is present almost to the Arctic Circle and grows in rocky ground often almost devoid of soil.

A perennial of climbing habit, bearing its flowers in symbodial spikes of 20 or more. The dark green leaves with short stipules have prominent veins and are about 2in. (5cm) long, terminating to a point. The fruit, a small round drupe or berry containing up to 20 percent volatile oil, is harvested not quite fully ripe and dried and ground so that it resembles allspice. The plant is native of Malaya and the East Indies and is grown in coffee and coconut plantations, usually against the trees for support because it enjoys semishaded conditions. *Piper methysticum*, of Southeast Asia and Polynesia, is also used for flavoring, but in this case it is the dried root that is used. Known as kava bush, the plant is perennial and makes a dense bush about 10—12 ft (3—4 m) tall.

PISTACIA VERA

PISTACHIO, GREEN ALMOND

Anarcardiaceae

78 | S Eur, W Asia
Warm Temperate Zones

PORTULACA OLERACEA

PURSLANE

Portulacae

79 | S Asia
Warm Temperate Zones

POTERIUM SANGUISORBA

SALAD BURNET

Rosaceae

80 | N Eur, N Asia
Temperate Zones

PRUNUS AMYGDALUS

ALMOND

Rosaceae

81 | C Asia, N Af
Warm Temperate Zones

A large genus of deciduous trees which includes cherry, plum, peach, and apricot. The almond is of the sub-genus *Amygdalus* and grows 20ft (6m) tall with smooth bark and broad lanceolate saw-edged leaves. The pink flowers appear early in spring before the leaves and on wood formed the previous year. The oval plum-like fruits are pale green tinted with red and contain a single deeply pitted yellow shell (the endocarp) which encloses the nut. When the fruit ripens, the outer covering opens to release the nut which is pointed at one end, round at the other, and covered in a thin brown tunic.

A genus of some 10 mostly deciduous trees native to the Canary Isles, islands of the Mediterranean, and the southwestern United States, growing in sandy soil close to the sea. Several species yield resins and oils, while *Pistacia vera* is grown for its edible seeds. It is a spreading, deciduous tree which attains a height and spread of 20—25ft (6—8m). Leaflets grow in 1—5 pairs, with pinnately compound leaves. A reddish-shelled fruit is borne containing a green or yellow edible seed. Long, hot, relatively dry summers are favorable, with rather cold winters for necessary chilling. Propagation is by budding on seedling rootstocks. It will require 4—5 years for the trees to bear fruit. The plant can be pruned to keep it small in the garden. The pistachio kernels, which contain 20 percent protein and 40 percent oil, are valuable foods. The nuts are removed, dehusked, placed in water, and left in the sun for drying.

An annual growing 6 in. (15 cm) tall, native of India and only half-hardy in cooler climes. A smooth spreading, fleshy herb with nearly opposite oblong leaves and bearing almost stalkless golden-yellow flowers with 4—6 petals which appear in mid-summer. It reached Britain and northern Europe early in the fifteenth century. The leaves are a welcome addition to summer salads, after removal of the stalks; with sorrel, they impart a sharp taste to broths and stews. Giles Rose, cook to Charles II of England, always included the leaves in salads he prepared for the king. The plant is used as an edging, seed being sown in spring and the plants thinned to 4 in. (10 cm) apart. Or sow in boxes indoors and plant out early in summer in a sunny position and in a well-drained soil. Golden purslane has yellowish-green leaves. In northern Europe, the young leaves are pickled to serve with cold meats.

An erect perennial growing 16 in. (40 cm) tall, the pinnate leaves divided into 4—12 opposite oval leaflets, serrate at the edges, and with a mild cucumber taste and smell. William Turner in the *New Herbal* (1543) described the leaves as "like the wings of little birds, setteth out when they intended to fly." The tiny purple-green flowers are borne in a capitate cyme. The upper female flowers forming red brush-like stigmas and the lower males their yellow stamens. Pollination is by wind agency. The flower heads have prickly wings to the calyx tube. The plant is present on downlands, growing in calcareous soils, and remains green all winter, being a valuable winter food for sheep. Seed is sown in boxes in spring, and the young plants are set out in summer in a well-drained soil. Begin to use the leaves in their second year. The lesser burnet is an umbellifer and in no way connected with this plant.

51

ROSMARINUS OFFICINALIS

ROSEMARY

Labiatae

82 S Eur, SW Asia, N Af
Warm Temperate Zones

An evergreen shrubby perennial; though native of the Mediterranean coastline and its islands, it possesses sufficient hardiness to survive the intense cold of a northern winter. It grows 6—7ft (2m) tall and enjoys a sunny wall. It has stalkless linear leaves, hoary on the underside, and its aromatic essential oil is stored in goblet-shaped cells immediately below the surface so that the scent is released with the slightest breeze or by one's clothes brushing against it. When there was no dry cleaning, rosemary bushes were grown near the entrance door of most houses so that all who entered would brush against the plant. The oil is used today in making perfume. The pale blue flowers appear in short axillary cymes early in spring and are much visited by bees. It takes its name from *ros marinus,* dew of the sea, for it grows best near the sea, in light calcareous soils and in full sun. The flavor of rosemary, which suggests incense to some, is fairly strong; discretion is advisable in its use for flavoring. The flowers make a pleasant addition to early salads, and a sprig (shoot) stuck into meat for roasting will impart its aromatic flavor. The plant has numerous medicinal uses and is propagated from seed or by cuttings. Plant in spring 3—4ft (1m) apart.

RUMEX ACETOSA, RUMEX SCUTATUS

SORREL, FRENCH SORREL

Polygonaceae

83 Eur, Asia
Temperate Zones

A tufted hardy perennial growing 12—16 in. (30—40 cm) tall with arrow-shaped leaves, the lower shortly stalked, the upper stem-clasping. The flowers are borne in spikes and are reddish-green, resembling those of the closely related rhubarb and dock. They are followed by hard, flat fruits. The plant is widespread on mountainous slopes and on wasteland and has been used in salads and as a substitute for spinach since early times. John Evelyn thought "it gave so grateful a quickness to a salad that it should never be omitted." The French sorrel, *R. scutatus,* is the best form. From the leaves a "green" sauce is made to serve with duck. But the leaves contain oxalic acid and should be used sparingly. Seed is sown in spring in shallow drills, thinning the plants to 6 in. (15 cm) apart. If not allowed to seed, the plants will remain productive for many years.

RUTA GRAVEOLENS

RUE, HERB-OF-GRACE

Rutaceae

84 S Eur
Warm Temperate Zones

A glaucous aromatic woody perennial growing 2ft (60cm) tall and present on limestone cliffs. Its leaves, of metallic blue-green, are divided into oblong obovate segments. The flowers are greenish-yellow with curved petals. It is a plant of considerable hardiness, retaining its leaves through winter in northern Europe and Asia. The leaves are rich in mineral salts and contain oil glands. When pressed, they release a pungent smell but with undertones of orange, for it is of the same plant order. Rue enjoys a calcareous soil and an open, sunny position. It is readily raised from seed sown in spring in shallow drills, thinning or planting out the seedlings to 20in. (50cm) apart; or propagate by cuttings of the half-ripened wood removed in summer and inserted in sandy compost. There is an attractive variegated leaf form and the variety Jackman's blue has the bluest foliage of all plants.

SALVIA OFFICINALIS

SAGE

Labiatae

85 S Eur
Temperate Zones

An evergreen of shrubby habit growing to 20 in. (50 cm) tall, with square stems as if covered in down and wrinkled oval gray-green leaves. The plant has, since earliest times, been reputed to give long life to those who ate it and takes its name from *salvia*, salvation. The purple irregular 2-lipped flowers appear in the axils of the leaves during late summer. The red-stemmed variety, *purpurea* is a handsome garden plant, the leaves also being shot with crimson; and *aurea* has golden leaves. *S. rutilans*, the pineapple sage, is more tender but is one of the most delicious of all herbs, its leaves having the smell and taste of ripe pineapples. It is propagated by cuttings but *S. officinalis* will also grow readily from seed sown in spring. Set out the plants 2 ft (60 cm) apart in a sunny position and in a well-drained calcareous soil. The plants may lose their leaves in a cold winter but will grow them again in spring.

SAMBUCUS NIGRA

ELDER, BLACK ELDER

Caprifoliaceae

86 Eur
W Asia, N Am

A deciduous shrub of considerable hardiness with which there are more superstitions and more uses than any other plant. It grows in any soil, in hedgerows, and on waste ground, reaching a height of 12–15 ft (4 m) with deeply furrowed pale gray bark that has a rather sharp smell. The dark green leaves have the same unpleasant smell. They are divided into 5 leaflets with saw-like, but not sharp, edges. The small creamy-white flowers are borne in flat-topped cymes and, when newly open (before fertilization) and warmed by the sun, emit a powerful musky smell which is retained after cutting. Pear growers in France place the fruits on layers of elder flowers to complete their ripening so that the fruits take on a muscatel perfume. The plant has hollow stems which were used to make musical instruments. The small juicy berries are first green, then red, before turning jet black when they are gathered for flavoring.

SATUREJA HORTENSIS, SATUREJA MONTANA

SUMMER SAVORY, WINTER SAVORY

Labiatae

87 S Eur
Warm Temperate Zones

Summer savory, *S. hortensis*, is an annual growing about 8 in. (20 cm) tall with branching stems and downy oblong linear leaves with short stalks; its pale lilac flowers are borne in clusters. It is present on cliffs and downlands, growing in calcareous soils, and is readily raised from seed sown in spring in shallow drills. Thin to 6 in. (15 cm) apart. If the plants are cut back in midsummer and the stems hung up to dry, there will be another cutting to make in autumn. The first growth will be ready to accompany broad beans, to which it imparts an aromatic flavor. *S. montana* is the winter savory, a perennial of spreading habit, growing 12 in. (30 cm) tall, its oblong leaves terminating to a point and bearing purple-pink flowers in loose racemes. The dried leaves are used with sage and thyme to make stuffings and used fresh to make a "butter" to serve with meat or fish. The plant remains green through winter and makes a pleasing edging to the herb garden. Propagate from cuttings or by root division in spring, planting 10 in. (25 cm) apart in sandy soil and in an open situation. If the plant is kept cut back, new growth will continually appear. There is not a great deal of difference in the taste of summer savory and winter savory.

SEDUM REFLEXUM

STONECROP SEDUM

Crassulaceae

 88 C + S Eur, W Asia

SESAMUM INDICUM

SESAME

Pedaliaceae

89 S Asia, C Af
*Tropical Zones
of the Old World*

TAMARINDUS INDICA

TAMARIND

Leguminosae

90 S Asia, C Af
Tropical Zones

TANACETUM VULGARE

TANSY

Compositae

 91 Eur, W Asia
N Am

A succulent evergreen with trailing stems and leaves arranged in 6—7 rows which are awl-shaped and swollen at the base. From the trailing stems, shoots arising to a height of about 10in. (25cm) bear the flowers. They are bright yellow with reflexed petals and are borne in terminal cymes. The stem leaves also have reflexed tips. It is a plant of rocky outcrops and is found on old walls; hence both its botanical and popular names are from the Latin, *sedere*, to sit on. The stonecrops require a sunny situation and a well-drained soil. Propagation is from pieces of the root. Other varieties include *S. cristatum*, coxcomb sedum.

An annual herb growing 3—4ft (1m) tall with spirally arranged lance-shaped leaves and pinkish-white flowers borne in the leaf axils. The fruit is a capsule provided with hooks, the wedge-shaped seed being surrounded with endosperm. The seeds contain oil and are whitish-brown and shiny. They have a nutty flavor and are widely used in countries of southeastern Europe and the Near East, to sprinkle over bread after baking. Ground sesame seeds are the basis of *halva*, a popular Near Eastern candy, and of *tahina*, a creamy paste used to flavor certain dishes and as a kind of dip. The seeds were exported from central Africa in early times and may have reached Europe following the Roman occupation of North Africa, for sesame seed was in great demand in ancient Rome. The oil extracted from the seed also has culinary uses and is an ingredient in the production of margarine.

A deciduous tree growing to 35ft (10m) high with pale gray bark and alternate leaves divided into 12—15 pairs of pale green leaflets. The scented reddish-purple pea-like flowers are borne in terminal racemes, the upper sepals and the 3 fertile stamens united. The seeds are borne in pendulous curved pods and are encased in pulp. The East Indian tama rinds number 6—12 seeds to a pod and are black after removal of the smooth brown tunic, which is done before the seed is dried and marketed. West Indian tamarinds have shorter pods containing 3—4 seeds. The ground seed is used in curry powders and to make chutneys, while the leaves yield a yellow dye. The pulp of the seed pods is used in cases of dysentery.

An erect hardy perennial growing 3—4ft (1m) tall with branched angular stems and dark green fern-like leaves divided into numerous pinnatifid leaflets with serrate edges which release a powerful balsamic smell when handled. This is due to the essential oil stored in minute glandular cells in the leaves. The tiny button-like flowers, which appear late in summer, have yellow disk florets and are borne in flat-topped terminal heads. Ray florets are absent. It takes its name from the Greek *athanasia*, immortality (for it remains long in bloom). The plant has a creeping rootstock and is propagated by lifting and dividing the roots in winter. It requires a well-drained soil and sunny position. Plant 20in. (50cm) apart. It is also grown from seed. The form *T. foliis crispis* is an attractive garden plant of dwarf bushy habit, used for summer bedding in Victorian times, its fern-like leaves for garnishing.

TARAXACUM OFFICINALE

DANDELION, BLOWBALL

Compositae

92 Temperate Zones

THEOBROMA CACAO

CACAO, COCOA, CHOCOLATE

Steruliaceae

93 S Am, Jamaica
*Tropical Zones
of the New World*

THYMUS VULGARIS

THYME, GARDEN THYME

Labiatae

94 S Eur
Warm Temperate Zones

A hardy perennial common everywhere, but an obnoxious garden weed unless controlled and so its culture should be confined to waste ground. The dark green lobed leaves arise from the long, fleshy root and have the lobes or teeth pointing backward. The flower stalks are hollow and leafless while the flowers are borne singly and are of brilliant gold. To make plenty of leaf, grow the plants in rich soil. In spring, sow seed singly, 2 in. (5 cm) apart in circles of 16 in. (40 cm) diameter, and 1 year later cover the plants with a large earthenware pot when they begin to make growth; this will blanch the leaves, reducing bitterness.

Its name means "food of the gods" and its seeds provide cocoa and chocolate. The tree grows 12—14 ft (4 m) tall with dark brown bark and lanceolate pale green leaves. The red flowers are produced all year, as are the fruits that follow them. The large reddish-yellow fruits are divided into 5 chambers, each of which contains a double row of large flattish seeds (beans) pointed at one end. It is usual to harvest the crop 3 or 4 times a year; the pods are then opened and the seeds left to dry in the sun. The beans contain about 50 percent of fat which is removed. The beans are mixed with sugar, roasted, and then ground to produce cocoa. When the fat is retained, the product is chocolate. The trees grow better in semishade and are usually under-planted as companions to taller trees grown for their commercial crop, thus obtaining two crops from the same ground.

An evergreen shrublet known as garden thyme, it grows 10 in. (25 cm) tall, with small oblong ovate leaves, dark green above, gray on the underside, and purple flowers borne in conical clusters. It is a plant of mountainous slopes and has been appreciated for its medicinal and culinary qualities since earliest times, being in demand for stuffing the richer meats. Thyme grows in light calcareous soil and in dry, sunny conditions, and there are many well-known varieties. The silver posie variety has rose-pink stems and leaves splashed with silver, while *aureum* has golden leaves. *T. citriodorus* is the lemon-scented thyme, the one most frequently cultivated and used in cooking, after *T. vulgaris*, while *T. nitidus* has narrower foliage and a pungent incense-like scent. *T. herba barona* is the baron-of-beef thyme for it was used to accompany beef when roasting, to which it imparts a distinctive

caraway flavor. *T. serpyllum* is the mountain thyme, a plant of almost prostrate habit found as far north as the Arctic Circle of which there are several varieties. It forms a mat of crimson flowers, borne in terminal heads. This wild thyme differs enough from the cultivated variety so that the French, who call the latter *thym*, give wild thyme a separate name, *serpolet*, in recognition of the difference. Its flavor has been described as "more concentrated and zestful" than that of its tamed cousin. The variety *alba* bears white flowers and *lanuginosa* is entirely covered in white hairs as if frosted. *T. fragrantissimus* has orange-scented leaves and its hybrid, lemon curd, is lemon-scented. These thymes are propagated from cuttings removed in summer and rooted in sandy com-

post. Move to small pots when rooted and plant out in spring in a well-drained soil. Thymes resent root disturbance and should be planted from pots.

TRIGONELLA FOENUM-GRAECUM

FENUGREEK, BIRD'S-FOOT

Leguminosae

95 SW Asia
Warm Temperate Zones

TROPAEOLUM MAJUS

NASTURTIUM, INDIAN CRESS

Cruciferae

96 S Am
Torrid + Temperate Zones

TUBER MELANOSPORUM

TRUFFLE

97 C Eur

A hairless annual growing 6 in. (15 cm) tall with stalked trefoil leaves, the leaflets spoon-shaped and pungent when handled. The pale pink pea-like flowers are borne June—July in the leaf axils and are followed by curved pods containing small brown oblong seeds. The seeds and leaves give off a celery-like smell. The seeds are sprouted in water or grown on damp flannel and, when 4 in. (10 cm) high, are cut and included in salads. The dried and ground seeds are included in curry powders and used to make condition powders for cattle. From its smell of newly mown hay, due to the presence of coumarin, the ancients named it *foenum-graecum* and would mix it with grass to dry for winter keep. The plant also has numerous medicinal uses. Seed is sown in shallow drills in spring, thinning the plants to 4 in. (10 cm) apart. It requires a well-drained soil and an open situation.

Of the same family as watercress, its leaves are equally rich in iron and sulfur and both leaves and flowers give a pleasant bitterness to salads. Native of Chile and Peru, it takes its botanical name from *tropaeolum*, a trophy, from the resemblance of the leaves to a shield and of the long spurred flowers to a Greek warrior's helmet. A trailing annual with round peltate leaves and bearing showy flowers of yellow, red, or orange. The 5 sepals unite at the base with the upper, forming a long free spur. In bloom throughout summer and autumn, the flowers are followed by large succulent deeply grooved seeds which are used as a substitute for capers. The plant requires an open, sunny situation but will grow in any soil and is decorative in a window box or hanging basket. Seed is sown in pots or boxes in spring, the plants being set out early in summer; or sow outdoors 10 in. (25 cm) apart.

Forms of *T. melanosporum* are among the most expensive and gastronomically appreciated members of the vegetable kingdom and grow underground in total darkness. Because of this, it is necessary for trained dogs to seek them out, drawn to them by their unusual smell. They are found mostly in deciduous woodlands of central Europe, and around the Piedmont district of northern Italy. The collection of truffles has often been in the same family for generations and even pigs have been trained to seek them out, burrowing into the leafy ground with their snouts and unearthing them. In Ireland, they are known as pignuts, the knobbly tubers often being uncovered when bogland is plowed. Strictly speaking, the species cited above is the black truffle or Périgord truffle, universally conceded to be the best, but the black truffles of Umbria, Italy, can give them a close race; it seems probable that they belong to the same species. *T. brumale*, the winter truffle, is a notch below, and *T. aestivus*, the summer truffle, found in Great Britain, several notches below. Several species of truffle are found in the United States, but they are hardly worth eating. The white truffle of Italy's Piedmont, *T. magnotum*, is very different.

VANILLA PLANIFOLIA

VANILLA

Orchidaceae

98 S Am
Tropical Zones

VIOLA ODORATA

VIOLET, SWEET VIOLET

Violaceae

99 S Eur
Temperate Zones

ZINGIBER OFFICINALIS

GINGER

Zingiberaceae

100 S Asia
Torrid Zones

A climbing epiphytic perennial of tropical forests where the plants pull themselves up tall trees by their aerial roots to reach the sunlight. Commercially, they are grown against posts and their climbing is restricted. The leaves are thick and fleshy and grow 10 in. (25 cm) long, while the yellowish-green flowers are borne in a dense inflorescence. They are followed by pods about 8 in. (20 cm) long which contain the beans from which vanilla extract is obtained by fermentation. Much used in perfumery and cooking, the odoriferous principle is vanillin. The fragrance is a stimulant to the mental system and was first used as a perfume by Francois Coty in his L'Aimant perfume. The pods resemble those of pole beans and are imported in bundles of 50 or more. A plant will begin to bear pods in its fourth year and continue to do so for 50 years. They are gathered in autumn just before fully ripe.

A perennial and the only species with scented flowers. It has a short rootstock and forms long runners (underground stems) which root at the leaf nodes. They can be detached and re-planted into moist soil to make a new bed. The stalked leaves are heart-shaped with glandular stipules; the flowers, white or purple-blue, are borne on leafless stems. The flowers are spurred, with 4 upper oblong petals and 2 side petals with or without a tuft of hairs. In bloom in spring, violet grows in open woodlands and in hedgerows, in semishade and in a moist soil. The plant was so highly regarded by the ancient Greeks that it became the symbol of Athens. The flowers are candied and used for sweetening, and are included in salads. They have numerous medicinal uses too. The plants were grown in pots on window sills in the shade, for their perfume counteracted the musty smells of medieval houses.

Native of China, India, and Southeast Asia, it is also cultivated in Jamaica and Queensland. It has a creeping rhizomatous rootstock from which arise 4—5 ft leafy stems (1.5 m) tall, the stems being enclosed in the leaf sheaths. The flowers are yellow and borne in a cone-like spike. Pieces of root about 2 in. (5 cm) long are planted in March, 4 in. (10 cm) deep and 10 in. (25 cm) apart. The stems die back the following March and the roots are lifted before they put out new shoots. They are then soft and succulent. One acre will yield about 4000 pounds (2000 kilos). The roots are washed and scraped and then dried in the sun. This is known as "white" or "uncoated" ginger. One root will produce about 8 tubers. As Shakespeare said, a piece of dried ginger was and still is known as a "race." The pale yellow Jamaican product is considered the best, for the roots have been scraped of their epidermis. Chinese ginger is usually the tuberous root of *Lapinia officinale*. If ginger is left too long in the ground it becomes fibrous, which is detrimental to its quality. The best ginger cuts clean and bright when it reaches the kitchen. Although some of the finest ginger is produced in Jamaica, the New World has no native varieties.

Medieval herb gardens were extensively planted, farmed, and gardened for medicinal, culinary, and aromatic purposes, as well as for their beauty. Herbs played a particularly important role in the preparation and seasoning of food and drink. Pictured above is such an herb garden from Brunschwig's *Liber de Arte Distillandi* (Strasbourg, Grüninger, 1500).

Growing and Processing

ROY GENDERS

Reference Section II

A tabulation of the 100 basic herb and spice plants, in which can be found classification data along with guidelines on propagation, planting or sowing, flowering, harvesting, and preservation. In specifying the parts of each plant that are used in seasoning, this section uses the following symbols:

 fruit / berry / cone

 leaf

 flower

 bud

 nut / bean

 bark

 seeds

 stem / shoots

 rootstock and tuber

 roots

bulb / clove

Growing herbs and spices might seem a purely utilitarian pursuit, which leaves no scope for artistry. But consider the herb garden. Its primary purpose may be to provide seasoners for the kitchen—that is, to cater to the aesthetic component of the sense of taste; but the herb gardener cultivates at the same time both the plant and the aesthetic elements proper to it. He arranges his plants in pleasing patterns, according to their respective heights, to the aspect of their foliage, to the colors of their flowers: he is appealing to the aesthetic component of the sense of sight. He does not neglect either one of the most subtle refinements of all: he is attentive to the fragrance of his plants, the aesthetic component of the sense of smell. The person who grows seasoners, like the cook, is practicing an art.

For the home gardener desiring to raise his own herbs or spices, the following pages offer a summary of our 100 selected plants. Roy Genders' chart offers a quick survey of the life cycle of each plant, from propagation and planting, to flowering, harvesting, and the preservation of the natural seasoners. These are of course norms and generalizations, rather than complete, exhaustive instructions. This section proposes an overview, for convenient classification of the plants. It is meant to be complemented by the Plant Lexicon and the chapter on gardening, the two sections immediately preceding, which contain advice on necessary climatic conditions for each plant and specific instructions for its cultivation, as well as a wealth of general background information. –*Ed.*

Few gardeners will be constructing herbal plots on the regal scale illustrated in this eighteenth-century German scene. But whether one is planting herbs in an outdoor garden, or simply in a windowbox or hanging basket, there is no escaping the need for planning and timing. By consulting the reference chart on the following pages, read-ers can quickly select plants of varying heights and complementary flowering season, to ensure a harmonious combination in a plot or pot.

REF. NO.	HERB OR SPICE	TYPE/HABIT	PROPAGATION FROM:	PLANT OR SOW	HEIGHT
72	ALLSPICE	Tree	Seed	Winter	35 ft (10 m)
81	ALMOND	Tree	Seed	Winter	20 ft (6 m)
11	ANGELICA	Perennial	Seed, division	Spring	6–7 ft (2 m)
73	ANISE	Half hardy annual	Seed	Early spring	20 in. (45 cm)
40	ASAFETIDA	Perennial	Seed	Spring	10 ft (3 m)
57	BALM	Perennial	Seed, root division, stem cuttings	Winter	2 ft (60 cm)
18	BAMBOO	Perennial	Stem cuttings	Autumn/winter	6–7 ft (2 m)
51	BAY	Tree	Stem cuttings, seed	Early summer	3–20 ft (1–6 m)
59	BERGAMOT	Perennial	Root division	Winter	2–3 ft (60–90 cm)
77	BLACK PEPPER	Perennial	Stem cuttings, seed	Spring	20 ft (6 m)
20	BORAGE	Biennial	Seed, root division, stem cuttings	Early summer	20 in. (50 cm)
74	BURNET	Perennial	Seed	Early spring	20 in. (50 cm)
93	CACAO	Tree	Seed	Winter	12–14 ft (4 m)
23	CAPER	Perennial	Stem cuttings, seed	Early summer	3–4 ft (1 m)
27	CARAWAY	Biennial	Seed	Midsummer	2 ft (60 cm)
37	CARDAMOM	Perennial	Root division, seed	Spring	6–7 ft (2 m)
13	CELERY	Annual	Seed	Spring	2 ft (60 cm)
12	CHERVIL	Annual	Seed	Spring	16 in. (40 cm)

FLOWERING TIME	PARTS TO USE	HARVEST	WHEN TO USE	HOW TO STORE
Summer	◈	Late Summer	All year	Dry, in containers
February–April	◈	Late Summer	All year	Dry, in containers
July–August	◈	Summer	Summer	Candied
	◈	September	All year	Store in containers
July–August	◈	Summer	Summer	Use fresh
	◈	September	All year	In seed containers
Summer	◈	Summer	All year	In glass jars
July–September	◈	Summer	Summer	Use fresh
			Winter (dried)	Dried and from freezer
August–October	◈	Summer	Summer	Use fresh
	◈	Autumn	All year	In containers
May–June	◈	All year	All year (fresh and dry)	Dry in containers
July–September	◈	Summer	Summer	Use fresh
			Winter	Dried and from freezer
Summer	◈	Late summer	All year	Ground, in containers
June–August	◈ ◈	Summer	Summer	Use fresh
July–August	◈	Summer	Summer	Use fresh
All year	◈	All year	All year	Ground, in containers
May–June	◈	Summer	All year	Seeds in pickle
June–July	◈	September–October	All year	In containers
Summer	◈	Late summer	All year	Dry or powdered
July–August	◈	Winter	Winter	Open ground
	◈	September–October	All year	In containers
May–July	◈	Summer	Summer	Use fresh
	◈	August–September	All year	In containers

61

REF. NO.	HERB OR SPICE	TYPE/HABIT	PROPAGATION FROM:	PLANT OR SOW	HEIGHT
25	CHILI PEPPER	Annual	Seed	Early summer	3–4 ft (1 m)
6	CHIVES	Perennial	Seed, bulbils or bulblets	All year	16 in. (40 cm)
29	CINNAMON	Tree	Stem cuttings, seed	Winter	35 ft (10 m)
30	CITRON	Tree	Grafting, seed	Winter	15 ft (4 m)
39	CLOVE	Tree	Stem cuttings, seed	Winter	70 ft (20 m)
32	CORIANDER	Annual	Seed	Early spring	12 in. (30 cm)
53	CRESS	Annual	Seed	All year	3 in. (7.5 cm)
76	CUBEB	Perennial	Stem cuttings, seed	All year	15 ft (4 m)
35	CUMIN	Annual		Early spring	16 in. (40 cm)
92	DANDELION	Perennial	Seed	Spring	8 in. (20 cm)
10	DILL	Annual	Seed	Early spring	2 ft (60 cm)
86	ELDER	Tree	Seed, stem cuttings, suckers	Winter	12–15 ft (4 m)
41	FENNEL	Perennial	Seed	Spring	5–6 ft (1.5 m)
95	FENUGREEK	Annual	Seed	Spring	6 in. (15 cm)
8	GALINGALE	Perennial	Root division	All year	3–4 ft (1 m)
5	GARLIC	Bulb	Seed, bulblets or bulbils	Spring/autumn	16 in. (40 cm)
100	GINGER	Perennial	Rhizomous division	March	4–5 ft (1.5 m)
28	GOOD-KING-HENRY	Perennial	Seed	Early spring	2 ft (60 cm)

FLOWERING TIME	PARTS TO USE	HARVEST	WHEN TO USE	HOW TO STORE
June–August	[symbol]	Summer	All year	Fruits in pickle
	[symbol]	Summer	All year	Seed in containers
July–August	[symbol]	All year	All year	Use fresh and from freezer
May–September	[symbol]	All year	All year	Dried
	[symbol]	Summer	All year	Dried
March–September	[symbol]	Summer	All year	Use fresh and from freezer
All year	[symbol]	August–November	All year	Dry, in containers
July–August	[symbol]	Summer	Summer	Use fresh
	[symbol]	September–October	All year	In containers
—	[symbol]	All year	All year	Use fresh
May–September	[symbol]	Late summer	All year	Store dry
July–August	[symbol]	September–October	All year	In containers
March–November	[symbol] [symbol]	Summer	Summer (fresh)	Use fresh
June–July	[symbol]	Summer	Summer	Use fresh
	[symbol]	Autumn	All year	In containers
July–August	[symbol]	August–October	Winter	As preserve
July–September	[symbol]	Summer	Summer	In freezer
	[symbol]	Summer	Summer	In freezer
	[symbol]	September	All year	In containers
June–July	[symbol]	Summer	All year	Dry, in jars
March–July	[symbol]	Autumn	All year	Dry, in containers
July–August	[symbol]	August–October	All year	In frost-free room
Summer	[symbol]	March	All year	In boxes or jars
July–August	[symbol]	Summer	Summer/winter	Use fresh and from freezer

REF. NO.	HERB OR SPICE	TYPE/HABIT	PROPAGATION FROM:	PLANT OR SOW	HEIGHT
33	HAZEL	Tree		Winter	16 ft (5 m)
42	HERB BENNET	Perennial	Root division	Autumn/spring	16 in. (40 cm)
46	HOP	Perennial	Cuttings from underground stems	Spring	16 ft (5 m)
15	HORSERADISH	Perennial	Root cuttings	Autumn/winter	2 ft (60 cm)
47	HYSSOP	Perennial	Seed, stem cuttings, division	Spring	16 in. (40 cm)
50	JUNIPER	Tree	Stem cuttings	Winter	40 ft (10 m)
52	LAVENDER	Perennial	Stem cuttings, seed, root divisions	Spring	1–4 ft (30--120 c
4	LEEK	Annual	Seed, bulblets or bulbils	Spring/autumn	2 ft (60 cm)
94	LEMON THYME	Perennial	Stem cuttings	Spring/early spring	4 in. (10 cm)
55	LEMON VERBENA	Perennial		Spring	6–7 ft (2 m)
44	LICORICE	Perennial	Seed, root division	Autumn	3–4 ft (1 m)
54	LOVAGE	Perennial	Seed, root division	Midsummer	3–4 ft (1 m)
22	MARIGOLD	Annual	Seed, special color types from cuttings	Spring	12 in. (30 cm)
9	MELEGUETA PEPPER	Perennial	Root division	Spring	6–7 ft (2 m)
56	MELILOT	Biennial	Seed	Late summer	3 ft (90 cm)
17	MUGWORT	Perennial	Root division, seed	Spring	3–4 ft (1 m)
21	MUSTARD, BLACK	Annual	Seed	Early spring	3–4 ft (1 m)
21	MUSTARD, WHITE	Annual	Seed	All year	4 in. (10 cm)

FLOWERING TIME	PARTS TO USE	HARVEST	WHEN TO USE	HOW TO STORE
March–April	[seed]	October–November	All year	Store dry
June–August	[root]	All year	All year	Use fresh
July–August	[flower]	Early summer	Early summer	Use fresh
	[seedhead]	September	Autumn	Store dry
June–August	[root]	All year	All year	Use fresh
July–September	[seedhead] [leaf]	All summer	Summer (fresh)	Store dry
Early summer	[berry]	Summer (2nd year)	Fresh	Use fresh
June–August	[seedhead]	September	Summer	Use fresh
			Winter	Store dry in containers
July–August	[flower]	All winter from open ground	Winter	Use fresh and in freezer
July–August	[leaf]	Summer	All year	Dry, in containers
July–August	[leaf]	Summer	Summer	Use fresh
June–July	[root]	October	All year	After drying
June–July	[leaf]	Summer	Summer	Use fresh
	[bark]	September	All year	In containers
All year	[leaf] [seedhead]	Summer	All year	Use fresh; flowers dry from containers
March–July	[bark]	Late summer	All year	In containers when ground
June–September	[bark]	Late summer	All year	In glass jars
July–August	[leaf]	Summer	Summer	Use fresh
			Winter (dried)	In dry room
June–August	[bark]	August–September	All year	In containers
—	[leaf]	All year	All year	Use fresh

REF. NO.	HERB OR SPICE	TYPE/HABIT	PROPAGATION FROM:	PLANT OR SOW	HEIGHT
62	MYRTLE	Tree	Seed, stem cuttings	Winter	6–8 ft (2 m)
96	NASTURTIUM	Annual	Seed	Spring	Trailing
60	NUTMEG	Tree	Seed and grafting	Winter	30 ft (9 m)
65	OLIVE	Tree	Stem cuttings, seed, suckers, seedlings	Winter	20 ft (6 m)
2	ONION	Bulb	Seed, bulblets or bulbils	Spring	18 in. (45 cm)
67	OREGANO	Perennial	Seed, stem cuttings	Autumn/spring	16 in. (40 cm)
24	PAPRIKA	Annual	Seed	Early summer	3–4 ft (1 m)
70	PARSLEY	Biennial	Seed	Early spring	12 in. (30 cm)
14	PEANUT	Annual	Seed	Spring	12 in. (30 cm)
58	PEPPERMINT	Perennial	Root division, stolons, runners	Winter	16 in. (40 cm)
75	PINE	Tree		Winter	100 ft (30 m)
78	PISTACHIO	Tree	Seed, budding, grafting	Spring	20 ft (6 m)
71	POKE	Perennial	Seed	Autumn	10 ft (3 m)
68	POPPY	Annual	Seed	Spring	20 in. (50 cm)
66	POT MARJORAM	Perennial	Seeds, stem cuttings	Autumn/spring	12 in. (30 cm)
79	PURSLANE	Half hardy annual	Seed	Early summer	6 in. (15 cm)
7	ROCAMBOLE	Bulb	Seeds, bulblets or bulbils	All year	2 ft (60 cm)
38	ROCKET	Perennial	Seed	Autumn	2–3 ft (1.5 m)

OWERING TIME	PARTS TO USE	HARVEST	WHEN TO USE	HOW TO STORE
ly–August	▨	Autumn	All year	Dry, in jars
ne–October	◆	Summer	Summer	Fresh
	▨	Summer	Summer	Seeds in pickle
year	⬤	All year	All year	Dry, in jars
ay–July	✹	Late summer	All year	Oil or fruit, in glass jars
ly–August	♧	September–October	All year	In dry room
ly–September	♠	Summer	Summer	Use fresh
			Winter (dried)	Dry, in container and in freezer
ne–August	✹	Summer	Summer	Use fresh
			Winter	From freezer
ly–September	♠	All year	All year	Fresh; dried or in freezer
	▨	Autumn (2nd year)	All year	
mmer	⬤	Late summer	All year	In containers
ly–September	♠	Summer	Summer	Use fresh
			Winter (dried)	Dry and rub down or chop for freezer
mmer	⬤	Autumn	All year	Dry, in jars
rly summer	⬤	Summer	All year	In glass jars
ne–August	⋏	Fresh	Summer	Use fresh
ly–September	▨	Summer; autumn	All year	In seed containers
ly–September	♠	Summer	Winter (dry)	Dry in containers; and in freezer
ly–September	♠	Summer	Summer	Use fresh
ay–August	♧	Autumn	All year	In frost-free room
mmer	♠	Summer	Use fresh	Use fresh

REF. NO.	HERB OR SPICE	TYPE/HABIT	PROPAGATION FROM:	PLANT OR SOW	HEIGHT
82	ROSEMARY	Perennial	Seeds, stem cuttings	Spring	5 ft (1.5 m)
84	RUE	Perennial	Root division, seeds	Spring	2 ft (60 cm)
26	SAFFLOWER	Annual	Seed	Early summer	30 in. (75 cm)
34	SAFFRON	Bulb	Root division	May	4 in. (10 cm)
85	SAGE	Perennial	Seeds, stem cuttings	Spring	20 in. (50 cm)
80	SALAD BURNET	Perennial	Seed, root division	Autumn/spring	16 in. (40 cm)
87	SAVORY, SUMMER	Half hardy annual	Seed	Early summer	8 in. (20 cm)
87	SAVORY, WINTER	Perennial	Stem cuttings, root division	Spring	12 in. (30 cm)
3	SCALLION, WELSH ONION	Perennial	Seed, bulblets or bulbils	Spring	6 in. (15 cm)
69	SCENTED-LEAF GERANIUM	Perennial	Stem cuttings	Early summer	20 in. (45 cm)
31	SCURVY GRASS	Annual	Seed	Early spring	12 in. (30 cm)
89	SESAME	Annual	Seed	Early spring	3–4 ft (1 m)
1	SHALLOT	Bulb	Seed, bulbils	Early spring	16 in. (40 cm)
83	SORREL	Perennial	Seed	Winter	12 in. (30 cm)
43	SOYBEAN	Annual	Seed	Spring	16 in. (40 cm)
58	SPEARMINT	Perennial	Root division, stolons, or runners	Winter	12 in. (30 cm)
48	STAR ANISE	Tree	Stem cuttings, seed	Winter	30 ft (9 m)
88	STONECROP	Perennial		Winter	10 in. (25 cm)

FLOWERING TIME	PARTS TO USE	HARVEST	WHEN TO USE	HOW TO STORE
March–June	(leaf)	All year	All year	Dry, in containers
	(flower)	March–June	Spring	Use fresh
	(seed)	September–October (in warm climate)	All year	In seed containers
July–September	(leaf)	All year	All year	Use fresh
Early summer	(flower)	Summer	Summer	Dry, in containers
	(seed)	Late summer	All year	Dry, in containers
August–September	(flower)	Autumn	All year	In containers
July–September	(leaf)	Summer	All year	Dried and from freezer
	(seed)	October	All year	In containers
June–August	(leaf)	Summer	Summer	Use fresh
July–August	(leaf)	Summer	Summer	Use fresh
July–September	(leaf)	Summer	Winter	In freezer
July–August	(leaf)	All year	All year	Use fresh
All year	(leaf)	All year	All year	Use fresh; and from freezer
May–June	(leaf)	Summer	Summer	Use fresh; and from freezer
May–July	(seed)	Late summer	All year	Dry, in jars
July–August	(bulb)	September–October	All year	In dry room
June–August	(leaf)	Summer	Summer	Use fresh
			Winter	From freezer
Summer	(seed)	Late summer	All year	Ground, in jars
August–September	(leaf)	Summer	Summer	Use fresh
			Winter (dried)	Dry and rub down, or chop for freezer
Spring	(seed)	Autumn	All year	Dry, in jars
July–August	(root) (leaf)	Summer	Summer	Use fresh

REF. NO.	HERB OR SPICE	TYPE/HABIT	PROPAGATION FROM:	PLANT OR SOW	HEIGHT
45	SUNFLOWER	Annual	Seed	Early spring	10 ft (3 m)
64	SWEET BASIL	Half hardy annual	Seed	Early summer	16 in. (40 cm)
61	SWEET CICELY	Perennial	Seed, root division	Spring	4–6 ft (1.5 m)
66	SWEET MARJORAM	Perennial	Seed, stem cuttings	Autumn/spring	16 in. (40 cm)
24	SWEET PEPPER (PAPRIKA)	Annual	Seed	Early summer	3–4 ft (1 m)
90	TAMARIND	Tree	Seed	Winter	35 ft (10 m)
91	TANSY	Perennial	Seed, root division	Winter	3–4 ft (1 m)
16	TARRAGON	Perennial	Seed, root division	Autumn/spring	2 ft (60 cm)
94	THYME	Perennial	Stem cuttings, root division	Spring	10 in. (25 cm)
97	TRUFFLE	Fungus		Spring	Underground
36	TURMERIC	Perennial	Root division	Spring	20 in. (50 cm)
98	VANILLA	Perennial	Stem cuttings	Spring	Climbing
99	VIOLET	Perennial	Seed	Spring/autumn	3 in. (7.5 cm)
49	WALNUT	Tree		Winter	100 ft (30 m)
63	WATERCRESS	Perennial	Seed, root division	Spring	8 in. (20 cm)
19	WINTER CRESS	Perennial	Seed	Spring	8 in. (20 cm)
36	ZEDOARY	Perennial	Root division	Spring	16 in. (40 cm)

LOWERING TIME	PARTS TO USE	HARVEST	WHEN TO USE	HOW TO STORE
te summer	▦	Autumn	All year	As cooking oil
uly–September	♠	Summer	Summer	Use fresh
			Winter (dry)	Dry in containers; and in freezer
lay–June	♠	Summer	Summer	Use fresh
	▦	September	All year	In freezer; in containers
uly–September	♠ ⟁	Summer	Summer	Use fresh
			Winter (dry)	Dry, in containers; and in freezer
une–August	▦	Summer	Summer	Use fresh
			Winter	From freezer
anuary–June	▦	Late summer	All year	Dry, in jars
uly–September	♠	Summer	Summer	Use fresh
			Winter	Dry in containers; and in freezer
une–July	♠	Summer	Summer	Use fresh
			Winter (freezer)	In dry room; and from freezer
uly–September	♠	Summer	Summer	Use fresh
			Winter (dry)	In dry room; in freezer
-	▦	All year	All year	Use fresh
ummer	▦	Late summer	All year	Dry or powdered
pril–June	⬬	Autumn	All year	As essence
larch–May	▦	Spring	Spring (fresh)	Candied
arly summer	⬬	Autumn	All year	Dry, in containers
une–August	♠	Summer	Summer	Use fresh
			Winter	From freezer
une–August	♠	Autumn; winter	Autumn; winter	Use fresh and from freezer
ummer	▦	Late summer	All year	Dry or powdered

The Art of Seasoning

NIKA HAZELTON

Happiness is a row of fragrant herbs on a sunny windowsill and a rack of pungent, aromatic dried herbs and spices. For here we have the elements of good cooking, the elements which transform the primitive gratification of hunger into a pleasurable, aesthetic experience.

All of us are familiar with at least a few fresh or dried herbs and with some whole or ground spices. I am thinking of parsley and chives that are used fresh, of thyme and sage that come to us most frequently dried, of stick cinnamon and ground mace, to mention just a very, very few of the flavorings that gladden our cooking. This book introduces a full hundred herbs and spices, which offer a wide range of choice.

The present chapter is intended as a general guide to the art of seasoning. Beginners and advanced cooks alike would do well to heed this basic advice before plunging into individual recipes.

This chapter and the Reference Section immediately following it are devoted to cooking. A general orientation to the uses of herbs and spices is provided, along with several multipurpose recipes, including ones for marinades, herbal bouquets, and vinegars. More elaborate recipes for complete dishes will be found in the Reference Section on pages 86–89.

The use of herbs in cooking, both for reasons of health and for taste, was practiced long before medieval times, but little pictorial evidence is available. Here, however, is a scene of a medieval kitchen from an early sixteenth-century print, *Küchenmeisterey* (Augsburg, Johann Froschauer, 1507).

The basics: Shown here are three fresh herbs, essential to almost any kitchen, which make up the basic herb bouquet: thyme and parsley (below), and bay leaf (right).

BOUQUET GARNI
Herb Bouquet

Essential in French cooking, a *bouquet garni* is a bunch of herbs tied together with string or, when any of the herbs are dried, wrapped in a piece of washed cheese cloth and tied with string. Herb bouquets are used to flavor soups, sauces, stews, braised dishes, and vegetables, and the reason for their packaging is to avoid their dispersal in the food liquid or their being skimmed off it, and to make their removal easy once the dish is finished. The classic combination is parsley, bay leaf, and thyme, but other herbs and vegetables may be added.

DRIED HERBS AND SPICES: SOME BASIC REMINDERS

Buy in small quantities and do not keep longer than one year at most. Especially dried herbs have a shelf life rarely longer than 4 to 6 months.

Store in tightly capped, airtight jars away from the light and heat and in a cool, dry place. A shelf near or above the kitchen stove will not do. If there is no cool place in your kitchen, store tightly covered in the refrigerator.

Open your herb and spice jars once a month and sniff for freshness. If stale, replace or your cooking will suffer.

Use dried herbs and spices with discretion and discrimination in any single recipe, particularly if you are not familiar with them. Remember that it is easy to add seasonings or flavorings to a dish, and very difficult if not impossible to remove them.

Avoid too many herbs and spices in the same dish unless a recipe calls for them. Use only one strong-flavored seasoning in a food which may be combined with several mild-flavored ones.

Do not flavor more than two dishes in a meal with herbs or spices. And do not forget that their purpose is to enhance the flavor of food and not to disguise it. If the taste of your cooking is overpowered by the seasoning, that dish is a failure.

Experiment with unfamiliar herbs and spices. Add a pinch or so to a little of the dish they are meant for and let stand at room temperature for 5–10 minutes so that the flavors are able to develop fully. Then taste and decide if you want less or more or none at all.

When you double or triple a recipe, do *not* double or triple the amounts of dried herbs and spices. These are the proper amounts: For double the recipe, use 1½ times the amounts called for. For triple the recipe, use twice the amounts called for.

ABOUT FRESH HERBS

Cooks newly beginning to flavor their foods with herbs may be mystified by the names of groups of herbs called for in many recipes. Here are the terms most frequently used and their explanations:

Sweet herbs are plants whose leaves, seeds, or roots make them suitable as seasonings, thanks to their aroma. Thyme, sage, chives, and mint are such sweet herbs.

Pot herbs are plants whose leaves and stems are used for food rather than seasoning. Cabbage, spinach, dandelion greens, and beet tops are pot herbs.

Salad herbs are any herbs used to flavor salads.

Herb bouquets are combinations of herbs used together to flavor soups, stews, braised meats, vegetables, and sauces; the combination depends on the dishes in which herb bouquets will be used. When fresh, the herbs are tied together with string; when dried, they are wrapped in a piece of washed cheesecloth and tied. The reason for tying the herbs is to prevent them from dispersing in the food and from being skimmed off, and also to make it easy to remove them. The most basic and common herb bouquet is the *bouquet garni*, essential in French cooking. A simple *bouquet garni* consists of 2 sprigs of parsley, ½ bay leaf, and 1 sprig or ⅓ teaspoon dried thyme. Other herbs to be added to a *bouquet garni* are always specifically mentioned, such as a medium bouquet with fennel or celery or marjoram.

Fine herbs (better known in the French form *fines herbes*) is also a combination of fresh herbs. However, these are minced and remain in the finished dish. A blend of parsley, chives, tarragon, and chervil are the standard *fines herbes* of French cookery, most often used in egg and cheese dishes.

Herbs and spices need not be restricted to *haute cuisine;* a cold picnic offers many opportunities to use them, in everything from the sesame seed crackers at far left, to truffles and olives with cream cheese, various herb butters and spreads, and watercress with tomato.

HOW TO USE FRESH HERBS

To prepare for cooking: Snip potted herbs frequently, for this promotes growth. But do not snip off more at one time than needed. Snip each stalk separately with scissors and never sheer off the top of potted herbs in a crew cut. Wash cut herbs gently in a bowl of cool water by swishing them up and down. Drain, shake dry gently, and pat dry with paper toweling. Crush, chop, or mince fresh herbs before cooking; this releases their flavor. Strip leaves off larger and coarser herbs before mincing, as their stems are tough. Wispy herbs like dill, fennel, and even parsley should be gathered in six to a dozen strands or heads and snipped straight across with a pair of sharp scissors.

Storing fresh herbs. Wrap loosely in damp paper toweling. Or wash, shake dry thoroughly, and pack into tightly closed jars, then refrigerate. Store whole herbs since minced herbs keep poorly.

Use leftover minced herbs to make herb butter (see pp. 131, 132).

Use whole herbs to make herb vinegar (see pp. 132–133).

If you are left with parsley stems having used the parsley heads elsewhere, tie the stems together and add them to slow-cooking dishes for flavoring. Discard the stems before serving.

Add fresh herbs to a dish during the last 15 minutes cooking time unless the recipe specifies otherwise.

To cold dishes in which fresh herbs are an essential ingredient (such as vegetable cocktails, salads, and cheeses) add herbs several hours or overnight before serving.

To salad dressings add fresh herbs about 15 minutes before serving.

Fresh herbs used as a garnish, such as parsley and chives, are sprinkled only at serving time over the dish they are to enhance.

Equivalents: One tablespoon minced fresh herbs corresponds to about ⅓ teaspoon ground and to about ½ tablespoon crushed dried herbs. However, this proportion depends on the kind and on the freshness of the dried herbs. Be sure to taste as you add either fresh or dried herbs to your cooking.

Cooking with fresh garlic. Unpeeled garlic cloves will give a mild, subtle flavor to your cooking. Add whole and unpeeled to your dish. When cooked, each clove may be squeezed firmly and the ensuing puree may be spread on bread or mixed into hors d'œuvres or into a salad dressing.

For a whiff of garlic, peel a clove or more and spear each clove with a toothpick for easy removal. Add to your food and cook for 10 to 20 minutes, remove and discard.

Warning! A crushed or mashed garlic clove has two to three times the strength of a minced one.

Though native to the Mediterranean islands of Corsica and Sardinia, where the climate is hot and dry, rosemary is hardy enough to withstand a winter of intense cold. As shown in this medieval print, it can be grown in tubs. It remains green throughout the year and, when used fresh, is delicious in salads.

ABOUT DRIED HERBS

Dried herbs will release more flavor to your food if you crush or crumble them well between the palms of your hands before adding them to your cooking; your body heat will release the herbs' flavorful essential oils.

Always reconstitute dried herbs for full flavor. Before using, soak dried herbs from 10 minutes to 1 hour in a liquid that you can add to your recipe, such as water, milk, bouillon, lemon juice, salad oil, wine, or vinegar. If possible, warm the liquid first. Or you may simmer dried herbs over low heat in a little butter for a few minutes. If you cannot add both liquid and herbs to your food, strain out herbs and use them alone.

When in a hurry and you want to add dried herbs to sauces, salad dressing, and mayonnaise, pour boiling water over dried herbs and let stand 1 minute. Drain and pat dry between kitchen paper before use. Or place measured herbs in a small tea strainer, dip in boiling water for 1 minute, then dip quickly in cold water, drain, and pat dry.

For long-cooking foods such as soups, stews, and casseroles, add herbs at the beginning of cooking time. This way they will blend in with the other ingredients. However, another school of cooks advocates adding dried herbs only during the last 30 to 45 minutes of cooking time or else their flavor will be lost. I subscribe to the first but you may prefer the second solution.

For quickly cooked foods, such as hamburgers, be sure to reconstitute your dried herbs as described above before blending them into your cooking.

In salad dressings, let dried herbs stand in the unchilled oil dressing for 15 to 30 minutes.

Both garlic and onion are available dried in varied forms. Garlic is found as instant minced, powdered, granulated, and garlic salt. Onion is available as flakes, instant minced, diced, chopped, sliced, powdered, granulated, and as onion salt. Instant minced garlic and onion, and onion flakes, diced, chopped, and sliced onions should be rehydrated for about 5 to 10 minutes with an equal amount of water. Drain before using. Fresh garlic and onions are infinitely preferable to dried ones. However, if for convenience's sake you must use the dried garlic and onions, treat them with great discretion for they are assertive and not always desirably so.

ABOUT SPICES

Sniff spices for freshness. Ground spices lose strength more rapidly than whole spices. If a spice smells stale, discard it for it will not flavor your cooking.

Keep spices dry, since moisture will cause deterioration. Never dip a moist spoon or knife tip into a spice jar. Discard spices that have begun to cake.

Pepper, black and white, whole and ground. The white variety is used for good visual effect in pale-colored dishes. A pepper mill is a must: fresh ground pepper has incomparably more flavor than storebought ground.

In cooking, put whole spices into a little cloth bag (such as a cheesecloth bag) or into a stainless steel metal tea ball; do *not* use tea balls made of any other metal. This way, spices are easier to remove from the finished dish. If no bag or tea ball is used, it will be necessary to strain the liquid.

FIRST AID FOR OVERSEASONED COOKING

Strain out bits of herbs and spices.

A raw, peeled, and quartered large potato simmered for 15 minutes in your cooking

Whenever possible use freshly ground rather than ready-ground or powdered spices. Freshly ground pepper or nutmeg make all the difference in flavor.

Grind whole spices just before using. A mortar and pestle, a pepper mill, a coffee grinder, a blender, or a food processor will do the job. For small amounts, use mortar and pestle or a pepper mill.

The flavor of whole spices, such as peppercorns, cardamom, coriander and cumin seeds, cinnamon sticks, whole cloves, and vanilla beans, is more pronounced than that of ground or powdered spices.

will absorb some of the excess seasoning. Remove potato pieces and discard.

If food is overly salty, first use potato as described and then stir a little sugar or brown sugar into your food. Start with 1/4 teaspoon and taste before adding more, up to 1–2 teaspoons depending on the food and the quantity.

If food is overly sweet, add about 1/2 to 1 teaspoon lemon juice, cider or white vinegar, tasting as you add.

If food is overly seasoned, prepare an *unseasoned* second batch and combine the two.

This engraving of an eighteenth-century manorial kitchen presents cookery as a somewhat diabolical, or at least a frenetic, art. The picture is from a guide to housekeeping published in Nuremberg in 1722, at a time when the French already wielded a strong influence on European cooking. The scene suggests a more adventurous, rather than "classical," cuisine, however, and one that was no doubt richly flavored. The woman seated at left appears to be working with a mortar and pestle.

SOUPS

Clear soups may be sprinkled at serving time with finely minced chives, watercress, mint, basil, or chervil. For a nice touch, add a dab of whipped cream to each helping of soup and concentrate your minced herbs on the whipped cream.

A chiffonade of fresh herbs improves both fresh and canned soups. Use any herbs at hand that harmonize with the soup's flavor. Allow 1 to 2 tablespoons fresh herbs to 1 pint of soup. Add a few tablespoons of the soup to the herbs and puree in a blender or food processor. Return the blended herbs to the soup and mix well. If you have no blender, simply mince the herbs very, very fine. Chives do not combine well with other herbs; they should be added separately.

Experiment with different spices in your soups. Add a dash of ground allspice to green or yellow pea soup, or a dash of ground mace or cardamom to cream soups and seafood chowders, and two to three cloves to vegetable soups. Add spices at the beginning of cooking; use discretion.

Most, if not all, soups will be improved both in appearance and in flavor by a sprinkling of minced parsley at serving time. Parsley is the one herb that will be compatible with the flavor of the soup, regardless of the other herbs that might already have been used in its preparation.

SAUCES

Sauces fulfill two functions: either to enhance a food gently or to be sufficiently assertive to add interest to foods with personalities that are not strong enough to stand on their own. However, a few basic principles apply to all sauces. Be careful about salting a sauce. Reducing a sauce concentrates the salt and if you are using stock or bouillon, this also will add salt. Add pepper near the end of cooking time because in a delicate sauce, the long cooking of pepper may develop a bitter taste. If sprigs of parsley or other herbs or whole spices are cooked in a sauce, lift them out before straining or pureeing the sauce or you will have a sauce flecked with unattractive dark spots. By the same token, use white pepper in a white or light sauce.

When preparing mushrooms to add to a sauce, cook the mushrooms in water to cover and add to the water a little salt and a

Tartar sauce, consisting of mayonnaise and herbs, can be made quickly using fresh ingredients. An egg yolk is beaten with a dash of dry mustard. Add droplets of salad oil one at a time, beating continually until a good consistency is obtained ($^3/_4$ to 1 cup oil will be needed). Combine with fresh chopped herbs (1 to 2 tablespoons), plus 1 tablespoon each of capers and chopped pickle if desired.

little lemon juice to avoid darkening. Drop the mushrooms, whole, quartered, or thickly sliced into boiling water and cook for 2 minutes after water has returned to boiling point. Drain into a bowl thoroughly and dry between paper towels. Use the mushroom liquid for the sauce or save it for use in other sauces, stews, or wherever a savory liquid is called for.

To flavor the milk for a white sauce or a béchamel add a small onion to the milk and

Fish combines well with such herbs as dill, fennel, parsley, balm, mint, or thyme. Spices such as ginger, mace, or allspice are appropriate seasonings for many shellfish.

bring to boiling point. Lower heat and keep the onion in the milk until you think the milk sufficiently flavored. Remove onion before using the milk. For a more pronounced flavor, stick the onion with 1 or 2 cloves and cook. A peeled garlic clove may be used instead or with the onion and treated as described above.

When a recipe calls for a dash of nutmeg, cloves, or other spice, add it to the sauce during the last 2 to 3 minutes of cooking time. Longer cooking may cause flavor to be lost or exaggerated, depending on the spice.

Uncooked sauces containing fresh herbs keep for about a week in the refrigerator; some, like pesto, can be frozen successfully. Use on vegetable salads, pasta, cold fish, or meats.

When making a sauce dominated by spices, such as curry, fry the spices in a little butter or oil for 2 to 3 minutes, stirring constantly. This will allow their full flavor to be released and captured in the sauce.

FISH

When steaming fish, add a bundle of fresh herbs to the liquid. Parsley, fennel, thyme, mint, and balm, single or in combination, are suited to the purpose.

Add fresh or dried herbs to fish cooked in foil.

Sprinkle sauteed fish with *fines herbes* during the last 3 minutes of cooking time providing no other herbs have been used. Vary the flavor of court bouillons with different herbs.

Add a dash of ginger, mace, or allspice to shellfish dishes.

Spread fish with herb mayonnaise before broiling.

EGGS AND CHEESE

When making an omelet, a frittata, or scrambled eggs, add half of the *fines herbes* or any other herbs or herb mixtures to the

beaten eggs before cooking. When eggs are almost set, sprinkle with the remaining herbs.

Give interest to bland cheeses such as cottage cheese or cream cheese by mixing with minced garlic, minced fresh herbs, reconstituted dried herbs, fennel, or aniseed. For a sweet cheese, use a pinch of sugar, grated nutmeg, ground cloves, and ground cinnamon or ground cardamom or mace.

A flavorful spread can be made from leftover cheeses.

Mash remaining bits of the same kind (that is, soft or hard cheeses), thin them a little with dry white wine, sherry, or brandy, and flavor with herbs or spices.

MEATS AND POULTRY

Whether you are grilling, broiling, roasting, or pan-frying meats, or cooking them by moist heat (that is in a liquid), add salt at the end or just before the end of the cooking because salting before browning draws out the juices. Pepper may be added earlier. Marinated meats require less salt, pepper, or flavorings. Taste as you add them to your cooking.

To distribute garlic evenly on roasts, mash a garlic clove into 2 tablespoons olive oil or melted butter. Spread over the meat's surface. If you wish to insert whole or halved garlic cloves, cut pockets into the meat and insert garlic making sure none shows on the surface. Any garlic bits on the surface of the meat will scorch and produce an unpleasant flavor. The same applies to any herb stuffing.

To add flavor to roasting meats, baste them with an herb baste made by simmering together for a few minutes white or red wine, or broth or a mixture of both, with garlic, onion, herbs, and spices. Keep the herb baste hot while basting, and when basting liquor is used up, use liquids in bottom of pan. Or rub seasoned salts into meat.

If you have a rosemary bush, use branches of this herb for brushing oil over roasting lamb. Use branches of any preferred herbs dipped into a basting sauce for basting roasting, broiling, or grilling meats. This also applies to barbecues and out-of-doors over-the-coals cookery.

Crush and press green or black peppercorns into steak before broiling.

When preparing kebabs, add a few bay leaves to the skewer, alternating them with the meats or vegetables. For pot roast, add either a few cloves or a few mustard seeds to the cooking liquid.

Use marinades (pages 133–134) to tenderize and flavor meats and poultry.

Use seasoned breadcrumbs for fried foods (see recipe above).

When cooking out of doors on an open fire, throw all the prunings and trimmings of the herb garden on the fire during the last few cooking moments. Their smoke will flavor the food deliciously.

Spread any food to be broiled or grilled with herb oil. This is made by soaking 1 or 2 preferably fresh herbs in a jar of olive oil. Let stand at room temperature for several days before straining and rebottling.

HERB AND SPICE VINEGARS

GENERAL RULES

Use only the best quality vinegars, such as cider or wine or white vinegars. (As a rule, white vinegars are sharper.)

It is preferable but not necessary (as shown in many recipes) to heat the vinegar before adding it to the herbs and spices. If you do, *heat only just below boiling point; do not boil.* Herb or spice vinegars mellow with time, losing their sharpness.

Do not use metal caps when bottling your vinegars; their chemicals do not agree and the vinegar may turn black.

The type of vinegar used will determine the flavor of the finished product.

Remove garlic from any herb or spice vinegar after 24 hours steeping or it will wreck the flavor of the vinegar.

FRESH HERB VINEGARS

Select herb leaves just before the plants are in full bloom. Gently bruise the leaves before placing in a jar. Start making herb vinegars with just one or two herbs. Combinations of more herbs require a good knowledge of the strength and flavors of each fresh or dried herb. Strongly flavored herbs will kill the flavor of milder ones.

Proportions for fresh herb vinegars
1 cup freshly minced herbs to 1 pint (2 cups) or 16 fluid ounces (U.S.).

DRIED HERB VINEGARS

It is preferable to heat the vinegar before adding to the dried herbs.

Proportions for dried herb vinegars
Infuse 10 days to 2 weeks. 2–3 teaspoons dried herbs (depending on strength) to 1 pint vinegar.

To make the dried herb vinegar, proceed as in *fresh herb vinegar.*

SPICE VINEGARS

The vinegar must be heated to just below boiling point.

In medieval times, herbs were usually gathered wild. Monasteries, however, cultivated them in great numbers, as shown in this 1490 drawing of a monastery garden. Although herb vinegars can be made with virtually any herb, the most popular choices are dill, shallot, and tarragon.

SHALLOT VINEGAR

Infuse 2 weeks

¼ pound shallots
1 quart white wine or white distilled vinegar

Peel and chop the shallots and place them in a wide-mouthed jar. Steep for 2 weeks. Strain through a fine sieve or cheese cloth. Pour vinegar into clean, preferably sterilized bottles. Use for vegetable and green salads or in nonsweet dishes that call for vinegar.

BASIC FRESH HERB VINEGAR

Infuse 10 days to 2 weeks

1 cup bruised or minced fresh herb leaves
1 pint best quality vinegar

Place herbs in wide-mouthed jar. Pour warmed or cold but not chilled vinegar over herbs and cover tightly. Stand in a warm place for 10 days to 2 weeks; shake or stir jar at least once a day. Taste at the end of 10 days. If stronger flavor is wanted, strain out herbs and replace with fresh herbs. Let stand for another week. Strain through a fine sieve or cheese cloth, bottle in clean, preferably sterilized bottles and cork tightly.

The seeds or spices must be crushed coarsely or bruised to release their essential oils. Do this with a mortar and pestle, or place the seeds or spices between waxed paper and pound with a rolling pin or a bottle. Combine seeds and spices carefully for congeniality.

Proportions for spice vinegars
Infuse 2 weeks. ½ ounce preferred seeds or spices to 1 pint vinegar.
To make spice vinegar, proceed as in *fresh herb vinegar*.

MARINADES

Marinades are liquids in which foods, especially meats, are soaked to tenderize them when tough, and to impart flavor. All marinades contain an acid such as vinegar, wine, or lemon juice which soften the tough fibers of the food. Marinades can be cooked or uncooked. Cooked marinades are preferable for foods that must marinate for 12 hours or more, as in the case of venison or in some beef dishes such as sauerbraten.

COOKED MARINADE FOR BEEF AND VENISON

About 8 cups

½ cup olive or salad oil
1 cup thinly sliced onions
1 cup thinly sliced carrots
½ cup thinly sliced celery
2 chopped garlic cloves
6 cups full-bodied dry red wine
1 cup red wine vinegar
1 cup water or
2 cups red wine vinegar
½ cup parsley heads, no stems
2 bay leaves
1 tablespoon allspice berries
1 teaspoon whole cloves
1 tablespoon crushed juniper berries
1 teaspoon peppercorns
1 tablespoon salt

Heat oil in a large saucepan. Add onions, carrots, celery, and garlic. Sauté vegetables over low heat for about 5 minutes until the onions are golden, but do not let anything brown. (This flavors the vegetables and prevents them from getting sour.) Add remaining ingredients and simmer covered over low heat for 1 to 1½ hours. Strain and cool. Refrigerate marinade; refrigerated, it will keep for weeks.

UNCOOKED LAMB MARINADE

About 1½ cups

1 small onion, chopped
1 garlic clove, minced
1 tablespoon minced fresh rosemary or crumbled dried rosemary
10 peppercorns
1 teaspoon salt
4 tablespoons olive oil
1 cup dry sherry or French vermouth

UNCOOKED MARINADE

About ¾ cup

Use for fish or chicken to be broiled

¼ cup salad or olive oil
½ cup dry white wine
1 tablespoon lemon juice
1 minced garlic clove
½ teaspoon grated lemon rind
½ teaspoon dried tarragon, thyme, or crumbled rosemary
½ teaspoon salt
½ teaspoon white pepper

Mix all ingredients thoroughly. Refrigerate for 2 hours or overnight in a covered jar. Marinate for about 3 hours, turning pieces at least once. During broiling, baste with marinade.

Any marinade container must be made of glass, china or ceramic, or stainless steel, and *never* of aluminum, iron, or any other metal.

Do not over-marinate any foods or their flavor will be lost. Marinate cubed meat as for kebabs for 2 to 3 hours; larger pieces of meat (5 to 10 pounds and more) overnight, for 24 to 48 hours and more, depending on the age of the meat. Make sure the food is totally immersed in the marinade and turn it occasionally. Allow about ⅔ cup marinade for every pound of food. Place marinating foods in the refrigerator if marination is for more than 1 to 2 hours.

Marinades often depend on the cook's tastes in flavoring herbs and spices. Go easy as you are trying out new combinations. Fresh or dried herbs are equally suited to marinades. When draining the food, wipe it clean of bits of herbs and spices before further cooking. Strain marinade and use for basting or in sauces.

When dry white wine for marinades is not available, use half the quantity called for of French vermouth and add water to bring up quantity. Since French vermouth contains herbs, go easy on the flavorings.

SALADS

Add minced or chopped fresh herbs to a salad just before tossing with the dressing, provided the dressing is plain. If you are using an herb dressing, omit salad herbs.

When using herb oils or herb vinegars, use salad herbs with discretion and only use herbs harmonious with the herbs flavoring the oil or vinegar.

The following herbs are suited for salads: parsley, chervil, tarragon, chives, dill, basil, mint, thyme, marjoram, and fresh dill and fennel sprigs.

Do not use too many different herbs; combine their flavor carefully, or they will cancel each other out.

In this illustration from the title page of a sixteenth-century German cookbook, the cook appears disgruntled, despite the copious food supplies in his kitchen.

A table virtually groaning beneath the weight of a profusion of fruit and pastries, from a late sixteenth-century painting by Lodovico Pozzoserrato. Renaissance cooks delighted in waffles and cakes, often spiced with cinnamon, nutmeg, and cloves. Today we often bake with allspice, which resembles these three flavors combined.

DESSERTS

Sweet herbs and spices can add new interest to desserts of many kinds. Sweet herbs suited for the purpose are rosemary, balm, rose geranium, bergamot, angelica, and sweet cicely. Sweet spices include nutmeg, vanilla, mace, cinnamon, ginger, cardamom, and aniseed.

The use of both sweet herbs and spices, when not specified in a recipe, is largely a matter of personal preference. Sweet herbs may be added to a fruit salad, to a sweet soufflé batter, to pies and cakes. When making a dessert that requires cooking, such as fritters, waffles, crepes, soufflés, and custards, herbs are added to the batter. They may be removed before cooking, as when flavoring a custard with bay leaf or rosemary, or they may be cooked into the finished dish. Whether to mince or not to mince fresh herbs used for this purpose depends on their size and on the cook's discretion. However, whole or minced herbs may be floated on a fruit salad, baked fruits, or fruit tarts. When using dried herbs, reconstitute them in a little water or fruit juice before adding to the food.

A sprinkling of spices adds new interest to familiar desserts. Sprinkle ground or freshly grated nutmeg on vanilla ice cream, yogurt, and other creamy desserts. Sprinkle ground ginger, mace, or cardamom on melon. Use crushed aniseed in cooked and uncooked fruit desserts such as rice pudding and fruit compotes. Add the crushed aniseed to cooked desserts before cooking them, and add to uncooked desserts half an hour or more before serving to develop flavors. Ground black pepper, a pinch or two of it, adds to the spices in a pudding or spice cake. Surprisingly, black pepper sprinkled on ripe strawberries accents their flavor. For fruit salads, make a sugar syrup with a preferred spice like whole cloves, cardamom, or aniseed. Cook for 10 minutes and strain onto fruit salad. Chill before serving.

To flavor sugar for desserts and cakes, bury a vanilla bean in a container filled with granulated or confectioners' sugar. Close tightly and let stand for a week before using.

Cooking with Herbs and Spices

PAULA WOLFERT

Reference Section III

A carefully balanced selection of recipes which put herbs and spices to good use. Unless otherwise stated all these recipes are © Paula Wolfert. They are arranged by category, in the sequence listed here and using the following symbols:

 soups

 sauces

 salads

 seafood

 egg and cheese dishes

 meat

 poultry

 vegetables

desserts and baking

It is a characteristic of man that he tends to add an aesthetic element to any activity he undertakes, even the most primitive and the most elementary. None of his preoccupations is more basic than the providing of food, a necessity for the preservation of life. It hardly requires adornment; but it receives it, through the art of gastronomy. There are many means by which the preparation of food has been elevated to a fine art: the most direct is by the use of seasoners. This is not even a development of civilization, with its sophisticated refinements. It antedates civilization, if, indeed, it is not one of the factors which developed it. We may be inclined today to think of prehistoric man as a brutish creature, devoid of subtle sentiments, whom we envisage as gulping down his food greedily, almost without tasting it; but

Singapore cooking, called *nonya*, is a blend of Indian, Indonesian, Malaysian, and Chinese influences. This chopstick-wielding group in an open-air restaurant in Singapore (*right*) is enjoying what is probably a highly spiced meal. Although Western cooking is traditionally tamer, master cooks—such as the Venetian Bartolomeo Scappi (*above right*)—often combine six or seven herbs and spices in a single dish.

Stone Age man was already seasoning his food. The recipes by Paula Wolfert collected here encompass a great variety of dishes, from soup to dessert, ranging from very simple to elaborate productions, and derive from a whole spectrum of national cuisines. Not all meant for timid eaters, none of them will cause the lips to blister. –*Ed.*

DISH	INGREDIENTS	DIRECTIONS

MEDITERRANEAN FISH SOUP

Serves 6

3 small white fleshed fish heads and spines, washed and with all traces of blood and organs removed
1 leek cut up
½ medium onion cut up
½ large carrot cut up
1 fennel stalk cut up
6 parsley sprigs
1 teaspoon fennel seeds
1 bay leaf and 1 pinch dried thyme
1 pound ripe tomatoes
3-inch dried orange peel
2 cloves garlic, halved
2 teaspoons salt
⅜ teaspoon pulverized saffron
1 tablespoon Pernod, flamed
2 medium-sized fillets of red snapper, or flounder, or sole boned
Garnish:
Julienned carrots
Julienned zucchini
Julienned turnips
Blanched orange zest—very little

Put fish heads and spines, cut-up vegetables, herbs, tomato, orange peel, garlic, and salt in 5-quart casserole. Add 3 quarts water and bring to a boil. Lower the heat to a simmer and cook uncovered for 30 minutes or until reduced to half. Skim off scum as it rises to the top.
Strain through a fine-meshed strainer. Add saffron and the Pernod. Bring to a boil and simmer for 2 minutes.
Meanwhile slice the fish, leaving the skin on, crosswise on a slight bias, into strips about 3 inches long and 1 to 1½ inches wide. Arrange 4 pieces of fish in each flat soup bowl.
Blanch the julienned vegetables in the simmering soup and refresh. Place in the center of each bowl.
Just before serving, pour very hot fish soup over the raw fish, just to cover. The hot soup will cook the fish.

MEXICAN FISH SOUP

Serves 4 to 5

¼ cup olive oil
½ cup finely diced onions
½ cup finely chopped celery
1 large clove garlic, finely sliced
¼ teaspoon red pepper flakes
¼ teaspoon ground cumin seeds
⅓ cup diced red bell pepper (pimiento)
½ cup diced green bell pepper
¾ pound mixed cubed fresh fillets of fish (red snapper, halibut, tilefish, etc.)
¼ pound fresh shrimp, peeled and deveined
3 tablespoons chopped fresh green coriander leaves
½ cup peeled, cubed, and seeded tomatoes
12 littleneck clams, shelled
½ cup dry white wine
3 cups fish stock or 1½ cup fish stock and 1½ cups clam juice
Lemon juice
Salt and pepper to taste

In a large skillet, heat the olive oil; add the onion, celery, garlic, pepper flakes, cumin, red and green bell peppers, and cook over medium heat for 2 minutes, swirling to blend flavors.
Add the shrimp, fish, green coriander leaves, tomatoes, clams and their liquor, and wine. Bring the pan juices to the boil. Add the fish stock and simmer 5 to 7 minutes, stirring often. Skim off the foam that rises to the surface. Add a dash of lemon juice, salt, and pepper. Serve at once.

ORIENTAL MEATBALL SOUP

Serves 4

4 ounces ground pork
1 tablespoon soy sauce
1 tablespoon sherry
1 slice boiled ham
2 scallions
1 quart chicken stock, well degreased
Salt

Mix ground pork with soy sauce and sherry. Form into 12 smooth equal-sized balls.
Dice the ham. Chop the green shoots and the white bulbs of the scallions to make 3 tablespoons.
Bring 1 quart water to a boil in a wide saucepan. One by one, gently drop in the meatballs. Reduce heat and poach for 5 minutes.
Use a slotted spoon to lift the meatballs out of the simmering water and let them drain on a flat dish. Discard the poaching water.
Heat chicken stock. Drop in the meatballs and cook 5 minutes. Season the stock with salt if necessary.
Add the diced ham and chopped scallions. Let them heat through. Serve at once.

DISH	INGREDIENTS	DIRECTIONS

ALMOND SOUP

Serves 4 to 5

2 tablespoons butter
½ cup chopped onions
2 tablespoons flour
1 quart boiling chicken stock
½ cup ground blanched almonds
½ cup heavy cream
Salt and freshly ground white pepper

Melt the butter in a saucepan, add the onions, and cook until soft but not browned. Stir in the flour. When blended add the boiling stock, stirring briskly. Allow to simmer a few minutes. Stir in the ground almonds. Cook at the simmer 20 minutes. Stir in cream and allow to heat through. Season with salt and pepper to taste. Serve hot.

RUSSIAN FISH SOUP

Serves 4

2 pounds fish trimmings: heads, tails, and bones of a sole, bass, red snapper, or any other white-fleshed fish
2 tablespoons butter
2 medium-sized onions, sliced
2 ribs of celery with leaves, sliced
½ cup sliced carrots
½ tablespoon salt
½ teaspoon cracked peppercorns
2 sprigs parsley
5 sprigs fresh dill
1½ quart water
1½ tablespoons tomato paste
½ teaspoon sugar
Juice of 1 lemon
1 cup sauerkraut juice
½ pound fresh salmon or sturgeon, boned, skinned, and cut into 2-ounce portions
12 capers, rinsed and drained
4 black olives, halved
¼ cup diced dill pickle
4 thin slices of lemon
2 tablespoons chopped fresh dill

Wash fish trimmings under cool running water; cut away any traces of blood, liver, intestines, or eggs; set aside.
In a heavy 4-quart saucepan melt the butter and sauté the onions, celery, and carrots for a few minutes, stirring. Add the fish trimmings, salt, peppercorns, parsley, and dill sprigs. Moisten with water and stir over high heat until it comes to a boil. Skim. Stir in tomato paste and sugar. Simmer, covered, for 30 minutes, skimming when needed; strain. Add lemon and sauerkraut juices. Return strained soup to a clean saucepan and reheat to a simmer. Poach fish pieces in the soup very gently for 5 minutes (7 minutes if the pieces are very thick.)
Arrange 1 piece of fish in each soup bowl; add to each bowl 3 capers, 2 olive halves, 1 tablespoon diced pickle, 1 lemon slice, ½ tablespoon chopped dill. If the soup is too sour for your taste, add pinches of sugar.

VIETNAMESE SOUR SOUP

Serves 4

1 ounce tamarind pulp
⅔ cup hot water
1-inch thick ring of fresh pineapple, cored and peeled
1 quart water
2 tablespoons Nuoc Mam (oriental fish sauce)
1 tablespoon lemon juice
1½ tablespoons peanut oil
¼ cup finely sliced shallots
2 cloves garlic, thinly sliced
6 ounces fresh or frozen shrimp, peeled and deveined
Sugar (optional)
Salt and freshly ground pepper
1¼ cups fresh bean sprouts
3 tablespoons roughly chopped fresh coriander leaves

Soak the tamarind pulp in hot water for 2 to 3 hours. Press through a sieve set over a small bowl. Using your fingers, separate the fruit and squeeze to release as much liquid pulp as possible. Discard the contents of the sieve, reserving only the strained liquid.
Finely dice the pineapple. In an enameled 3-quart saucepan combine 1 quart water, fish sauce, tamarind, and lemon juice, and bring to boil. Add the pineapple and simmer gently, uncovered, for 10 minutes.
Heat the oil in a small skillet, fry the shallots and garlic in it, stirring, until golden brown and crisp; drain. Set aside. Add the shrimp to the soup and continue to cook 3 to 5 minutes longer. If the soup is too sour for your taste, stir in a small amount of sugar. Taste for salt and pepper. Bring soup to boil; stir in the bean sprouts; then immediately remove from the heat.
Ladle into individual bowls, scatter crisp shallots and garlic over each serving, and top with coriander leaves. Serve hot.

BASIL SAUCE FOR ROAST LAMB OR CHICKEN

Serves 6

2 cups extra rich chicken stock
1 tablespoon finely chopped shallots
½ clove garlic, finely chopped
½ cup dry white wine
½ cup white port
1¼ cups heavy cream
Salt and freshly ground white pepper
2 dozen medium-large basil leaves (2 tablespoons finely chopped leaves)

In a saucepan combine chicken stock, shallots, garlic, white wine, and port. Reduce almost to a glaze. Add the cream and reduce again to a napping consistency. Strain; return to the saucepan, season with salt and pepper, and fold in the basil.

DISH	INGREDIENTS	DIRECTIONS
CHIVE BUTTER FOR GRILLED FISH Makes 1 cup	1 bunch fresh chives 16 tablespoons sweet butter, softened to room temperature Salt and pepper Lemon juice to taste	Puree fresh chives in workbowl of food processor. Add butter, tablespoon by tablespoon, and process to combine. Rub through a sieve. Chill. In a small saucepan bring 2 tablespoons water to the boil. Quickly beat in the chive butter piece by piece over medium-high heat. The butter must foam and start to boil. Boil 5 seconds, whisking. Pour into a small bowl. Season with salt, pepper, and if desired, a drop of lemon juice.
CLASSIC WHITE BUTTER SAUCE Makes about 1 cup serving 5 to 6	1/4 cup dry white wine 2 tablespoons white wine vinegar 2 tablespoons finely chopped shallots 12 tablespoons unsalted butter; firm but not cold and cut into tablespoons 1/4 teaspoon coarse salt Scant 1/4 teaspoon ground white pepper	In a 1 1/2 or 2 quart non-aluminum saucepan combine the wine, wine vinegar, and chopped shallots. Bring to a boil, lower the heat and cook, uncovered, until reduced to a glaze, in about 5 minutes. Remove the saucepan from the heat. Touch the bottom of the inside of the pan with your index finger. It should be just hot enough to withstand the heat for 2 seconds. Quickly whisk in 2 chunks of butter. When soft and creamy return the saucepan to very low heat. Whisking constantly, continue adding chunks of butter, a few at a time. Add more butter only when the previous addition has been absorbed. The consistency of the mixture must be creamy and thick. Remove pan from heat whenever butter appears to be melting rather than thickening and foaming. Strain the sauce into a bowl. Season with salt and pepper. Set in a warm, but not hot, place until ready to serve.
GREMOLATA (Recipe by Nika S. Hazelton)	2 tablespoons minced parsley, preferably Italian parsley 1 medium garlic clove, minced 1/2 teaspoon grated lemon rind	Mix ingredients and sprinkle on food during the last 5 minutes of cooking. Simmer covered over very low heat to let flavors be absorbed by the food. An Italian mixture of seasonings for sauces and pan gravies. The classic use is in Osso Buco, a dish of braised veal shanks. Do not use gremolata in white sauces or creamed dishes.
PESTO Fresh Basil Sauce Makes 1 cup (Recipe by Nika S. Hazelton)	2 cups loosely packed fresh basil leaves, no stems 2 garlic cloves, or to taste, chopped 1/4 cup pine nuts or walnuts (optional) 2 tablespoons grated Romano cheese and 2 tablespoons grated Parmesan cheese (or 4 tablespoons either Romano or Parmesan) 4–6 tablespoons olive oil Salt, freshly ground pepper	Put the basil, garlic, and nuts into the container of a blender or food processor. Blend at low speed for a few moments or until ingredients are coarsely chopped. Add cheese and half of the olive oil and blend again. Scrape the mixture down from the sides of the container. Turn speed to low and trickle in remaining olive oil while blending. By hand, stir in salt and pepper to taste. To refrigerate pesto, turn into a jar and add a thin film of olive oil to cover the top.
OLIVE AND CAPER RELISH Makes approximately 1 cup	1 two-ounce tin anchovy fillets, rinsed and drained 1 cup black Mediterranean-type olives, pitted, and roughly chopped 2 tablespoons capers, rinsed, drained 1 tablespoon lemon juice 1/2 teaspoon Dijon mustard Freshly ground black pepper 2 tablespoons cognac 1/4–1/2 cup fruity olive oil	Blend anchovy fillets, olives, capers, lemon juice, mustard, freshly ground pepper to taste. Add cognac until pasty. Still blending, pour in just enough olive oil in a steady stream to obtain a smooth, thick sauce. Scoop into a pretty pottery bowl and chill well before serving.
SAUCE BÉARNAISE (FOOD PROCESSOR METHOD) Serves 4 to 6	3 tablespoons dry white wine 1/4 cup tarragon vinegar 2 tablespoons minced shallots 3 tablespoons finely chopped fresh tarragon or tarragon leaves packed in vinegar, divided 2 egg yolks 1/2 teaspoon salt 1/4 teaspoon white pepper Cayenne pepper 12 tablespoons unsalted butter, melted and kept hot	In a small non-aluminum saucepan, combine the white wine, vinegar, shallots, and 1 tablespoon tarragon. By boiling, reduce to 1 1/2 tablespoons. Scrape into the workbowl of a food processor; add the egg yolks, salt, and pepper, and process 1 minute. With the machine on, spoon the hot butter through the feed tube. Taste and readjust the seasoning. Add a pinch of cayenne for a sharper taste if desired. Fold in remaining 2 tablespoons tarragon.

DISH	INGREDIENTS	DIRECTIONS

 SPAGHETTI WITH OLIVE SAUCE

Serves 10 to 12

½ pound juicy black Greek olives, rinsed, pitted, and finely chopped
½ pound green olives, rinsed, pitted, and finely chopped
2-ounce tin anchovy fillets, rinsed and mashed
1 tablespoon capers, rinsed and drained
2–3 tablespoons chopped pickled or raw mushrooms (optional)
2 tablespoons chopped parsley
2–3 fresh basil leaves, chopped (optional)
2–3 cloves garlic, finely chopped
Freshly ground black pepper
Olive oil
2 pounds spaghetti
Salt

Combine olives, anchovies, capers, mushrooms, herbs, garlic, and pepper in the mixing bowl. Pour over enough olive oil to cover. Allow to stand and marinate 2 hours, turning the ingredients often and adding more oil if necessary to keep the olive mixture completely covered.
Cook the spaghetti in boiling salted water until tender. Meanwhile in a saucepan heat the olive and oil mixture but do not allow it to boil. Drain the spaghetti, pour over the sauce and serve at once. Serve without grated cheese.

 SPICE MIXTURE FOR COFFEE

Makes ⅓ cup mixture

2 whole nutmegs (about 4 teaspoons ground nutmeg)
4 blades cinnamon (about 1 teaspoon ground cinnamon)
6–8 dried rosebuds
½ teaspoon ground cloves
1 tablespoon ground ginger
½ teaspoon ground galingale or 2 small pieces
2 allspice berries (about ⅛ teaspoon ground)
¾ teaspoon ground white pepper
3 blades mace (about ½ teaspoon ground mace)
15 white cardamom seeds or pods
1 teaspoon fennel seeds
1 teaspoon aniseed
1 tablespoon sesame seeds

Combine spices in an electric spice grinder or blender. Sieve and bottle carefully to preserve the freshness and aroma.
When making coffee, add ¼ teaspoon to every ½ cup ground coffee grinds before making coffee in your usual fashion. (It makes no difference whether you are making black Turkish-style coffee or American roast.)

 CARROT SALAD

Serves 4

1 pound carrots
1 clove garlic
⅛ teaspoon ground cinnamon
¼ teaspoon ground cumin
½ teaspoon sweet paprika
Pinch of cayenne pepper
Juice of 1 lemon
⅛ teaspoon granulated sugar
Salt, olive oil, chopped parsley

Wash and peel carrots. Boil whole in water with the garlic until barely tender. Drain. Discard the garlic and dice or slice the carrots.
Combine the spices with the lemon juice, sugar, and salt to taste, and pour over the carrots. Chill. Sprinkle with oil and chopped parsley just before serving.

 COOKED TOMATOES AND SWEET GREEN PEPPER SALAD

Serves 6

16 red, ripe tomatoes (about 4 pounds), peeled, seeded, and chopped
Olive oil for frying
9 sweet green peppers, grilled, cored, seeded, and chopped
2 cloves garlic, peeled and chopped
1 teaspoon paprika (optional)
Salt and cayenne to taste

Fry the tomatoes in a small amount of oil, mashing and turning them with the spoon as they cook down. When they are very thick add the chopped green peppers, garlic, optional paprika, and some salt and cayenne to taste. Continue to reduce the mixture until all the liquid has evaporated and it starts to fry in the released oil. (At this moment you must give the dish your full attention, turning the tomatoes and peppers over and over in the skillet to avoid scorching.) When everything is very thick and has reduced to about 1½ cups, remove from the heat and drain. Serve cool.

 CUCUMBER SALAD

Serves 4

2 cucumbers, peeled, seeded, and grated
1 tablespoon granulated sugar
1 teaspoon vinegar
1 tablespoon olive, salad, or peanut oil
¼ teaspoon salt
⅛ teaspoon thyme or oregano; or a mixture of two
Handful of cured black olives

Drain off excess liquid from the cucumbers, then combine with the sugar, vinegar, oil, and salt. Crush the herbs between your fingertips and sprinkle over the cucumbers. Mix well with two forks, then chill. Decorate with the olives just before serving.

DISH	INGREDIENTS	DIRECTIONS

 GREEK MIXED SALAD

Serves 6

Assorted salad greens (Boston, bibb, romaine, escarole, and watercress)
1/2 clove garlic
1 crisp cucumber, sliced, salted
1 diced green pepper
1 jar pitted black olives
4 tablespoons imported olive oil (virgin is best)
1 tablespoon red wine vinegar
Freshly ground black pepper
1 can anchovy fillets, drained and cubed
Dried oregano, crumbled between fingertips to release oils
1/4 cup feta cheese, crumbled

Wash greens and dry well. Tear into bite-size pieces. Rub wooden salad bowl with garlic. Salt cucumber 1/2 hour. Drain and pat dry. Toss greens with cucumber slices, green pepper, and olives. Mix oil and vinegar, pepper, anchovies, and a good pinch of oregano in a small mixing bowl; blending well. Toss dressing with the salad and garnish with feta cheese and more oregano.

 ORANGE AND GRATED CARROT SALAD

Serves 4 to 6

1 pound carrots
1 navel orange
1 teaspoon ground cinnamon
2–3 tablespoons lemon juice
1 1/2 tablespoons granulated sugar
1 teaspoon orange flower water
Pinch of salt

Clean and grate the carrots. Peel and section the oranges, reserving the juice. Mix orange juice with the remaining ingredients. Stir in the orange sections. Toss with the grated carrots. Chill before serving. Partially drain if necessary.

 PURSLANE SALAD

Makes 6 cups

2 quarts purslane
1 or 2 small dried red chili peppers
1 teaspoon salt
10–12 cloves garlic
1 cup chopped parsley
1 cup chopped green coriander
Salad oil
1/4 pound cured black olives
2 teaspoons paprika
2 teaspoons ground cumin
Juice of 2 lemons
Lemon wedges

Wash the greens under running water. Drain and cut small. Fill the bottom of a steamer with water and bring to a boil. Fasten on the perforated top, add the greens, and steam, covered, for 30 minutes. Remove from the heat and allow to cool, uncovered. When cool enough to handle, squeeze out as much moisture as possible.
Pound the chili pepper in a mortar with 1 teaspoon salt and the garlic. Gradually add the chopped parsley and coriander and continue pounding until it becomes a paste.
Heat 3 tablespoons oil in the casserole and slowly cook the olives with the paprika and cumin 2 to 3 minutes. Add the herb paste and the lemon juice, cover, and cook 5 minutes. Pour in 1/2 cup oil, add the greens and cook together, stirring frequently, for 20 minutes, or until all the moisture has evaporated and the mixture is very thick. Salt to taste. Serve with lemon wedges.

 TUNISIAN MIXED SALAD

Serves 4 to 6

1 cup peeled, seeded, and diced ripe red tomatoes
1 cup chopped onions
1 cup seeded, de-ribbed and diced sweet green peppers
1 tablespoon seeded and finely chopped hot green chili pepper
1 cup peeled, cored, and diced raw green apple
1 1/2 tablespoons vinegar
4 1/2 tablespoons olive oil
1 tablespoon pulverized dried mint leaves
Salt to taste
Freshly ground black pepper to taste

Combine the tomatoes, onions, peppers, and apple in a serving bowl. Add the vinegar and oil and toss well.
Sprinkle with the pulverized mint, salt, and pepper. Mix thoroughly. Serve at room temperature.

 ZUCCHINI AND CARAWAY SALAD

Serves 4 to 6

1 1/2 pounds small firm zucchini, trimmed
1 1/2 teaspoons chopped garlic
1 1/2 teaspoons ground caraway seed
4 tablespoons olive oil
1 tablespoon wine vinegar
Salt and freshly ground pepper to taste
Cayenne pepper to taste

Boil the zucchini until just tender. Place in workbowl of food processor or jar of electric blender and puree. Combine with garlic, caraway seed, oil, vinegar, and seasonings, mixing well. Chill before serving.

DISH	INGREDIENTS	DIRECTIONS

 SEAFOOD SAUSAGE LE PLAISIR

Makes 6 sausages

¾ pound fresh or frozen sea scallops
⅓ pound fresh or frozen shrimps
1 tablespoon finely minced shallots
1½ tablespoons unsalted butter
1 heaping tablespoon finely minced carrots
1 tablespoon finely minced celery rib
½ teaspoon crumbled thyme leaves
Salt and freshly ground pepper
18 fresh well-dried and shredded sorrel leaves
2 yards sausage casings, soaked 1 hour in water
2 cucumbers
Sugar and 1 teaspoon butter for glazing
1 recipe White Butter Sauce (see p. 140)
2 tablespoons finely chopped fresh peeled tomato
Chopped parsley

Rinse and dry scallops. Cut into small cubes. Puree in food processor. Peel and devein shrimp. Cut into small pieces. Soften shallots in butter. Add carrots and celery and sauté gently 1 minute. Sprinkle with thyme, salt, and pepper. Cool. Mix seafood, vegetable mixture, and sorrel and force into sausage casings. Knot sausages.

Peel, seed, and cut cucumbers into small olive shapes. Cook in salted boiling water 1 minute; drain and pat dry. Glaze in a skillet with ½ teaspoon sugar and 1 teaspoon butter.

Steam sausages 10 minutes or poach 15 minutes. Spoon white butter sauce onto serving plates. Place one sausage on each. Decorate with glazed cucumber, "dots" of tomato, and parsley. Serve hot.

 SEAFOOD, HAM, AND OKRA GUMBO

Serves 6 to 8

1 ham hock
⅓ cup bacon fat, lard, or vegetable oil
⅓ cup flour
1¾ cups chopped onion
1 green bell pepper, chopped
⅓ cup thinly sliced green scallion shoots
2 tablespoons finely chopped parsley
2 cloves garlic, peeled and chopped
1 pound small tomatoes, sliced
1 pound fresh okra, chopped or one 10-ounce package frozen okra, defrosted and chopped
¼ teaspoon cayenne pepper
Salt, preferably rock salt
1 teaspoon dried thyme leaves
Crab Boil (see below)
Juice of 1 lemon
12 live, medium-sized, hard-shelled blue crabs (optional) or substitute 2 cups cooked lump crabmeat
2 pounds raw shrimp

"CRAB BOIL" For Louisiana Gumbos

6 allspice berries
2 crumbled bay leaves
Pinch of grated nutmeg
5 dried hot peppers, crumbled
2 teaspoons coriander seeds
1 tablespoon black mustard seeds
2 cloves
Mix and wrap in a cheesecloth bag. Enough for the gumbo.

The day before you plan to serve the gumbo, simmer the ham hock in 3 quarts water for 2 hours. Then make the gumbo soup base. Heat the bacon fat in a 4-quart saucepan and blend in the flour, stirring. Cook over low heat, stirring constantly, until the mixture turns a nice chocolate brown. Do not allow the flour to burn.

Add the onion, green pepper, scallion, parsley, and garlic and cook, stirring, for 10 minutes. Add tomatoes, okra, cayenne, 2 teaspoons salt, and the thyme. Add the ham hock and 1½ quarts of its cooking broth. Bring to a boil, cover, and simmer for 1 hour. Cool and allow to ripen in the refrigerator overnight.

The following day, bring 4 quarts water to a boil in a large pan; add the Crab Boil mixture, the lemon juice, 1 tablespoon salt and boil for 10 minutes, covered. Add the crabs, bring back to the boil, and boil crabs for 12 minutes or more, depending upon their size. Remove the crabs and allow to cool. Add the shrimp and bring to the boil again. Remove from the heat and let stand 10 minutes, covered. Remove the shrimp and let cool. Boil down the cooking liquid to half. Add 2 cups of this liquid to the gumbo. Remove the ham hock from the gumbo: discard the fat and the bone and cut the meat into bite-size pieces. Add to the gumbo. When the crabs and shrimp are cool, they can be shelled and added to the gumbo. Reheat to boiling and serve hot.

 FRIED HALIBUT OR POLLOCK WITH PARSLEY SAUCE

Serves 4

¾ cup roughly chopped parsley
½ teaspoon chopped garlic
Juice of ½ lemon
Salt and freshly ground black pepper
4 one-inch-thick halibut or pollock steaks
Flour seasoned with salt and pepper for dredging
½ cup olive or vegetable oil
2 tablespoons chopped onion
1 tablespoon flour

Place the parsley and the garlic in the blender jar. Add ¼ cup water. Whirl until smooth. Thin with another ¼ cup water. Add lemon juice, salt, and pepper. Set aside.

Dip the fish steaks into seasoned flour and shake off any excess. Fry in hot oil until nicely browned on both sides. When cooked remove to a warmed serving dish. Pour off half the oil. Cook the onion in the remaining oil and pan drippings until soft and golden. Add the flour and cook until light brown, stirring. Add the parsley mixture. Cook, stirring, 2 minutes. Pour over the fish and serve at once.

DISH	INGREDIENTS	DIRECTIONS

 CHINESE STEAMED FISH

Serves 6

2 pounds sea bass
2 Chinese black mushrooms (cloud ears)
1 scallion, bulb and green shoot
1 slice boiled ham
2 slices ginger
2 tablespoons soy sauce
1 tablespoon sherry
1 tablespoon vegetable oil
1/4 teaspoon each: salt, pepper
1/2 teaspoon sugar

Wash whole fish under cold running water. Wipe dry. Score with a sharp knife; make 1-inch diagonal slits at 1-inch intervals on both sides.
Soak cloud ears in warm water 30 minutes. Slit the scallion in half and cut on diagonal, into strips 1 inch long and 1/4 inch wide. Shred the ham and ginger into matchsticks. Wash cloud ears thoroughly to remove sand. Pat dry, then cut into matchsticks.
Place the fish on an oven-proof platter which must be a bit smaller in diameter than the steamer so it can be easily removed. Leave the head and tail on the fish if it will fit. Spoon soy sauce, sherry, and vegetable oil over fish.
Sprinkle with salt, pepper, and sugar. Scatter ginger, cloud ears, scallion, and ham on top.
Steam over 2 inches of boiling water 15 minutes with tightly covered lid. Serve fish whole as soon as possible.

 POTTED SALMON

Makes about 1 to 1 1/3 cups

Court-bouillon: 1/2 cup dry white wine; 1 small carrot, scraped and cut into rounds; 1 small celery rib, sliced; 1 small onion, sliced; 6 black peppercorns; herb bouquet: parsley, bay leaf, and thyme
5 ounces fresh raw salmon
1 shallot, peeled and halved
9 tablespoons unsalted butter, cut into chunks
5 ounces smoked salmon, picked over for small bones
2 teaspoons Armagnac or Cognac
1 teaspoon fines herbes
Salt and freshly ground white pepper
Thin slices of buttered toast

Make a court-bouillon in a small saucepan with the ingredients listed here. Bring to a boil, reduce the heat, and cook at the simmer 10 minutes. Slip in the sliced salmon and poach it until the flesh flakes easily when prodded with a fork. Remove; drain, discard any skin and bones. Cool and break the flesh into large pieces.
Finely chop the shallots. In bowl of food processor blend butter, shallot, smoked and cooked salmon until well mixed but gritty in texture. Add Armagnac, herbs, salt, and pepper. Let ripen 2 hours in refrigerator before serving. Serve with hot buttered toast.

 SEA SCALLOPS IN PAPILLOTE WITH WATERCRESS AND TOMATOES

Serves 4

1 pound red ripe tomatoes
2 tablespoons olive oil
Salt and freshly ground pepper
1 bunch watercress with thick stems removed
1 cup heavy cream reduced to half
16 sea scallops
2 ounces unsalted butter

Peel, core, halve, and seed the tomatoes. Cut into small cubes. Soften in hot olive oil, stirring, for 4 minutes. Drain in a colander to remove excess moisture. Season cooked tomatoes with salt and pepper.
Wash and dry watercress leaves and pat dry on paper towels. Mix the tomato and reduced heavy cream.
Have ready four 12 by 16 inch pieces of foil. On half of each sheet, place a few of the watercress leaves. Spread about 2 tablespoons of the tomato mixture over the leaves and top with 4 sea scallops. Cover with two more tablespoons of tomato and a few more leaves. Dot each package with butter. Fold securely around the edges, leaving some room for steam to expand during baking.
Bake on a cookie sheet in a preheated 500 degree oven for about 5 minutes, or until the foil package puffs up. Serve at once.

 ARTICHOKE FLAN

Serves 6

1 package frozen artichoke hearts (9 or 10 ounces)
1 lemon
Flour
1/4 cup olive oil
6 eggs
1 teaspoon salt
1/4 teaspoon pepper
1/4 cup milk
1/2 teaspoon summer savory

Thaw the artichokes and drain dry on paper towels. Sprinkle with juice of 1 lemon for flavor. Preheat the oven to 400 degrees. Dust the artichokes with flour. Heat the olive oil in a skillet and fry the artichokes until golden brown on all sides. Arrange, cut side up, on the bottom of an ovenproof skillet. In a mixing bowl, beat the eggs with salt, pepper, milk, and savory until frothy. Pour over the hot artichokes and cook over moderate heat for 30 seconds to set eggs on the bottom. Then transfer skillet to preheated oven and bake for 8 to 10 minutes, or until eggs are firm.
Remove from the oven and let the flan rest a few minutes. Use a spatula to loosen the sides and bottom and turn out onto a round serving dish. Cut into wedges and serve at room temperature.

DISH	INGREDIENTS	DIRECTIONS

 EGGS IN BRIOCHE WITH MUSTARD TARRAGON SAUCE

Serves 4

4 stale brioches
¾ cup dry white wine
3 tablespoons finely chopped shallots
1 tablespoon finely chopped parsley
1 tablespoon finely chopped fresh tarragon or 1½ teaspoons dried tarragon
Dried mustard
⅓ cup heavy cream
8 tablespoons unsalted butter, cut into 8 pieces
Salt and freshly ground pepper
4 fresh eggs

Remove the tops of each brioche about ⅕ of the way down and reserve. Scoop out the centers without piercing the outside. Be sure each hollow is large enough to hold one egg.
In a small, heavy non-aluminum saucepan, combine the wine, shallots, parsley, and tarragon. Bring to the boil, lower heat, and cook slowly until the liquid is totally evaporated and the shallots are very moist and soft but not browned. Add 1 teaspoon mustard and the cream and reduce quickly to 2 tablespoons. While the pan is still hot, beat in the butter, tablespoon by tablespoon, off the heat. The butter should be foamy and thick, not oily. Readjust seasoning, adding more mustard if necessary. Set aside.
Break an egg into each brioche, season lightly with salt and pepper. Bake in a preheated 400 degree oven for 7 to 10 minutes, or until the whites are set.
Spoon a little sauce over each egg; set the top of the brioche in place and serve at once.

 SCRAMBLED EGGS WITH CHERVIL

Serves 4

8 very fresh eggs
5 tablespoons butter, plus enough to coat bowl
Salt and freshly ground pepper
2 tablespoons heavy cream
2 tablespoons finely minced chervil

About 1 hour before serving, break the eggs into a fine wire strainer set over a bowl. Gently crush the yolks with the back of a wooden spoon. Let them drip; do not press or beat the eggs, though you can stir them from time to time if desired. Butter the sides and bottom of a glass or ceramic mixing bowl. Set over a saucepan filled with simmering water. Add the eggs, salt, pepper, and 1 tablespoon butter. Cook slowly over simmering water, stirring constantly with a rubber spatula. Be sure to move the spatula along the sides and bottom of the bowl to avoid curds forming. When the eggs begin to thicken add remaining butter tablespoon by tablespoon. When the eggs begin to hold together with as few curds as possible, but still very creamy and saucelike, remove the pan from the heat, still stirring. Fold in the cream and half the herbs.
Spoon equal amounts of scrambled eggs into small ramekins and garnish each with a pinch of the remaining chervil.

 CHILI CON CARNE

Serves 4 to 5

1¾ cups finely chopped onion
4 tablespoons vegetable oil
1 pound ground lean beef
½ pound ground lean pork
1¼ teaspoons finely chopped garlic
¼ cup chili pepper powder
2 tablespoons oregano
1 tablespoon cumin seeds
1 quart fresh tomatoes: peeled, seeded, and chopped
Salt and pepper
1 whole clove
1 tablespoon red wine vinegar
½ tablespoon sugar
2 tablespoons grated chocolate

Soften the onion in the oil in a deep pan. Add the meat and stir to break up. Add garlic, chili pepper powder, oregano, cumin, and tomatoes. Bring to the boil, stirring. Simmer uncovered 1½ hours. Skim off fat before seasoning with salt, pepper, and clove. Stir in vinegar and sugar and cook 15 minutes longer. Add the chocolate and bring back to the boil. Serve hot with garnishes of chopped onion, sour cream, and cooked kidney beans.

LAMB STEW WITH MARJORAM

Serves 4 to 5

3 pounds lamb shoulder, cut into 1½-inch chunks
3 tablespoons salad oil
1 cup grated onion
¼ teaspoon pulverized saffron
1 teaspoon ground black pepper
Salt to taste
1 teaspoon chopped garlic
5 tablespoons chopped parsley
2½ pounds zucchini, preferably small ones
2 teaspoons marjoram

Trim and discard excess fat from the lamb. In a casserole brown the meat on all sides in oil. Add grated onion, spices, salt, garlic, and parsley. Toss to coat the meat. Add 2 cups water and cook at the simmer, covered, 2 hours or until the meat is almost falling off the bones. Add small amounts of water whenever necessary.
Top and tail the zucchini and cut into ¾-inch slices. Salt lightly and let drain 20 minutes, then rinse and drain again. Sprinkle with 1 teaspoon marjoram and set aside.
Remove meat from the casserole and arrange in a shallow baking dish. Degrease the sauce. Add the zucchini and cook 10 minutes. Spread zucchini over the meat. Boil down the sauce to thicken. Pour over the meat and reheat in a hot oven. Serve at once, with a small sprinkling of remaining marjoram.

DISH	INGREDIENTS	DIRECTIONS

LAMB STEAKS WITH OLIVE SAUCE

Serves 6

Two 1¼ pound lamb steaks
(each 1½ inches thick)
Salt
Grapeseed or vegetable oil
1 cup chicken or lamb stock
¾ cup juicy black Mediterranean style
olives, rinsed, pitted, and chopped
1 ounce anchovy fillets, rinsed
and mashed
1 tablespoon finely chopped parsley
½ teaspoon finely chopped garlic
Lemon juice to taste
⅛ teaspoon cayenne pepper

Lightly season the lamb with salt. Brush both sides of lamb steaks with oil. Set aside until 35 minutes before serving.
In a saucepan combine stock, olives, anchovy fillets, parsley, garlic, 1 tablespoon lemon juice, and cayenne pepper. Heat, stirring, until flavors blend. Correct the seasoning. Keep hot. Broil lamb steak 4 inches from heat, 3 minutes each side. Let rest in warm place 20 minutes. Meanwhile preheat oven to 475 degrees. Place lamb in baking dish and set in oven to roast 8 minutes for rare, 9 or 10 minutes for medium-rare, and 11 minutes for well done.
Cut immediately, slightly on the diagonal, into thin slices. Surround with the sauce and serve immediately.

LIVER BROCHETTES WITH BAY LEAVES

Serves 3 to 4

10 imported bay leaves
1 pound calf's liver, cut into 1-inch cubes
Salt and freshly ground black pepper
Pinch of grated nutmeg
Vegetable oil
1 lemon, quartered

In a mortar pound 3 of the bay leaves until almost a powder. In a mixing bowl toss the liver cubes with the ground bay leaves, salt and pepper, grated nutmeg, and 3 tablespoons oil. Allow to stand 1 hour.
Cut the remaining 7 bay leaves into 1-inch pieces. Thread seasoned liver cubes alternately with bay leaves. Brush with oil. Broil quickly on all sides, 2 or 3 inches from a broiler flame until the first drops of light pink liquid ooze up. Serve at once with lemon quarters.

MME CHU'S STAR ANISE BEEF

Serves 6

2 pounds boneless stewing beef cut in
1-inch cubes
2 scallions
2 tablespoons vegetable oil
½ cup dry sherry
¼ cup soy sauce
2 thin slices ginger
1 whole star anise or eight sections
1 teaspoon salt
1 tablespoon sugar

Wash the beef and pat dry with paper towels. Slice scallions in half and cut into 2-inch lengths on the diagonal, using both green shoots and white bulbs.
Heat the oil in a saucepan over high heat. Using a wooden spoon to turn the meat, sear well on all sides, a few pieces at a time. Add sherry, let boil 1 minute, then add soy sauce and 1 cup water.
Mix in the ginger, scallions, star anise, salt, and sugar. Cook for 3 minutes. Bring again to boil. Reduce heat to simmer and cover pan. Cook for 30 minutes. Stir to baste the meat and continue cooking for 30 minutes longer. Remove ginger slices and whole star anise. Serve hot.

MIDDLE EASTERN LAMB TARTLETS

Makes 16

Tartlet crust:
⅔ cup cream cheese
8 tablespoons sweet butter
2 cups all-purpose flour
½ teaspoon salt
Filling:
2 tablespoons butter
½ cup finely chopped onions
1 pound ground lamb
Salt and freshly ground black pepper
⅓ teaspoon ground allspice
2 tablespoons chopped parsley
½ cup pine nuts
⅓ cup unflavored yogurt

To make the crust: Blend the cream cheese and butter together. Work in the flour and the salt. Press to knead the dough in order to incorporate the flour evenly. Wrap in plastic wrap and chill at least 2 hours. Roll out between sheets of plastic wrap and cut out sixteen 2½-inch rounds. Make small rims to hold in the following filling. Fill the tartlets and bake in a preheated 350 degree oven 30 minutes. Serve hot.
To make the filling: melt the butter in a skillet and in it cook the onions, without browning, until soft. Add the meat and continue cooking 3 to 4 minutes breaking up any lumps of meat with a fork. Add salt, pepper, and allspice. Mix in the parsley and the pine nuts. Allow to cool, then stir in the yogurt. Fill, bake, and serve hot.

RIB STEAKS IN THE STYLE OF ROME

Serves 4 to 5

2 boned rib steaks, 1 inch thick
1 tablespoon finely chopped fresh
rosemary, or ½ tablespoon dried
2 cloves garlic, peeled and chopped
½ cup olive oil
¼ teaspoon freshly ground black pepper
Salt
Lemon quarters

The day before serving pound the slices of meat between sheets of wax paper until somewhat thinner. In a mortar pound the rosemary and the garlic to a paste. Stir in the olive oil and season with pepper and a little salt. Marinate the meat overnight in the oil mixture, turning the meat once or twice. Remove the meat and pat dry with paper towels. Broil 4 minutes on each side or until done to taste. Place on a warmed serving dish, sprinkle with lemon juice, and serve at once.

DISH	INGREDIENTS	DIRECTIONS

ROAST LAMB, ARAB STYLE

Serves 10

1 forequarter lamb (10 pounds)
1½ tablespoons ground coriander seed
4 to 5 cloves garlic, peeled and mashed
2 teaspoons ground cumin
1 teaspoon sweet paprika
6 tablespoons sweet butter, softened
Salt to taste

Carefully remove extraneous fat from the lamb, then make deep incisions under the foreleg bone along the breastplate. Blend all the other ingredients into a paste and rub into the meat. Let stand 10 minutes.
Preheat the oven to 475 degrees.
Place the lamb, fatty side up, in a large roasting pan. Place on the middle shelf of the oven and roast 15 minutes. Reduce the heat to 350 degrees and continue to roast for about 3 hours, or until the meat can easily be removed from the bones with your fingers. Baste every 15 minutes with the juices in the pan. Serve at once, while still burning hot. Eat with your fingers and have a bowl of ground cumin and salt ready for those who like to dip their meat.

CHICKEN LIVERS ON CROUTONS

Makes 12

8 ounces chicken livers, picked over to remove green bile
1 small onion, finely chopped
¼ cup butter
1 California bay leaf or 2 European bay leaves
½ teaspoon crumbled sage leaves
¼ teaspoon freshly ground black pepper
½ cup dry white wine
3 tablespoons cognac
3 fillets of anchovies, rinsed, drained, dried, and chopped
2 teaspoons capers, drained and chopped
12 slices of French or Italian bread

Roughly chop the livers. Soften the onions in half the butter for 1 to 2 minutes. Add the bay leaves and the sage. When the onions turn golden, add the roughly chopped livers. Stir with a wooden spoon over moderate heat for 2 to 4 minutes. Add pepper. Pour in the wine and cognac and raise the heat. Let bubble for 5 minutes. Remove bay leaves when livers and sauce are almost dry.
Blend the chopped anchovies and capers with the remaining 2 tablespoons butter. Reheat chicken livers and when hot beat in the anchovy butter mixture. Blend well. Pile on toasted bread rounds and serve at room temperature. Serve with drinks.

CHICKEN WITH FORTY CLOVES OF GARLIC

Serves 4 to 5

3½-pound ready-to-cook chicken
Salt and freshly ground black pepper
2 bouquets garnis of Provençal herbs: bay leaf, parsley, thyme, celery leaves, savory, and a little rosemary
¼ cup olive oil
40 cloves of garlic, unpeeled
2 tablespoons anisette, pastis, or anisina
Flour and water paste

Preheat the oven to 350 degrees.
Rub the chicken with salt and pepper. Stuff with one of the herb bouquets, then truss the chicken. Place in the casserole. Combine oil, garlic cloves in their skins, anisette, salt and pepper, and remaining herb bouquet and dump over the bird. Cover and seal the casserole with a ribbon of flour and water paste. Set in the oven to bake 1 hour 15 minutes.

CHICKEN WITH MOROCCAN SPICE MIXTURE

Serves 4

2½ to 3 pound chicken, quartered
¼ cup vegetable oil
1½ cups finely chopped onions
Salt and freshly ground black pepper
2 teaspoons of Moroccan spice mixture (below)
2 ripe tomatoes, peeled, seeded, and chopped
4 sprigs each: fresh green coriander and parsley
2 tablespoons lemon juice
1 cup Greek green-cracked olives

MOROCCAN SPICE MIXTURE FOR LAMB AND CHICKEN STEWS
1 tablespoon each: ground ginger
ground black pepper
ground turmeric
½ tablespoon ground cinnamon
1 teaspoon grated nutmeg

Brown the chicken quarters in hot oil. Add the onions and stir-cook 3 to 4 minutes. Add salt, pepper, and spice mixture. Cook over medium heat 5 minutes, tossing and turning the chicken quarters often. Add the tomatoes. Cook over high heat until the pan juices are well reduced. Add ½ cup water and cook over moderate heat, stirring, until evaporated. Add another 1½ cups water, a little at a time, stirring constantly. When the pan juices are thick, add the herbs. Cover tightly and cook over low heat until the chicken is tender.
Add lemon juice and olives and cook 5 minutes longer to blend flavors.

DISH	INGREIDENTS	DIRECTIONS

 FRIED CHICKEN WITH SESAME SEEDS

Serves 4

4 leg and thigh pieces of chicken, halved
Salt and freshly ground black pepper
1 egg, lightly beaten
⅔ cup all-purpose flour
1 cup sesame seeds
2 teaspoons paprika
Oil for frying

Preheat the oven to 350 degrees.
Rub the chicken pieces with salt and pepper. Beat the egg with ½ cup water in a shallow bowl. Combine flour, sesame seeds, paprika, and salt to taste in a plastic bag, mixing well. Place the chicken pieces, 2 or 3 at a time, in the egg mixture then in the plastic bag. Close and shake until the chicken is nicely coated with the sesame seed mixture. Remove to a dish. Repeat with the remaining pieces of chicken.
In hot but not smoking oil brown the chicken pieces on both sides. Transfer to a baking sheet, set on the middle shelf of the preheated oven to finish the cooking in about 20 minutes.

 GINGERED CHICKEN STEW WITH CHICK PEAS

Serves 6 to 8

1 pound dried chick peas
2 chickens, quartered
1 teaspoon ground Jamaican ginger
1 rounded teaspoon freshly and finely ground black pepper
1 teaspoon salt
¼ teaspoon pulverized saffron
3 tablespoons finely chopped parsley
Pinch of ground cinnamon
1 leek, thinly sliced
¼ cup butter
1 cup thinly sliced onion
Salt

Soak chick peas overnight in water to cover.
Rub chickens with a mixture of ginger, black pepper, and salt. Drain chick peas, place in saucepan, cover with fresh water and cook, covered, 1 hour. Drain and submerge in a bowl of cold water. Rub chick peas to remove their skins. Place spiced chicken in deep casserole. Add saffron, parsley, cinnamon, leek, and butter. Cover with 1½ quarts water and bring to a boil. Reduce heat, cover, and simmer 1 hour, turning the chickens frequently in the resulting sauce.
Remove chickens when tender and keep warm.
Add finely sliced onions, peeled chick peas, and cook until the onions are soft and the sauce has reduced to a thick gravy. Reheat the chickens in the sauce. Taste for salt and serve hot.

 ITALIAN ROAST SQUAB WITH JUNIPER BERRIES

Serves 6

½ cup long grain rice
6 squabs and their livers
4 slices prosciutto or Canadian bacon
12 juniper berries, toasted in a dry skillet until shiny
Salt and freshly ground black pepper
6 slices bacon
4 ounces unsalted butter
⅓ cup dry white wine
⅓ cup chicken stock

Boil rice for five minutes; drain.
Puree livers with prosciutto in workbowl of food processor. Crush juniper berries in a mortar and rub through a sieve. Mix drained rice, pureed livers, and juniper berries. Season with salt and pepper. Stuff the squabs with this mixture. Place 1 strip of bacon across each breast and truss each bird. Rub roasting pan with 2 tablespoons butter. Rub each bird with 1 tablespoon butter. Roast at 350 degrees for about 1 hour. Degrease pan. Deglaze pan with white wine. Add stock and boil down to intensify flavors. Strain juices over the squabs.

 GRATED POTATO CAKE STUFFED WITH LEEKS

Serves 6

1 pound leeks, whites plus 1-inch shoots, roots trimmed, well-washed, and dried
5 tablespoons unsalted butter
½ cup heavy cream
Salt and pepper
2 pounds potatoes, peeled
¼ cup clarified butter

Thinly slice the leeks. Melt 2 tablespoons butter in a heavy casserole. Add leeks, cover, and cook gently for 6 minutes. Uncover. Add remaining butter and stew the sliced leeks 5 minutes longer. Add the cream and boil down to thicken. The leeks must not be runny. Season with salt and pepper. Cool.
Grate the potatoes or cut into very thin matchsticks. Rinse in several changes of water. Drain; spread them out on a kitchen towel to dry. Roll the towel and potatoes up like a rug and squeeze tightly to extrude all excess water. Potatoes will keep in this state for at least an hour.
Heat clarified butter in a large skillet. Spread out half the potatoes to cover bottom. Top with braised leeks, leaving an inch margin around the edge. Cover with remaining potatoes and pat into a cake-like form, about 10 inches in diameter. Cover and cook 5 minutes, shaking the pan often to keep the potatoes from sticking. The bottom should be golden and crusty. Invert and continue cooking, uncovered, over low heat 10 to 15 minutes, or until the potatoes are tender. Sprinkle with salt. Serve hot, cut into wedges.

 PUREED GREEN CELERY WITH CORIANDER SEED

Serves 8

2 bunches celery with green leaves attached
¾ pound peeled potatoes
3 tablespoons sweet butter
⅛ cup heavy cream
¼ teaspoon ground coriander seed
Salt and freshly ground pepper

Wash each celery rib and cut into 2-inch pieces. Do not remove green tops or scrape away strings. Cook the ribs with the potatoes in boiling salted water. Drain, and let cool slightly. Rice potatoes or rub through a food mill. Puree celery stalks and leaves in workbowl of food processor. Combine in a gratin pan. Add butter, cream, and seasoning to taste. Reheat in a 350 degree oven. Serve with grilled lamb.

DISH	INGREDIENTS	DIRECTIONS

 ARTICHOKE HEARTS IN RED WINE

Serves 6

1 cup cubed, blanched lean salt pork
6 raw artichoke bottoms, quartered
1 cup cubed prosciutto
1½ cups chopped onions
½ cup chopped mushrooms
⅔ cup minced scallions
1 cup sliced carrots
2 teaspoons sliced garlic
2 teaspoons tomato paste
1 bottle coarse full-bodied red wine
2 bay leaves
1 sprig of thyme
3 parsley sprigs
6 black peppercorns
Salt
¾ cup brown sauce (or gravy)
Pinch of sugar
2 tablespoons olive oil
1½ tablespoons brandy
2 tablespoons sweet butter
½ tablespoon minced parsley

In a skillet, lightly brown the salt pork. Add the trimmings of the raw artichokes, the prosciutto, onions, mushrooms, scallions, carrots, and garlic. Sauté 1 minute, stirring. Blend in tomato paste. Add red wine, herbs, peppercorns, and salt to taste. Reduce heat and cook gently 1½ hours. Stir in the brown sauce. Simmer 5 minutes longer. Strain, pressing down on the vegetables to extract all their juices. You should have about 2 cups sauce. Reduce if necessary. Adjust seasoning adding a pinch of sugar if necessary to balance flavors.
In a clean skillet, sauté artichoke pieces in hot olive oil until lightly browned around the edges. Add brandy and reduce to a glaze. Add red wine sauce and simmer 15 minutes. Swirl in butter to thicken. Sprinkle with parsley.
Serve with grilled meat or poultry or alone as a first course.

 PAELLA

Serves 8

¾ cup olive oil
1 cup grated onion
½ pound boneless pork shoulder cut into 1-inch cubes
3-pound chicken, cut into 8 pieces
1 teaspoon finely chopped garlic
2 cups peeled, seeded, and chopped tomatoes
2 bay leaves
4 sprigs fresh parsley
Salt and freshly ground black pepper
½ teaspoon pulverized saffron
12 mussels, well scrubbed
½ pound small clams, scrubbed and soaked in cold water 30 minutes to eliminate sand
¼ pound sweet green peppers, seeded, deribbed, and cut lengthwise into thin strips
¼ pound green beans, trimmed and cut into 1-inch lengths, or 9 ounces frozen artichoke hearts, thawed
3 cups raw imported Spanish or Italian rice
7-ounce jar roasted red peppers, drained and cut into thin strips
½ pound shelled and deveined shrimp
¼ pound fully cooked chorizo sausage, skinned and thinly sliced
2 lemons, quartered

In a large casserole heat ⅓ cup olive oil and in it cook ½ cup grated onion for 2 minutes, stirring. Add the pork and chicken and sauté for 5 minutes, stirring. Then add the garlic, tomatoes, herbs, salt, pepper, and saffron. Cover and cook over medium heat about 25 minutes, stirring from time to time.
Meanwhile steam the mussels and clams in 1 cup water until they open, about 5 minutes. Discard any that do not open. Reserve the mussels, clams, and cooking liquor and discard the shells. Strain the liquor.
Add the green peppers and green beans or artichokes to the casserole. Cook, covered, 5 to 10 minutes longer.
Meanwhile heat the remaining olive oil in the paella pan and cook the remaining ½ cup grated onion 1 minute. Add the rice and cook, stirring until all the grains are coated, 8 to 10 minutes.
Add the mussel and clam liquor plus 7 cups water to the casserole. Bring to the boil. Slowly pour the bubbling sauce over the rice. Then slide the remaining contents of the casserole evenly over the sizzling rice. Add the red peppers, shrimp, chorizo slices, mussels, and clams. Stir once. Cook, uncovered, over brisk heat until the liquid is absorbed and the rice is tender, about 20 minutes. Rotate and shake the pan from time to time to cook the rice evenly. Allow the contents to rest 5 minutes before serving. Serve directly from the pan with the lemon wedges.

 STUFFED TOMATOES

Serves 4

8 firm red tomatoes
Salt
¼ loaf French or Italian bread
2 cloves garlic, peeled and crushed
Olive oil
2-ounce tin anchovy fillets
¼ cup pine nuts
¼ cup yellow raisins plumped in water, then drained
2 tablespoons chopped fresh parsley
Freshly ground pepper

Cut a slice off the top of each tomato, scoop out the pulp and seeds, and discard or reserve for some other use. Salt the shells and set them upside down to drain.
Thinly slice the bread, rub with garlic, and cut into ¼-inch cubes. Brown lightly in olive oil and set aside to drain on paper towels.
Drain, rinse, drain, and mash the anchovies. Mix with remaining ingredients. Stuff tomatoes, cover with tops, and fit into baking dish. Bake 20 minutes in a hot oven. Serve hot.

DISH	INGREDIENTS	DIRECTIONS

ANDRÉ DAGUIN'S PEPPER COOKIES

Makes 7 dozen

1½ cups all-purpose flour
¼ cup sugar
4 tablespoons (½ stick) unsalted butter
¼ cup olive oil
⅞ teaspoon freshly ground white pepper
1 small egg, lightly beaten

In the workbowl of a food processor fitted with the metal blade, combine the flour, sugar, butter, and olive oil and process for 10 seconds. Add the pepper and egg; blend again until just combined. Form the dough into a ball; wrap in waxed paper or plastic wrap; and chill overnight.
Line a baking sheet with parchment paper and preheat the oven to 350 degrees.
Roll the dough out between floured sheets of waxed paper or plastic wrap to a 9 by 12 inch rectangle. Beginning at the wide end, fold the dough up ¾ inch and over itself using the paper or wrap as an aid. Cut along the width of the fold and then cut the resulting strip into ¾-inch pieces.
Repeat the process with the remaining dough.
Transfer the cookies to the prepared baking sheet, and bake in the preheated oven for 10 minutes, or until the cookies are just golden, not brown. Cool on racks. They will keep a long time in an airtight jar or metal container.

CLOVE ORANGE ICE

Makes 1½ quarts

2¾ cups granulated sugar
2 cups water
2 whole cloves
1 quart orange juice, strained
½ cup strained lemon juice
½ tablespoon grated orange rind

Combine sugar, water, and cloves in a large saucepan. Cook, stirring, over medium heat until the sugar is dissolved. Boil the syrup for 5 minutes. Strain into a mixing bowl and let cool. Combine orange juice, lemon juice, and grated rind. Stir into sugar syrup. Set in the freezer compartment until the mixture is mushy but set around the edges of the bowl. Use an electric beater and beat until smooth. Return to the freezer for 4 to 5 hours. Beat again, pour into mold, and freeze it until almost firm.

FILBERT CRISPS

Makes 45 crisps

5 tablespoons unsalted butter, softened
1 cup sugar
½ cup egg whites (about 4 egg whites)
¾ cup ground hazelnuts
2 teaspoons grated orange rind
⅔ cup cake flour

Preheat the oven to 425 degrees.
Place the butter and the sugar in the mixing bowl; beat until creamy. Beat in the egg whites. Fold in the ground nuts and the grated orange rind. Using a rubber spatula gently stir in the flour 2 tablespoons at a time. Pack into a pastry bag. Drop small rounds of batter onto the greased baking sheets, leaving 3 inches between each round. Using a knife dipped in cold water, flatten each into a thin oval shape. Bake until the edges are golden brown—about 10 minutes.
Use a spatula to detach the crisps and allow to cool on wire racks. Store in an airtight tin.

SAUTÉED APPLES WITH LEMON OR ORANGE MARMALADE

Serves 4

2 large tart green apples
3 tablespoons unsalted butter
4 tablespoons imported lemon marmalade
Grated nutmeg
Confectioners sugar

Peel, core, and slice the apples into 12 pieces each.
In a small skillet, melt 1½ tablespoons butter.
Add the apple slices and sauté them, turning them often, for 1 minute or until they are barely soft. Push the apples to one side of the skillet, add the marmalade and remaining 1½ tablespoons butter, and mix with the pan juices.
Fold in the apple slices and cook over high heat, turning the apple slices constantly until caramelized around the edges.
Sprinkle with grated nutmeg and confectioners sugar. Serve hot.

SWEET AND SOUR CHERRIES WITH MACE

¾ pound firm, not too sweet cherries
1 cup red wine vinegar
⅔ cup sugar
Ground mace

Wash and prick each cherry once or twice with a needle. Trim each stem, leaving about 1 inch attached. Heat the vinegar in an enameled or stainless steel pan, add the sugar and cook, stirring, over low heat until the sugar is dissolved. Raise the heat and boil for 3 to 4 minutes. Stir in a good pinch of ground mace. Cool slightly.
Place the cherries in a ¾-quart preserving jar and pour the liquid over them. Seal closely and leave at least 6 weeks before using.

DISH	INGREDIENTS	DIRECTIONS

MOROCCAN BREAD

Makes 2 six-inch round loaves

1 package active dry yeast
1 teaspoon granulated sugar
3½ cups unbleached flour
1 cup whole-wheat flour
2 teaspoons salt
½ cup lukewarm milk
1 teaspoon sesame seeds
1 tablespoon aniseed
Cornmeal

Soften the yeast in ¼ cup sugared lukewarm water. Let stand 2 minutes, then stir and set in a warm place until the yeast is bubbly and doubles in volume. Meanwhile, mix the flours with the salt in a large mixing bowl.

Stir the bubbling yeast into the flour, then add the milk and enough lukewarm water to form a stiff dough. (Since flours differ in their ability to absorb moisture, no precise amount can be given.) Turn the dough out onto a lightly floured board and knead hard with closed fists, adding water if necessary. To knead, push the dough outward. (It will take anywhere from 10 to 15 minutes to knead this dough thoroughly and achieve a smooth, elastic consistency. If using an electric beater with a dough hook, knead 7 to 8 minutes at slow speed.) During the final part of the kneading, add the spices. After the dough has been thoroughly kneaded, form into two balls and let stand 5 minutes on the board.

Lightly grease a mixing bowl. Transfer the first ball of dough to the greased bowl and form into a cone shape by grasping the dough with one hand and rotating it against the sides of the bowl, held by the other hand. Turn out onto a baking sheet that has been sprinkled with cornmeal. Flatten the cone with the palm of the hand to form a flattened disk about 5 inches in diameter with a slightly raised center. Repeat with the second ball of dough. Cover loosely with a damp towel and let rise about 2 hours in a warm place. (To see if the bread has fully risen, poke your finger gently into the dough—the bread is ready for baking if the dough does not spring back.)

Preheat the oven to 400 degrees.

Using a fork, prick the bread around the sides 3 or 4 times and place on the center shelf of the oven. Bake 12 minutes, then lower the heat to 300 degrees and bake 30 to 40 minutes more. When done, the bread will sound hollow when tapped on the bottom. Remove and let cool. Cut in wedges just before serving.

HONEY CINNAMON CAKE WITH WALNUTS

1¼ cups sugar
¾ cup honey
1¼ teaspoons ground cinnamon
Juice of ½ lemon
1¾ cups chopped walnuts
1½ cups all-purpose flour, sifted
1 teaspoon double-acting baking powder
4 tablespoons sweet butter, softened to room temperature
4 eggs, separated

To make the syrup: Cook ¾ cup sugar and ¾ cup water in a small saucepan, stirring. Bring to the boil. Simmer 5 minutes. Stir in the honey, ¼ teaspoon ground cinnamon, and the lemon juice. Cook at the simmer 5 minutes longer. Allow to cool completely.

Preheat the oven to 350 degrees.

Combine 1¼ cups nuts, remaining cinnamon, flour, and baking powder. Set aside. Cream remaining ½ cup sugar with butter until light and fluffy. Add egg yolks, one at a time, beating well after each addition. Beat in the walnut mixture. Separately beat the egg whites until stiff. Gently fold the egg whites into the walnut mixture. Put the mixture into the prepared cake pan. Sprinkle the top with the remaining ½ cup chopped walnuts. Set in the oven to bake until the cake tests done.

Remove the cake from the oven. Cut into diamond shapes in the cakepan. Pour cool syrup over the hot cake. Cover and allow to stand overnight before serving.

Seasoning Around the World

WAVERLY ROOT

Flavor is the gift of Asia. Of the two most important categories of plants which add tastiness to food, spices and herbs, the first are almost solely Asiatic; the second, though also Asiatic, come from a part of Asia which shares its largesse with Europe.

The great majority of the principal spices of the world (cinnamon, cloves, ginger, mace, nutmeg, pepper) are natives of an area which extends from India to the Molucca Islands. The great majority of the principal herbs of the world (anise, basil, bay leaf, chervil, coriander, cress, fennel, fenugreek, marjoram, mint, oregano, rosemary, sage, tarragon, thyme) come from an area which starts in Iran but spreads through Asia Minor along the northern shore of the Mediterranean into southern Europe. The onion-garlic family, whose members are important seasoners, is believed to have originated in Central Asia. Citrus fruits serve as flavorers too: they probably started in China.

Seasoners are not the most decisive factors in shaping the character of a cuisine, but they are the most spectacular. They force themselves first upon our attention. When we enter a strange country, we learn at once what sort of cooking we may expect from the nature of the condiments we find waiting for us on restaurant tables.

In France there used to be, on each table, a four-place cruet containing olive oil, vinegar, salt, and pepper, to permit the diner to make his own salad dressing in accord with his own taste, a habit now, unhappily, in decline. In Italy there is grated Parmesan cheese, in Germany, probably, grated horseradish. Scandinavia offers chopped dill or dill-mustard sauce; England, mustard or Worcestershire sauce; and the United States, of course, ketchup (which is of Asiatic origin, as is Worcestershire sauce).

Everywhere in Latin America you will find tiny hot chilies chopped into vinegar or vegetable oil or both, to which Brazil will add a shaker of manioc meal. Everywhere in southeastern Asia you will find a salty liquid derived from fermented fish which is identical with the all-purpose seasoner of ancient Rome, *garum;* in the Far East, soybean sauce. (In India, there is nothing; Indians do not eat in the restaurants. They are for foreigners.)

Ethiopia offers its fiery red *berberé* sauce, perhaps the hottest all-purpose seasoner in the world, with the possible exception of the Latin American chili condiment. But you have only to move on to North Africa to meet its complete antithesis. In the luxury restaurants of the Maghreb (Tunisia, Algeria, Morocco) your eyes will delight in the graceful shape of a tall slender vase, often of silver, which looks as though it were meant to hold a single orchid; but even an orchid stem could not pass through the narrow opening at its top. It is designed to release its precious contents only drop by drop. It holds rose water.

Abundant, colorful spices displayed in an open-air market in Guatemala city.

SEASONERS AND STAPLES

If Asia is the principal source of the world's seasoners, why doesn't food everywhere taste Asiatic? Twice during the world's history it did. When the Roman Asiatic Army returned to Italy in 185 B.C. bringing strange flavorers with it, Roman food foundered in Asiatic excess. When the Crusaders returned from Asia Minor in the Middle Ages, Europe wallowed briefly in Oriental spicing. "Modern Indian cookery probably comes closest to medieval," Anne Willan wrote. But Eastern spices were soon tamed by incompatibility with Western staples: wheat married less easily with vivid seasoning than rice, meat less easily than fish.

EUROPE

The basic grain of Europe is wheat and its basic meat beef, both of which accord best with what we might call reasonable unsensational seasoning. Italy, which uses much rice and prefers veal to beef, is accordingly a country which spices its food with bravura. In Central and Slavic Europe, rye bread and pork encourage flavors sometimes strong and sour, while the pungent spicing of Scandinavia developed in function of its fish, especially the herring.

FISH
Dill

MEAT
WHEAT
Basil
Garlic
Olive oil
Couscous

Okra
Baobab

MILLET
Berberé sauce

MAIZE

Dried lemons

Asafetida
Pepper
Ginger
Cardamom

Cinnamon

WHEAT

Ginseng

Soybean sauce

RICE

FISH

Nuoc Mam

Nutmeg
Cloves

RICE
FISH
Seaweed

ROSEMARY, "dew of the sea" (because it grows well on coasts), is an herb much used in European cooking.

SWEET PEPPERS, common vegetables in Europe, are natives of America, brothers to the more pungent chilies.

GINGER, widely [in] Asia, probably [origi]nated in India, f[rom?] name comes fro[m] Sanskrit sring[a] "horn-root."

NUTMEG, original[ly] confined to a few sma[ll] islands in the Molu[c]cas, was the last Asia[]tic spice to reach Euro[]pe, in 1190.

AFRICA

South of the Sahara, Africa originally knew few cereals, but ate much game; consequently seasoning was bland before the sixteenth century.

INDIA

When the Aryans invaded India from the north, where dairy cattle were important, they brought with them a cuisine which cooked with butter, in the form of ghee (but the poor used sesame or mustard-seed oil, the very poor, safflower oil); the south continued to use vegetable oils or coconut milk. The north ate wheat, the south rice. These differences made the south even more receptive than the north to imaginative seasoning.

Indian food is colorful. Ingredients for a holiday meal assembled at Jangri, southern India—wheat flour, sugar syrup, saf-from—are a joyful yellow.

SOUTHEAST ASIA

The diet of Southeast Asia is dominated by rice and fish—two foods which cry out for vivid subtle seasoning and here receive it. The "salt" of this region is a liquid made from fermented fish, almost identical, curiously, with the all-purpose seasoner of ancient Rome, garum, made from fermented fish too.

The water buffalo shown tilling a flooded Asiatic rice in this eighteenth-century woodcut is not quite outdated yet.

ANGLO-SAXON cooking is anything but reticent in its seasoning, partly because of the forthright nature of its staples—wheat (oats in Scotland, potatoes in Ireland), beef (with Worcestershire sauce), and mutton (with mint sauce), but even more, perhaps, because of climate. Cold, damp winters help make the Briton one of the world's greatest overeaters of sugar, a warming energy-building food.

THE FAR EAST

Except in the distant north, rice is the basic cereal in the Far East and in Southeast Asia too, for that matter); and the area harbors the world's greatest fish eaters, the Japanese. Both rice and fish demand assertive spicing, and get it in the form of that universal all-purpose seasoner, the salty soybean sauce.

NORTH AMERICA

Hearty foods—wheat and beef—and for much of the United States rigorous winters, encourage the use of strong seasoners rather than subtle ones: for instance, the white mustard, whose plant is shown above. A unique North American seasoner is maple sugar.

Mustard

MAIZE

Maple sugar

WHEAT

MEAT   Peanuts

Chili

LATIN AMERICA

Maize (bland), cassava flour (insipid), and the potato (modest) are the staples of Latin America; the sharp bite of the native chilies lifts their low taste thresholds. Subtropical and tropical climates are consistent with chilies too, and also with the luscious, aromatic velvety vanilla and allspice.

MAIZE

Vanilla
Allspice
Cassava

POTATO

MEAT

The eating habits of large part of the world were changed when sugar cane was transplanted from its native Asia (India?) to the West Indies, with such success that sugar, previously a luxury food, decreased in price and became available to everybody.

A familiar scene in every Latin American market is the chili seller, his brightly colored wares spread out on the ground before him. It is familiar too in other warm countries, for the New World chili has conquered the Old World.

Cardamom, Cinnamon, Ginger,
Lemon, Mung bean
sprouts, Pepper, Poke,
Sesame, Tamarind, Turmeric,
Zedoary root

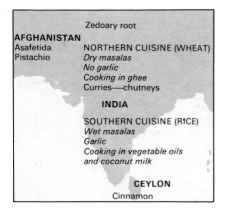

IMPORTED SEASONERS USED
COMMONLY IN INDIA

Anise, Asafetida, Chili, pepper,
Coriander, Cress, Cumin, Dill,
Fennel, Fenugreek,
Garlic (in south only), Mustard,
Onion, Peanut, Pistachio, Saffron

INDIA

For Westerners, the taste of India is the taste of curry; but curries are only one manifestation of what really characterizes Indian cooking—the skillful use of spices. India probably uses more different seasoners than any other area in the world; and it uses them more subtlely.

"The variety, the combination, and the use of spices are the major factors that distinguish Indian cooking from any other cuisine in the world," Santha Rama Rau has written. "Through the choice of spices, through their proportion and blending, a good Indian cook expresses imagination, ingenuity, individuality, subtlety, adventurousness"; and she reminds us that in some parts of India a bride stands barefooted on the stone used for grinding spices, while in others she brings her own private mortar and pestle with her to her husband's home. "Indian cooks," wrote Caroline Bates, "combine spices as painters mix colors, striving for the proper proportion, balance, and nuances of tone and grinding different mixtures... for every dish.... Indian cooking owes its distinctive character to the refined use of spices."

Most Westerners know by now that curry powder does not come from a single plant, like cinnamon or nutmeg, but is a mixture of seasoners; many persons, however, still think that it is an invariable mixture, compounded always of the same spices in the same proportions. Actually no standardized curry powder exists in India except what is called, disdainfully, "railway curry." Dining cars are ill equipped for subtlety; the conditions under which they operate oblige them to stock a single mixture which, being designed to go with everything, does not go well with anything. No Indian housewife would use the same powder for every curry she cooks, any more than a Western housewife would flavor everything from soup to desserts with the same seasoners. The difference between the Indian cook and the

Western cook is that the latter puts the different herbs and spices called for by her recipe into the dish separately, one by one; the Indian cook assembles all the seasoners first, works them into a common blend, and puts the resulting mixture into the dish. The ideal is that the flavor of the curry should be the flavor of the *blend*; the different ingredients which have gone into it should not be individually identifiable. What the Westerner calls a curry powder, the Indian calls a dry masala; there are wet masalas too, semiliquid pastes compounded also of a variety of flavorers. Curries are not all hot, as Westerners are inclined to think: they run from the fiery to mixtures so bland that foreigners with taste buds less finely attuned than those of Indians find it difficult to perceive their savor at all. This is true also of chutneys—relishes—which range from sweet jam-like kinds made chiefly with fruit through sweet-and-sour varieties to hot spicy sour concoctions never found outside India. A wide variety of spices accounts also for the soul of achars, Indian oil pickles. There is a marked difference in India between the cuisines of the north and the south. The basic cereal of the north is wheat: the south and the east eat rice. The common cooking fat of the north is ghee, clarified butter; that of the south is vegetable oil (but never olive oil, which would falsify the subtle seasonings of Indian cooking by adding another flavor of its own) or sometimes coconut milk. As a result, the south uses many more herbs and spices than the north, and prefers them, if possible, fresh. The north, where many dishes call for slight seasoning or none at all, is often content with dried seasoners. Garlic is popular in the south, but is rarely eaten in the north, where orthodox Hindus frequently refuse to use it at all.

The spice which goes oftenest into curries is turmeric, whose aromatic, slightly bitter, and somewhat musty flavor represents for many Westerners the typical taste of curry; when it is not turmeric it is probably coriander, second only to turmeric in frequency of use, though it is not native to India, or even fenugreek, which may not be native either, though in this case there is room for doubt. The widely used chilies, which make hot curries hottest, are also foreign.

After these, the seasoners most used are black pepper, cumin, cardamom, aniseed, dill, mustard, sesame, fennel, saffron, ginger, and mung bean sprouts. India also employs a number of flavorers not much found elsewhere: the seeds of the jackfruit, which might be described as the poor man's breadfruit; powdered pumpkin rind; *tamarind,* sharp but refreshing; *anvla,* a fruit which looks like a gooseberry but is sharp in taste; *asafetida,* whose gum is the part used; *camphor,* combined in a dessert with bananas; *tamarish manna,* an excretion provoked when insects damage the twigs of this tree; a small dark-brown flower called *badiani khatai;* a South Indian fruit, *kokum,* described in Sanskrit literature as resembling in color and texture the mouth of a beautiful woman (but not, one hopes, in taste, for it is extremely acid); and we might add also the flavoring of the Bengal *undhya* ("upside-down"), a vegetable dish flavored with salt, red pepper, cumin, coriander, fenugreek, fennel, ginger, and garlic, turned out of its cooking pot onto moistened hay, which gives it, unexpectedly, a smoky flavor. The hay is not eaten, but as its function is to contribute taste, it is entitled to be called a condiment.

Tejpat, used in Indian cooking, is often mistranslated as "bay." Bay leaves, however, are never used in curries.

SOUTHEAST ASIA

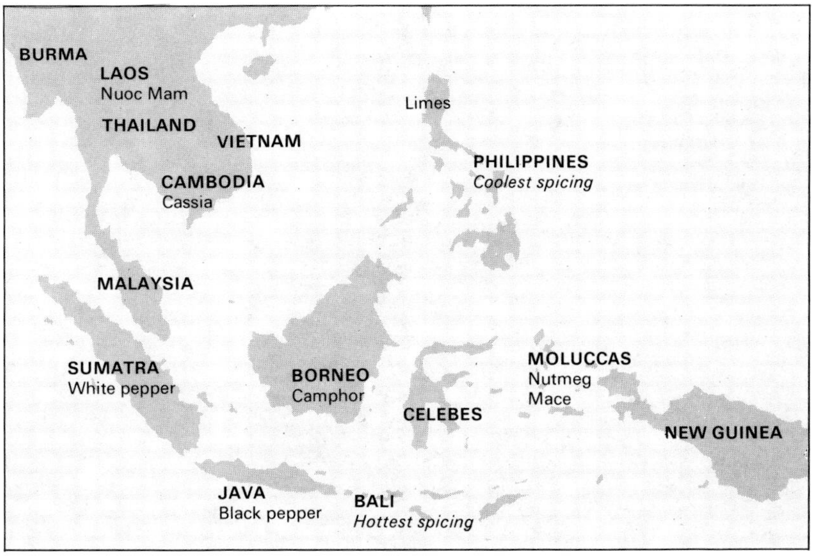
BURMA
LAOS
Nuoc Mam
THAILAND
VIETNAM
CAMBODIA
Cassia
Limes
PHILIPPINES
Coolest spicing
MALAYSIA
SUMATRA
White pepper
BORNEO
Camphor
CELEBES
MOLUCCAS
Nutmeg
Mace
NEW GUINEA
JAVA
Black pepper
BALI
Hottest spicing

The chief unifying elements in the cooking of Southeast Asia are a cereal (rice) and a seasoner (*nuoc mam* in Vietnam, *tuk trey* in Cambodia, *nam pla* in Thailand, *ngapi-yet* in Burma, *patis* in the Philippines, *bagoong* in Hawaii) which has been described as "a smelly liquid redolent of rancid fish, unpleasing to Western palates." Actually the fish is not rancid, but salted and fermented; the liquid pressed from it, which Indochinese gourmets enrich with ground *karung,* a water bug which looks like a cockroach, is the salt of Southeast Asia, used to bring out the taste of many kinds of foods, just as salt is used in the Occident.

Northern Burma bows to Chinese influence by using soybean sauce as its universal seasoner, but in the south this gives way to the ubiquitous fermented fish condiment, along with another almost as common, a salty shrimp paste. Indian influence causes Burmese meals to be built around curries, sometimes cooled by cooking in coconut milk, though the normal cooking fats are sesame or peanut oil. Many Burmese dishes are too acid to please Westerners.

Thailand bows to Chinese influence by us-

SEASONERS
OF SOUTHEAST ASIA

Burma

Coconut milk, Curries, Fermented fish sauce, Peanut oil, Sesame oil, Shrimp paste, Soybean sauce (in north)

Malaysia

Candlenut, Coconut milk, Chilies, Lemon grass

Thailand

Chilies, Coriander (leaves), Curries, Fermented fish sauce, Lemon grass, Lotus (root, seeds), Mung bean sprouts, Peppermint, Pessicary, Saffron, Soybean sauce

Indochina

Bamboo shoots, Cassia, Curries, Fermented fish sauce, Ginger, Jellyfish, Lemon grass, Lily petals, Soybean sauce, Star anise, Water chestnut, Water convolvulus

Indonesia

Bay leaf, Black pepper (Java), Chilies, Cloves (Moluccas), Coconut milk, Coffee (Java), Garlic, Ginger, Keluak nut, Mace (Moluccas), Mung bean sprouts, Nutmeg (Moluccas), Onions, Peanut oil, Sesame seeds, Soybean sauce, Turmeric, White pepper (Sumatra)

Philippine Islands

Chilies, Fermented fish sauce, Garlic, Lime, Onions, Shrimp paste, Tamarind

ing water chestnuts, lotus roots or seeds, and soybean sauce (on salads); to Indian by using much curry *(khaeng phed)*; and to regional preferences by employing the characteristic fermented fish sauce. Its original native seasoning was probably mild, which has survived in its bland soups, flavored with musky coriander leaves or with a herb popular in many parts of Southeast Asia—citronella or lemon grass.

"The delicate perfume of an herb or a leaf constitutes perhaps the greatest contribution of Vietnam to the universal cuisine," according to *The Song of Pounded Rice,* a Vietnamese cookbook. Some are indeed delicate, like a number of borrowings from China (water chestnuts, star anise, bamboo shoots, mung bean sprouts); the ever-present basil; *nghe,* described as a sort of saffron, though it seems closer to safflower; the water convolvulus, which tastes like a cross between cabbage and kale; and its own spe-

cialty, dried lily petals. Others are more authoritative, for Vietnamese cooking is distinguished by the wide range of its seasoners. *Rau ram,* or persicary, also known in English as lady's-thumb, is peppery. Among mints, Vietnam prefers the sharp purple-stemmed varieties derived from peppermint and goes them one better with a local type called *tia to,* whose lacy purple leaves are sharp in odor and flavor. What appears to be a variety of chives is stronger than European chives, and the ginger-like root called *rieng* outdoes ginger. The strangest seasoner in the Vietnamese pantry is *sua*—jellyfish.

Laotian seasoners are much like those of Vietnam, used with greater finesse. Each spice or herb is cooked separately for its optimum time until the moment arrives when they all go into the pot together. Laos sometimes strews over its dishes an aromatic herb not thought of as a seasoner in the West—

Since the staple food everywhere in Southeast Asia is rice, a bland grain that greatly profits from spicing, the peoples of this area have developed a genius for seasoning. Although new strains of "miracle rice" have been introduced, most Asiatics dislike their flavors and textures. Modern machinery has also been introduced, but most rice paddies are still worked by hand. Recent studies have shown, however, that there is no significant difference in yield between rice farms that use tractors and those that stick to bullocks and hand labor.

marijuana. Cambodia sprinkles flowers on its rice.

The cuisine of Malaysia is modeled on that of India, but uses mild sweet spices where India might prefer stronger ones. One of its favorite seasoners is the mild-flavored candlenut, and the cooling coconut milk is often used for cooking.

It is Indonesia which eats the hottest, spiciest food of Southeast Asia. Bali, where Indian influence is strong, likes the most fiery food of all. Its standard seasoning mixture is *tabia bun*, made from turmeric, sesame seeds, bay leaves, onion, garlic, ginger, and two pungent roots which seem to have no names in European languages, *kentjur* and *laos*. Borneo produces a flavorer of minimum use—camphor.

Yet the favorite seasoners of Indonesia are, inconsistently, mild: soybeans, peanuts, and mung bean shoots, in that order. A local condiment which is less restrained is the black bitter *keluak* nut; the Moluccas, contrarily, grow a milder nut, the *kenari*, which has been compared to the almond. These are the original Spice Islands, once the only habitat in the world of mace, nutmeg, and cloves. They still produce 70 percent of the first two, but export more than they use, while the clove trade has been lost to Zanzibar.

The Philippine Islands enjoy the coolest cuisine of Southeast Asia. The fermented fish sauce and spicy shrimp paste are still found here, but both are blander than anywhere else. A favorite seasoner is lime juice or peel, from a local variety, the *calamansi*. Philippine food strikes Westerners as being basically sour.

The chief links between the cooking of Southeast Asia and the Pacific Islands are coconuts and rice, the latter a comparatively recent arrival. Before its advent, the basic food of the Islands was *poi*, the sour purplish paste pounded from the taro root, a discourager of seasoning; the Pacific Islands

were in any case poor in native spices or herbs, though Hawaii, like the Philippines, has developed its own citrus fruit, the Kaffir lime; its favorite nut is the macadamia, which is anything but pungent. What faint flavoring Pacific foods have is often applied from the outside—by the leaves in which meat, fish, vegetables, or fruit are wrapped for cooking. The broad leaves of the native *ti* plant are the most popular for this purpose, but the slightly musty savor they exude, while appreciated in fish, is inappropriate for fruits, which are therefore wrapped in banana leaves. Peculiar to Tahiti are the leaves of the wild *fafa* plant, employed especially to envelop chicken, because, it is explained, "they don't scratch the throat."

Southeast Asia is all islands and peninsulas; no spot is very far from the sea. The area therefore eats more fish than meat; besides, fish is cheaper. Like rice, fish calls for seasoning, and demands even more imperiously that it should be ingenious and subtle. Thus the basic foods of the region conspire to encourage the development of the art of using herbs and spices skillfully, which is characteristic of this part of the world.

Tumeric is widely used in India for coloring sweet dishes and curries. Commercial tumeric is used for coloring mustard and pickles.

THE FAR EAST

NATIVE SEASONERS
USED IN THE FAR EAST

China
Bamboo (shoots, sprouts),
Birds' nests, Cassia,
Chinese cabbage,
Chinese celery cabbage,
Cloud ear fungus, Ginger,
Ginseng, Jujube, Longan,
Lotus (root, seeds), Shark fins,
Soybean sauce, Star anise,
Szechwan pepper,
Tiger lily buds,
Water chestnut

Japan adds:
Bonito (dried), Burdock root,
Chrysanthemum, Giant radish,
Gingko nut, Japan pepper,
Sea urchin (pickled), Seaweed,
Shi-i-take mushroom, Yuzu (lime)

"There are dishes of all flavors," explained the Chinese poem *The Summons of the Soul* (third century B.C.), "bitter, salt, sour, hot, and sweet." Among the examples of fine foods cited in the same poem was "seethed tortoises highly seasoned, but not so much as to spoil the taste." This is the basic principle of Chinese cooking—plenty of condiments, but used always to accent the natural flavors of food, not to call attention to their own tastes.

The universal seasoner of the Far East is the salty, pungent soybean sauce; but the Chinese use it with commendable moderation. Soybeans appear as condiments in many other forms also—as bean sprouts; as soybean cake; as soybean "milk," often given to

eaten only unripe, when their flavor is agreeable.

Soybean sauce, made from beans fermented with the aid of bacteria and yeast, does not have to be as pungent as the liquid we are accustomed to encountering on the tables of Chinese restaurants. There are many kinds, some of them flavored by other substances—aromatic leaves, ginger, citronella, onions, fermented fish, or even fermented chicken. In China as in India, olive oil is not used as a cooking fat, though peanut oil, sesame seed oil, and even the not quite neutral soybean oil are common.

China is unlike India in using standardized seasoning mixtures. Five-Spice Powder, in its commonest form, is compounded of finely ground star anise, Szechwan pepper, fennel, cloves, and licorice root. Master Sauce starts with a small amount of Five-Spice Powder in soybean sauce, and adds more star anise, ginger, tangerine peel, salt, and sugar; it is kept for repeated cookings, growing richer with time from the flavors of the foods which have been cooked in it, and kept "alive" by regular replenishing of its seasoners. Hoisin Sauce is a sweet-and-spicy combination of seasonal vegetables with soybean sauce, chili pepper, garlic, sugar, and salt. The chutney-like *duk* sauce is made from red plums. Oyster sauce has no fishy taste, and indeed not much flavor of its own, but it brings out other flavors.

Northern Chinese cooking (Peking, Honan), versatile and vinegary, also likes the scorched meat of Mongolia, where meat is cooked very simply, but is served accompanied by a host of relishes, sauces, and seasoners, echoed in Peking when coriander leaves, vinegar, shrimp sauce, sesame jam, chili oil, mashed bean curd, and soybean sauce are placed on the table, with a bowl for each diner in which he can mix for himself the seasoning of his heart's desire.

Coastal food (Shanghai) is only lightly spiced. It is characterized by much use of the

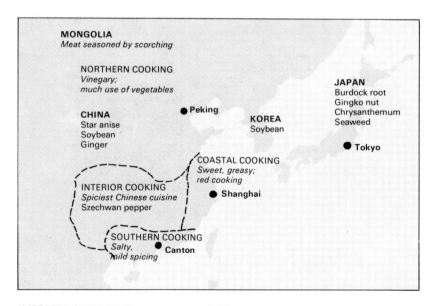

MONGOLIA
Meat seasoned by scorching

NORTHERN COOKING
Vinegary;
much use of vegetables

CHINA
Star anise
Soybean
Ginger

● Peking

KOREA
Soybean

JAPAN
Burdock root
Gingko nut
Chrysanthemum
Seaweed

● Tokyo

COASTAL COOKING
Sweet, greasy;
red cooking

INTERIOR COOKING
Spiciest Chinese cuisine
Szechwan pepper

● Shanghai

SOUTHERN COOKING
Salty,
mild spicing   ● Canton

IMPORTED SEASONERS
USED IN THE FAR EAST

Cashew, Chives, Clove, Coriander,
Fennel, Garlic, Gourds,
Hemp seed, Horseradish,
Licorice, Mustard seed, Onions,
Poppyseed, Rape seed, Scallions,
Sesame seed and oil, Walnuts

children instead of cow's milk, scarce in cattle-poor China, which is why the soybean is called "the cow of the East"; but soybean curd, which looks like custard, is "meat without bones" for those who think it tastes like beef extract. Other Chinese liken it to strong cheese, little liked in China, and call one type *chou tofu*, stinking curds. Soybean grains, bitter if mature, are

FENNEL

SZECHWAN PEPPER

LICORICE ROOT

STAR ANISE

CLOVE PLANT

The ingredients of Chinese Five-Spice Powder, a basic blend used either on its own or as a foundation for complicated sauces.

technique called "red cooking," the color produced by braising foods in the standard combination of soybean sauce, wine, star anise, ginger, and sugar. This cuisine is relatively sweet and, in the opinion of Chinese from other regions, greasy, for lard is the usual cooking fat.

Southern cooking (Canton) is in many opinions China's best; but when this assessment comes from Americans it is partly a tribute to familiarity, for American Chinese cooking is a branch of Cantonese—the first Chinese to settle in the United States. The flavoring, though a trifle salty, is on the cool side. Garlic sauce is used, but black bean, oyster, and lobster sauces are more characteristic.

The cooking of the interior (Szechwan) has a worldwide reputation for hot spicing which is not entirely deserved; its chief characteristic is the wide variety of seasoners used rather than their strength; it also tends to be oily. One reason for this reputation may be the success of Szechwan pepper (*fagara*, not the same as Indian pepper) in forcing itself upon your attention. Ordinary pepper registers its effect immediately and then fades away; Szechwan pepper, barely tasted when swallowed, develops a rapid crescendo which can leave you gasping. Szechwan cooking is hot only in comparison with other Chinese cuisines; it has resisted the more violent influences of its neighbors, India and Vietnam. One of its superficial characteristics is much use of crunchy bamboo shoots, which are certainly mild enough.

Bamboo shoots are much liked elsewhere in China too, and so are dried mushrooms (the meaty Japanese *shi-i-take* or the southern Chinese cloud ear or tree ear); dried tiger-lily buds, alias "golden needles"; black and white sesame seeds; dried jujubes; lotus leaves, roots, fruits, and seeds; "dragon's eyes," the lichee-like fruit which looks like russet-yellow grapes and tastes sweet or sub-acid; orange peel; dried shrimps; baby fish, squid, and scallops, used curiously as condiments; minced smoked ham; the licorice-flavored star anise; ginger; icicle radish; water chestnuts; scallions and green onion sprouts; soybean and mung bean sprouts; black vinegar; Chinese cabbage, Chinese celery cabbage, and Chinese parsley (which is coriander, used more for its leaves than for its seeds); but, strangely, little Chinese cinnamon, no doubt because this is the sharp coarse cassia, and China prefers the subtler spice of Ceylon.

Japan, once tributary to China in many domains, was once its gastronomic satellite also, and its seasoning, consequently, was dominated by soybean sauce. But when, in the ninth century A.D., Japan withdrew into self-imposed isolation, it became bad form to put soybean sauce on the table. The ascetic military tradition stamped it as an effete luxury, and besides it was Chinese, an unwelcome reminder of the abandoned servitude. The soybean survived all the same, but the sauce (*shoyu*) made from it, less sharp in Japan than in China, has been relegated to a secondary role as one ingredient among many in marinating mixtures, in cooking liquids, or in dips.

Instead of the Chinese Five-Spice Powder the Japanese have Seven-Pepper Powder, of quite different ingredients—mustard seeds, sesame seeds, poppy seeds, rape seeds, hemp seeds, dried tangerine peel, and pepper leaf (*sansho*), which comes from the prickly ash, whose leaves and bark also serve as a substitute for ordinary black pepper.

At breakfast the Japanese begins his day with an extremely bitter pickle, usually in the form of the tiny very sour red plum called *umeboshi*, guaranteed to wake one up as effectively as a cold shower; and he is accustomed to cleansing his mouth at the end of each meal with another pickle, plum, ginger, cucumber, or, likeliest of all, the giant white radish called *daikon.*

In the typically Japanese tempura cooking (more prosaically, deep frying), flavor is imparted to foods by the liquids in which they are cooked. Since the role of the cooking oils is now precisely that of contributing taste, the Japanese do not rule out olive oil as the Chinese and Indians do, but they use it in discreet quantities. Each tempura cook has his own favorite blend: one may use 85 percent cottonseed oil, 10 percent olive oil, and 5 percent sesame seed oil, another 75 percent peanut oil, 20 of sesame seed oil, and 5 of olive oil. Tempura-cooked food is usually placed before the diner accompanied by several little bowls containing such condiments as lemon juice, chopped horseradish, or a sharp sauce made from dried bonito. *Sashimi,* the Japanese specialty of fillets of raw fish, are served with *wasahi,* a soybean sauce rendered uncharacteristically pungent by the addition of a hot variety of fresh ripe horseradish, especially in summer, when the fish served is likely to be red-fleshed and oily, like tuna; in winter white-fleshed fish are eaten with *ponzu,* a dip of soybean sauce and the lime-like *yuzu* juice.

A favorite dry seasoner for sprinkling over cooked vegetables is *katsuobushi,* the tuna-like bonito dried until it is as hard as wood; it has to be shaved into flakes with a special kitchen tool. Combined with *kombu* (kelp), this becomes *dashi,* which not only flavors vegetables, but is used as the basis for fish stock. A similar concoction is *tsukudani,* tiny fish and kelp boiled down until all the liquid has been eliminated, when it is powdered for sprinkling over rice dishes. Japan uses half a dozen different kinds of seaweed to flavor salads and soups.

Other condiments much used in Japan are dried *shi-i-take* mushrooms; chestnuts, cashew nuts, and gingko nuts (which taste like dried almonds that have somehow acquired a vaguely fishy flavor); Chinese cabbage; the mild rice vinegar; *kanpyo,* dried gourd, sold in strips; *gobo,* burdock root; *shirataki* and *konnyaku,* both made from a sort of yam; mustard, chives, scallions, and onions; fresh ginger and *shoga,* pickled red ginger; *takano tjume,* small whole red peppers, probably the hottest condiment in the Japanese repertory; pickled sea urchin; bamboo shoots and lotus roots; *junsai,* "the slippery vegetable," because it is difficult to hold onto the viscous coating of its spindle-shaped edible part; *goma,* black or white sesame seed; and *goma-abura,* sesame seed oil; the icicle radish, which tastes about as *daikon* does; and even, but rarely, the leaves of Japan's national flower, the chrysanthemum.

Korea lies between China and Japan gastronomically as well as geographically, but unlike them has taken chilies to its bosom, producing dishes much hotter than either of its neighbors. Like them also, it makes heavy use of the soybean; its fermented *hamanatto* is exported to Japan, where it is more popular than that country's own *natto.* Its seasoners are much like those of its neighbors—bean sprouts, sesame seeds, nuts—and in addition one peculiar to itself: *insam,* which resembles ginseng.

Daikon, a large white radish, is used more in Japan than in other countries. It is eaten raw, cooked, or grated, and the juice is used in bean curd stew.

In the year of the Hegira 623 (A.D. 1226), Chamseddine Mohamed ben el Hassan el Baghdadi offered in his cookbook, *Kitab el-Tabih,* 159 recipes for "meats, poultry, fish, vegetables, dairy products, and sweets, seasoned with a variety of aromatic herbs, such as coriander leaves, parsley, mint, pennyroyal, fennel, rue, serpolet, dill, thyme, and bay leaf, and with exotic spices from China, the Islands of the Sound, the Indies, and East Africa: saffron, coriander, cumin, pepper, ginger, cinnamon, cloves, cardamom, mace, betel, musk, nutmeg, camphor, and hyacinth. He perfumed his dishes also with rosewater and orange-flower water, with the bitter juice of the sumac and of pomegranates, and with the tears of mastic gum. He also used lemon, vinegar, and honey. He mixed fruit and meat, the sweet and the sour, and sesame seeds, dates, grapes, and dried apricots, pistachios and all kinds of nuts." Add to this two other seasoners which became available only with the discovery of America, allspice and chili pepper, and this is a nearly complete list of the seasoners used today in what we might call, for want of a better name, Byzantine cooking, for it comes down to us from the heavily flavored food of Assyria and Babylonia through the Byzantine and Ottoman empires.

Despite their possession of an almost unlimited number of herbs, many of them sharp, and spices, many of them hot, the peoples of the Middle East have developed a seasoning essentially cool. Green herbs, aromatic and basically refreshing, but sometimes considered strong by Westerners because of their unfamiliarity, dominate the pungent spices, with an occasional exception like that of the Yemenites who brought back a hotly spiced cuisine from southwestern Arabia when they returned to Israel after an exile which had lasted 2,500 years. Thus garlic, though common, is used with discretion, least so perhaps in Greece

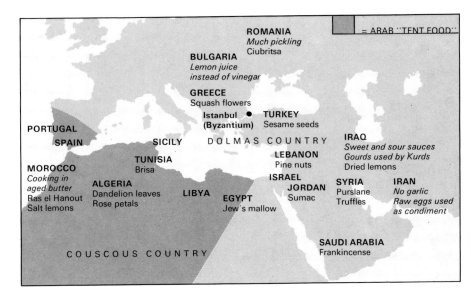

(where it probably arrived from the north, not the east) and Lebanon, the Middle Eastern country most altered by foreign influences; but even there it is eaten almost only fresh, when it is not as strong as after it has been dried. Iran considers it vulgar. As for the stinging chili peppers imported from America, they are most indispensable to the cooking of Bulgaria, on the fringe of this culinary area. Bulgarian cooking is spicier than that of its neighbor, Romania, whose cuisine is dominated by a local herb, *ciubritsa,* which resembles tarragon.

Though Middle East seasoning is not violent, it is complicated. A clue to the attitude toward flavoring is to be found in the fish recipes in Lebanese cookbooks, which describe in detail the herbs and spices which should go into each dish, but commonly begin "Take a five-pound fish," without bothering to specify what kind of fish should be used; obviously the seasoning is more important than what Westerners would consider the principal ingredient; the function of the fish is to carry the seasoners. Among familiar herbs, the favorites are dill, mint (especially pennyroyal), coriander

SEASONERS OF NEAR AND MIDDLE EAST

Almonds, Bulghur, Chilies, Ciubritsa ("tarragon"), Coriander (leaves), Dill, Fennel, Fenugreek, Gourds, Lemons (dried), Mastic, Mint, Pine nuts, Pistachio, Pomegranates (juice, seeds), Quince, Sumac, Tamarind, Tree wormwood

SEASONERS OF NORTH AFRICA

Coriander (leaves), Cumin, Dandelion leaves, Garlic, Jew's mallow, Jute, Lemons, Salt, Onions, Ras el Hanout, Saffron.

leaves, fennel, and fenugreek. The most used nuts, often powdered or broken into small bits for seasoning purposes, are first of all the pine nut, followed by pistachios, almonds, and walnuts. Much use is made of the mouth-twisting quince, pomegranate juice and seeds, the grated rind of tamarind, which adds a sour taste, and citrus fruits, of which limes and lemons undergo a transformation peculiar to this region: they are dried until they become black, as hard as rock (and almost weightless), and are put into stews, their rinds pierced with tiny holes to release their concentrated bitter acidity into the dish. The chief cooking fat is olive oil, except where Bedouin influence is strong, when it becomes mutton fat.

To the more or less familiar condiments the Middle East adds a few of its own. Dried sumac leaves, particularly popular in Jordan, give a sour woodsy taste to the dishes in which they are used. *Shaybah* ("old man") is a dried curled grayish leaf, in English tree wormwood. A leaf used fresh is *kurrath*, which is chopped fine for seasoning, like chives, and indeed belongs to the same family. Jew's mallow, a sort of jute, apparently acquired its name in Syria, for it was Jews who cultivated it there; jute proper is eaten in Egypt. The licorice-like flavor of mastic, which oozes from the lentisk tree and is sold in the form of small, irregularly shaped pebbles, is appreciated throughout the region. *Habbah sawda* is called in English black caraway, but is probably nigella. *Mahlab* is a condiment made from black cherry kernels, which gives a fruity flavor to bread. Grains of wheat are converted into a seasoner by being boiled, dried, and cracked into small bits; they are eaten almost everywhere in the Middle East under one form or another of the name "bulghur." You may class as a seasoner, if you wish, a food dear to Yemenites—baked desert locusts.

A few local specialties: Iran, the Kurdish condiment of gourd cooked in syrup sprinkled with chopped walnuts and cinnamon. Greece, its well-known egg and lemon sauce, *avgolemono;* its equally well-known carp roe, *taramosalata,* which becomes a dip when beaten into lemon juice and olive oil, with grated onion or garlic optional; its less well-known heavy garlic sauce, *skordalia,* in which the garlic is abetted by olive oil, lemon juice, sometimes walnuts or almonds, and, improbably, mashed potatoes; and its *vlita,* mustard-flavored greens with olive oil, thyme, and much garlic. Syria, purslane, not a strange plant, but this seems to be the only place where it is used in the Middle East.

Egyptians like their food spicy, in revolt perhaps against the uninspiring nature of the beans which in various guises constitute a large part of their diet. We are now in Africa, not only geographically, but also gastronomically, for it is here that we first meet with the most widespread dish of North Africa, couscous. It is comparatively rare in Egypt, and sometimes sweet, but the usual version is seasoned with brown gravy containing onions, fresh coriander leaves, and gum mastic. This is restrained flavoring for couscous, a dish which welcomes vivid seasoning. In the rest of North Africa it gets it.

Couscous is a dish of unlimited versatility —a versatility achieved almost solely by its seasoning. Basically it is steamed semolina, cooked in a pair of pots. The grain is in the upper pot, whose bottom is pierced with small holes to permit the passage of vapor from the bouillon boiling in the bottom one. Tunisia, Algeria, and Morocco, have each their own type of couscous; within them are sub-types for their Arab, Berber, and Jewish ethnes, and within these, sub-sub-types which correspond to different localities or tribes. The most important factor which differentiates one from another is the seasoning, applied at four stages. The semolina acquires its first flavoring from the steam rising from the bottom pot, whose contents vary with the wealth of the cook. If he is poor, it will be a bouillon of vegetables, enlivened, according to his means, with parsley, coriander, raisins, saffron, marrow, and much black and red pepper. If he is well-to-do there will be meat in the pot, most likely chicken or mutton. The second seasoning occurs when, after the cooking, some of the bouillon is poured over the grain, which dowers it with a pronounced flavor when, as in Tunisia, it is given heightened spicing with *brisa,* a condiment made of crushed dried hot red peppers, cumin, and salt. The third seasoning is then often added by pouring also over the semolina a thin hot sauce which gives further fire to the whole. The fourth seasoning consists of little sauces of varicolored highly spiced pastes offered as side dishes; some of them are so hot that nobody dares put them directly on the couscous. Instead a large tablespoon is filled with the bouillon and a minute amount of one or the other of these condiments is dissolved in it. Its sting thus adulterated, it may be added safely to the dish.

Couscous is purely Arab, the most characteristic dish of the nomad cuisine whose very name translates as "tent food." The variety of foods which can be conveniently carried on the march is limited. To relieve the monotony of the diet, much use is made of herbs and spices, whose small compass and minimum perishability, once they have been dried, makes them eminently portable. The result is often hot, but can on occasion be extremely subtle, with delicate blends of many herbs often perceived initially as unpleasant by Western palates, but this is a function of their unfamiliarity. The marriage of rustic nomad Arab food with the sophisticated Byzantine cuisine reached its zenith in Morocco, where Islam established itself at the period when Arab culture had attained its highest level—in philosophy, in mathematics, in medicine, and in gastronomy. Morocco is the home of *ras el hanout,* which means "head of the shop," the best thing it has to sell. It is a blend of some thirty herbs and spices which has the reputation of being aphrodisiac, as it ought to be if it is true that one of them is cantharides. Legend has it that its formula is a secret of the spice merchants of Fez, but many of its constituents are generally known, among them ginger, cinnamon, black pepper, red pepper—and rosebuds!

Morocco is also the capital of the various dishes made from the fine many-layered pastry which was the invention of the Saracens—*brik,* a raw egg enveloped in a turnover, a trap for unwary eaters, and *bastilla,* in which pigeon is the most important of the several ingredients tucked into the pastry leaves. These dishes are elaborately flavored. Moroccan *bastilla* is apt to contain parsley, coriander, ginger, turmeric, cumin, and onions, with perhaps a little saffron as well; before serving, it is sprinkled with chopped almonds, cinnamon, and sugar. A third Moroccan contribution is *msir,* the celebrated salt lemon. Preserved in brine, it is the North African counterpart of the dried lemon (or lime) of the Middle East, but it is more subtle. Half a lemon in a stew will flavor it more elegantly than salt.

North Africa favors both garlic and onion in its cooking, and makes lavish use of black and red pepper. Many of its dishes are elaborately, not to say extravagantly, seasoned. Snails, for instance, appear in a sauce which contains green anise seeds, caraway, licorice, thyme, green tea, sage, mint, bitter orange rind, sweet marjoram, hot red pepper, and gum arabic. Desserts are surprising and ingenious too. The Algerian cake called *ybba* is made of flour, olive oil, honey rose petals, and dandelion leaves. Dates are stuffed with a paste of pistachio nuts flavored with rose water.

Cumin and coriander seeds are the spices most used in North Africa. The most used herbs, coriander leaves and mint, often flavor tea. In a pleasant custom that is dying out, three different types of mint tea are ceremoniously presented.

Spain-Portugal
Almonds, Chilies, Chocolate,
Coriander (leaves),
Cumin (native),
Olive oil (strong),
Turmeric, Vanilla

CONTINENTAL EUROPE

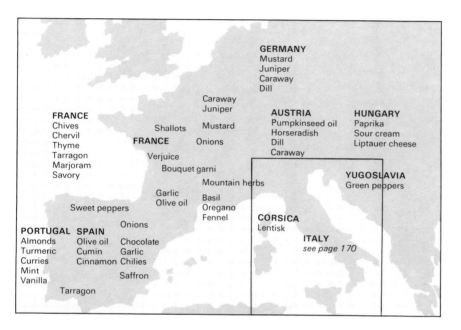

GERMANY
Mustard
Juniper
Caraway
Dill

Caraway
Juniper

FRANCE
Chives
Chervil
Thyme
Tarragon
Marjoram
Savory

Shallots

Mustard

FRANCE
Verjuice
Bouquet garni

Onions

AUSTRIA
Pumpkinseed oil
Horseradish
Dill
Caraway

HUNGARY
Paprika
Sour cream
Liptauer cheese

Mountain herbs

Garlic
Olive oil

Basil
Oregano
Fennel

YUGOSLAVIA
Green peppers

Sweet peppers

CORSICA
Lentisk

ITALY
see page 170

Onions

PORTUGAL
Almonds
Turmeric
Curries
Mint
Vanilla

Tarragon

SPAIN
Olive oil
Cumin
Cinnamon

Chocolate
Garlic
Chilies

Saffron

Italy
Borage (Genoa),
Cockscombs (Padua),
Ginger (south),
Marrow (Padua),
Mastic (Sardinia),
Myrtle (Sardinia),
Parmesan cheese,
Pomegranate juice,
Squash (flowers, seeds),
Truffles (white, black),
Vinegar of Modena

France
Bouquet garni, Caraway (Alsace),
Juniper (Alsace),
Truffles (black),
Verjuice (Touraine)

Germany
Anchovies, Hops, Juniper,
Peppercorns, Poppy seeds

Hungary
Lard, Liptauer cheese,
Paprika, Sour cream

Italian cooking is individualistic almost to the point of anarchy. Its diversity is such that no single seasoner can be cited as characteristic of Italy as a whole; yet Italy as a whole is characterized by great skill in the art of seasoning. This is a function of the kind of foods Italy eats, foods of which the principal characteristic seems to be that they are designed to serve as a background for flavoring. The universal pasta acquires its character from its stuffing or its sauce; the almost as universal *risotto* looks to condiments to lend it an interest which rice unadorned fails to inspire; and even the favorite meat of Italy is the most bland, the one which lends itself with least resistance to the intrusion of other savors than its own—veal.

The finesse with which Italians apply tastiness to such foods is achieved with relatively conservative means. In her *Italian Food,* Elizabeth David describes the contents of "the Italian store cupboard" as (among herbs) sweet basil, sweet marjoram, wild marjoram (another name for oregano), sage, thyme, mint (especially peppermint), rosemary, fennel (roots and seeds), celery, parsley, bay leaves, myrtle, borage, and juniper, and (among spices) nutmeg, cloves, cinnamon, vanilla, coriander seeds, saffron, black pepper (preferably freshly ground at the table; red pepper is not mentioned), and salt (preferably sea salt, of which there is no lack in Italy). Among other seasoners she lists garlic ("It is a mistake to suppose that all Italian food is heavily garlic-flavored"), but neither onions nor shallots; anchovies; dried mushrooms; pine nuts; white truffles (Umbria has excellent black ones); tomato paste; Parmesan cheese, of course; and also of course, olive oil.

The individualism which deprives Italy of any single characteristic flavoring bestows instead typical types of seasoning on its different regions, and even on single cities. Strangely enough, the two cities which were the greatest traders in Oriental spices after the Crusades, Venice and Genoa, make the most moderate use of them today. The city of Venice is content with its *salsa veneta,* of flour, butter, egg yolks, lemon juice, wine vinegar, minced onions, and cooked strained spinach, but some localities in its hinterland allow themselves somewhat more latitude: they use *pevara,* a pepper sauce to which cinnamon and cloves are added in Treviso. Vicenza bastes roast turkey with pomegranate juice, and Padua is wildly eccentric: the three condiments which are its trademarks are squash flowers, marrow, and cockscombs. As for Genoa, and its province of Liguria, "the most salient feature of Ligurian cooking is a presence—of aromatic herbs. Its second most important characteristic is an absence—of spices." The perfume of Genoa is basil. It is grown on every windowsill and is the soul of *pesto,* Genoa's famous sauce, in which it is combined with two kinds of cheese, garlic, and usually pine nuts—one of the three Genoa prefers, along with walnuts and hazelnuts. (A recipe for *pesto* appears on page 140.) Genoese ravioli has borage in its stuffing; the city uses bay leaves, oregano, sweet marjoram, fennel, mint, sage, rosemary, parsley, and wood mushrooms grown in Liguria, and it imports capers.

For the rest, it may be said that Italian taste favors herbs over spices, except in sausages; but the country follows what seems to be a general rule in the northern hemisphere: its seasoning is hottest in the south and becomes progressively cooler as one moves northward. On this principle, Sicily ought to use the most violent seasoners of Italy, but Sicily is a special case: its history has been largely non-Italian. It owes to the sweet tooth of the Saracens, who once ruled it, a penchant for the sort of spices which accord with sweetness—cinnamon, nutmeg, anise, and pistachio—and it is nontypical in its use of such condiments as sesame seeds, squash seeds, and the edible pods of the carob. Sicilian flavoring is assertive rather than hot; it is just across from it on the mainland that the most explosive foods are found. Almost all the dishes of the Basilicata are hot with pepper, and ginger is so ubiquitous in Calabria that its presence is taken for granted even when it is not named: a "strong" dish there is understood as one dominated by ginger.

In Apulia we are almost as far south, but there is more subtlety, as in the reputed preserved figs of Bari, stuffed with bay leaf, fennel seeds, and almonds. However, Apulia can go off the deep end on occasion; usually it prefers onions to garlic, but in its *spaghetti alla zappatora* it uses much chopped garlic along with the tiniest hottest red chilies it can find. We may doubt that this form of pasta enjoys much social standing: its name means "ditch diggers' spaghetti." The food of the Abruzzi is still hot. Wild.thyme, which develops particular pungency in the higher altitudes of this region, is preferred to cultivated thyme, and locally grown poppy

seeds and saffron are used extensively. Red pepper goes into soups, and the typical Abruzzi sausage, called crazy liver or alternatively *diavoletto,* devilish, owes the second name to its fiery spicing. Naples is the capital of garlic and flavors its pizza with oregano instead of the milder marjoram. Off the coast lies Sardinia, whose dominant flavorer is myrtle, backed up by borage, saffron, and mastic gum from the lentisk tree. The north begins with Rome, which dislikes garlic; its own characteristic seasoner is wild mint. In Italy, Rome alone eats the potherb named *misticanza,* though it is not unknown in England, where it is called rockets. The capital also likes pine nuts and rosemary (which flavors its Easter specialty of milk-fed lamb), but this herb is more characteristic of Florence, where it flavors roast pork. One honored Florentine dish, *pollo alla diavola,* takes its name from the hot ginger sauce with which it is served, but this is uncharacteristic of Florence and of Tuscany, where the cuisine is sober.

One is tempted to describe the seasoning of the rest of northern Italy as dominated by the two M's—Modena and Milan. Though Modena has competition in its own region of Emilia-Romagna from the area which produces the commonest condiment of Italy, the Parmesan cheese which, grated, goes onto pasta and into minestrone, and from Bologna, whose *ragù* (chopped meat, tomato, parsley, marjoram, nutmeg) is a remarkable sauce for *tagliatelle,* it can still claim to cover the widest gamut in its flavoring. The griddle cake called *crescentina* is given the subtlest of seasonings by being fried between two chestnut leaves, the pig's foot sausage called *zampone* is given one of the strongest with its spicing of nutmeg, cinnamon, cloves, salt, and pepper. It is Modena also which makes the finest vinegar of Italy, *aceto balsamico,* herb-flavored to begin with, and then aged in a process during which it passes successively through a series

Perhaps no country in Europe is more sensitive to seasoners than Italy. Each region possesses its own special favorites.

PIEDMONT
White truffles
Milan •
Saffron

Padua
Marrow • Venice
• Salsa Veneta

• Modena •
Genoa Herb vinegar

Bologna
Ragú

Pesto
Basil
Borage
Pine nuts

• Florence NORTHERN
Fennel COOKING
Rosemary

Perugia •
Black truffles

Saffron
Wild thyme
Poppy seeds

Rome •
Dislikes garlic
Wild mint
Rockets

SOUTHERN
COOKING

SARDINIA
Myrtle
Borage
Mastic
Saffron

Naples
Garlic
Oregano

Onions
Fennel
Bay leaves
Almonds

SICILY
Nutmeg
Anise
Pistachio
Sesame
Carob
Citrus fruits

Ginger
Citrus fruits

of twelve barrels, each of which communicates to it some of the taste of the wood of which it is made—oak, chestnut, mulberry, juniper, etc.

A trademark of Milan is a dish, or more exactly a combination of two dishes, whose fame has spread around the world—*osso buco* accompanied by *risotto alla milanese*. The veal shank which is *osso buco* is distinguished by its gremolada sauce, flavored with parsley, rosemary, sage, garlic, crushed anchovy, and grated lemon peel, to which some cooks add carrot, celery, and sweet marjoram. The Milanese rice is rich with saffron.

The diversity of Italian seasoning is endless, but let us stop with Piedmont, which uses more garlic than other parts of Italy. Its characteristic condiment is *bagna calda,* a hot dip for cold vegetables. It is composed of butter and olive oil mixed, much garlic, and thinly sliced white truffles, found almost nowhere else.

A country of which large parts were governed for eight centuries by the Moors might be expected to indulge in high heady spicing; Spain is on the contrary almost ascetic in its seasoning.

The list of Spanish herbs and spices is not long. Cloves and cumin (the latter native to Spain) are used sparingly. Among the herbs besides parsley, one finds occasionally a probable heritage from the Moors, mint (in the mint-flavored rice of Estremadura), tarragon (in Seville salads), bay leaves (in the tiny oyster-like *ostiones* of Cadiz), and in the Pyrenees, wild thyme and rosemary. Aragon, which uses more garlic than its neighbor, Castille, whose food is classic and sober, eats what seems like a dubious combination—calves' tongue with chocolate. Of the foods they found in America, Spaniards have adopted, besides chocolate, the tomato, whose ubiquity in sauces has perhaps also helped to discourage the development of other condiments, and chilies,

which provide the heat for that spiciest of Spanish products, the fiery red *chorizo* sausage. Garlic is found everywhere in Spain, even in Castille, which usually prefers onions, in the comparatively mild form of one version or another of *sopa de ajo,* garlic soup.

The most used eastern spices are cinnamon, which is combined with chocolate, and saffron, which is combined with rice in the ubiquitous *paella.* Even the Spanish onion is sweet and bland.

The best-known gastronomic trademark of the Basques is *piperade,* the sauce which derives its very name from "pepper," but it is made with mild sweet peppers. Catalonia is more receptive to heat. It uses a great deal of garlic, and with many foods places on the table two bowls of sauce, of which one contains *ali-oli* ("garlic-oil"), and the other the sharp reddish-brown *romesco,* redolent of hot chili pepper. Nevertheless a Catalan saying maintains that *"la cocina catalana no admite trampas en lo cocina,"* which means that the region frowns on disguising the natural flavor of foods beneath an overlay of heavy seasoning.

The Portuguese, who, after all, were among the first to ferry Oriental spices to the West, are more receptive to exotic florid seasoners than Spaniards. The great days of Vasco da Gama have dowered southern Portugal, the Algarve, with curries redolent of turmeric, a spice little used elsewhere in Europe; the Algarve also grows large quantities of almonds, much used to flavor Portuguese dishes. From the other half of the world, Portugal acquired vanilla, much more favored here than in Spain, though it was the Spanish who met it first in Mexico. The New World is also represented on Portuguese tables by a porcelain jug containing a dark-red sauce made of olive oil and hot chilies, *piri-piri.*

Portugal's favorite herb is coriander, much grown in the province of Alentejo, used

The Italian-speaking part of Switzerland favors Italian cooking. Here, the town of Ascona, on the shores of Lake Maggiore, holds a festival in honor of risotto.

chiefly in the form of its fresh green leaves. Mint, bay leaf, cumin, and black pepper are also common; lemon juice is often applied to meat.

The cooking of southern Europe has oozed into southern France across frontiers which in any case have not always been in the same place. The *pesto* of Genoa is the *pistou* of Nice, both animated by fresh basil, but the French sauce is not as sharp as its Italian cousin. At the other extremity *piperade* is as characteristic of the French Basque country as of the Spanish Basque country, and the Catalan *ali-oli* is the southern French *aillioli*—the garlic mayonnaise which is called "the butter of Provence." Contrary to an impression which is general in America, garlic is not a trademark of French cooking in general, it is a regional phenomenon which characterizes the cooking of that part of France which once spoke the *langue d'oc*. There are not many exceptions to this rule—snails with Burgundian snail butter, for instance, or the slivers of garlic thrust into slits cut into a leg of lamb. Also typical of southern French cooking is skillful use of the wild herbs which are never so flavorful as when they grow in the higher altitudes of Provence or in the brush of Corsica.

Like the rest of Europe, France plunged into an orgy of heavy spicing after the Crusades; an almost universal condiment was cameline sauce, made of ginger, cinnamon, cloves, nutmeg, and vinegar. A revulsion against this tendency began with the advent of the *paquet*—chives, thyme, chervil, parsley, and only one hot spice (a single clove) wrapped up together in a strip of fat, placed as a whole in a dish to provide all the flavoring it was felt to need. Its modern descendant is the *bouquet garni,* the little bunch of herbs (parsley, thyme, and bay leaf is a common combination) which flavors many dishes with characteristic moderation.

Most of the survivors from the days of high seasoning are local. Saffron has almost disappeared except in the *bouillabaisse* of Marseilles (a southern phenomenon again). The acid verjuice pressed from green grapes, so widely used in medieval and Renaissance times, is making its last stand in the Touraine, which also defies much of the rest of northern France by combining fruit and meat (prunes with roast pork); French purists inveigh against such dishes as duck with orange or trout with almonds. Burgundy still uses the ancient *saupiquet* sauce, meaning that it is strongly seasoned, for this word *sau* (from the modern *sel,* salt) refers to a meaning of salt commoner in earlier times as standing for spices in general. The capital of Burgundy is also, of course, the capital of mustards, many of them herb-flavored. Local peculiarities stemming from a later period include the caraway (in bread and on cheese) and the juniper berries (in sauerkraut) which have seeped into Alsace from the east, and the extensive use of onions which is the trademark of a city with a high gastronomic reputation—Lyons.

As a rule, however, French cooking and French seasoning remain remarkably uniform throughout the whole region which extends northward from the Gironde. Hot spices are rare, herbs are familiar and reassuring—marjoram, savory, tarragon, parsley, thyme, chervil, chives, and occasionally sage (one must look to the south for oregano, basil, and fennel). Salads are soberly seasoned with the classic French dressing of olive oil, vinegar (or lemon juice), salt, and pepper, often enlivened with chopped aromatic herbs. Sausages, the last refuge of spiciness in some countries, are as a rule mildly flavored in France, but fairly high seasoning remains in stuffings for poultry or meat (in breast of veal, for instance). On the whole, French flavoring, unobtrusive and thoughtfully employed, might be described as the seasoning of sanity.

"The Germanic peoples...had no real

Fines herbes is made by mincing fresh herbs—such as oregano, thyme or garlic, savory or tarragon—and then combining them. Adding *fines herbes* to ordinary butter that has been allowed to warm to room temperature makes a delicious spread for hot French bread.

Famous Alsatian sauerkraut is seasoned with spicy juniper berries. Germany adds peppercorns, caraway, allspice, and bay.

Schnitzel (boned and breaded veal scallop) is looked upon as a typically Austrian dish, but it was actually adapted from Italy's *costaletta alla milanese* during the Austrian occupation of Lombardy. Garnish with parsley. Add lemon slices and capers.

contribution to make to the art of cookery," wrote Richard Barber in *Cooking and Recipes from Rome to the Renaissance,* which makes short shrift of ham, bacon, and sausage. "German cooking is distinguished by its colossal character," Georges and Germaine Blond remarked in their *Histoire pittoresque de notre alimentation,* by which they seem to have meant that it is excessive in quantity and in kind. This might well be a result of Germany's climate, which, despite its two openings to the sea, is basically continental; continental climates call for hearty rather than for subtle foods. Germany's favorite foods are unlikely to encourage sensitivity to fine nuances in seasoning: rye bread, particularly in northern Germany (consider the nature of pumpernickel); herring, fresh, smoked, dried and pickled (the runner-up in the fish category is probably smoked eel); cabbage and potatoes (the Germans were the first Europeans to accept the potato whole-heartedly in the late sixteenth century when almost everybody else was afraid to eat it); and beer in soups and stews. Consistently, German seasoners tend to be those with a sledgehammer effect.

The commonest is perhaps horseradish, eaten preferably fresh and grated. Caraway is frequently used; for one thing, it marries well with rye bread. A favorite condiment is the salty fillet of anchovy; the favorite herb is perhaps the sourish dill. Others which turn up often include marjoram (in dumplings), bay leaves, and savory, while hops are sometimes also eaten as an herb. The favorite spices include mustard, capers, whole black peppercorns, poppy seeds (especially in Silesia), and juniper berries.

A country like Germany, once a mosaic of many small states each with its own peculiarities, must necessarily show many local differences in seasoning preferences. The trademark of Munich is *Radi,* salted white radish served sliced paper-thin;

another Munich specialty, *Leberkäs,* which despite its name contains neither liver nor cheese, is a meat loaf of finely ground beef, pork, and bacon flavored with onion, marjoram, and nutmeg, as well as pepper and salt. Northern Bavaria makes a marjoram-flavored pork sausage, *Schweinswürstl.* In the Rhineland, pheasant is cooked with a stuffing which includes mushrooms, onions, chervil, parsley, tarragon, and grated lemon rind. In Baden salads are enlivened with dandelion greens, sorrel, watercress, and chervil. Frankfurt seems particularly receptive to herbs: one of its specialties is chervil soup, but its most characteristic contribution to condiments is its green herb sauce. Pomerania's black sauce is made from goose blood, vinegar, flour or groats, salt, nutmeg, cloves—and sugar.

One might be tempted to consider Austrian seasonings as relatively simple, if one happened to make contact with its cooking first through one of its two most characteristic dishes, *Backhendl,* fried chicken, often served with no other condiment than a slice of lemon, or, in a more orgiastic mood, with fried parsley. This is an opinion which would have to change on acquaintance with the other characteristic dish, *Tafelspitz,* boiled beef: it comes with grated horseradish mixed with vinegar, or applesauce, or whipped cream (!), plus one cold sauce (of chives, gherkins, or anchovies) and one hot sauce (of dill, tomato, mushrooms, onions, or cucumber). A seasoning not much found elsewhere is pumpkinseed oil, used in salads. This is a specialty of Styria, which has a number of ideas of its own, including capon stuffed with its own liver, stale bread, rosemary, parsley, marjoram, and pepper—a dish attributed, it is true, to the influence of Yugoslavia. Austria shares with Germany a predilection for onions, especially liked in the Tyrol, Italian as well as Austrian (but

Austria uses a little more garlic than Germany does), wild mushrooms, marjoram, dill, savory, black peppercorns; caraway, and horseradish. Austrian roast pork with caraway seeds, garlic, and mustard, or alternatively with horseradish, seems to be of Bohemian origin, also exemplified by the version of the spicy Czech sausage served, with mustard, in Vienna, though there its heat is toned down.

Polish practice may have contributed to a use of marjoram in Austria even more extensive than in Germany. Yugoslavia has exercised considerable influence on Austrian seasoning too, though it is often difficult to pin down, since Yugoslavian flavoring is in itself difficult to describe, because of its five principal ethnes, to say nothing of the effect of the long Venetian presence on the Dalmatian coast. It may be noted, at least, that Yugoslav food is basically peasant; strongly spiced meats are placed on the table backed up with relishes of chopped onion and small green peppers.

The country which contributed the most flavor to the cooking of the Austro-Hungarian Empire was probably Hungary; one thinks at once of paprika: modern Hungarian cooking is indeed based on paprika, lard, and onions. There is also a lavish use of sour cream as a condiment, and it may be that Liptauer cheese, though its name is German and its range covers much of Central Europe, is a Hungarian invention. This is not, traditionally, as many persons assume, a single separate cheese served ready to be popped into the mouth. It might instead be described as a dish composed entirely of condiments, accompanied by just enough cream cheese to serve as the glue to hold them together. An order for Liptauer cheese brings to the table a host of small saucers, containing, respectively, the cheese, butter, crushed anchovy, caraway seeds, mustard, paprika, capers, onions, and anything else which appeals to local fantasy.

Although American in origin, paprika has become the national spice of Hungary, and it is difficult to envision Hungarian cooking without it. The country's best paprika supposedly grows in the neighborhood of Szeged. Women thread the individual peppers into long strings that are hung to dry against sun-drenched walls. Famous European dishes that feature paprika include *Rosenpaprika* and Hungarian goulash.

SLAVIC AND SCANDINAVIAN SEASONING

NORWAY
Beech smoking
Syr
Lye
Caraway
Seaweed
Nettles

SWEDEN
Jellied salmon fins
Saffron

DENMARK
White pepper
Radish
Mustard
Allspice
Clove
Anchovy
Caraway

POLAND
Dill
Marjoram
Caraway
Garlic
Cinnamon
Cloves
Juniper

FINLAND
Rose hips
Orange peel
Cranberries
Pine needles
Reindeer mallow

ESTHONIA
Caraway
Lingonberries

LITHUANIA
Garlic
Nutmeg
Pepper

UKRAINE
Sunflower seeds

CZECHOSLOVAKIA
Horseradish
Mustard
Caraway
Dill

SOVIET UNION
Dill
Parsley
Nettles
Angelica
Horseradish
Raw onions
Vinegar
Quince
Persimmon
Pomegranate
Kliukvy
Mushrooms

Mallow
Sorrel

GEORGIA
Marigold petals
Saffron
Fenugreek
Mint
Coriander
Tarragon
Cress
Oregano
Savory
Thyme

ARMENIA
Bulghur
Pumpkin seeds
Pine nuts
Allspice
Cumin

FAVORITE SEASONERS OF NORTHERN EUROPE

Slavic

Angelica, Dill, Horseradish, Kliukvy (''cranberry''), Nettles, Onion (raw), Parsley, Persimmon, Pomegranate, Quince, Sunflower seeds, Vinegar

Scandinavian

Allspice, Bay leaf, Berries, Capers, Chives, Cinnamon, Cloves, Cumin, Dill, Ginger, Horseradish, Marjoram, Mushrooms, Mustard, Nutmeg, Nuts, Onion, Parsley, Pepper (black, white), Thyme, Vinegar (strong)

If you pass, in Central Europe, from the territory of Teutonic cooking into that of Slavic cooking, you may not immediately perceive a marked difference, even in flavoring, which is the most sensitively variable factor in food and the one most intimately responsive to the nuances of ethnic character. You will still be in the presence of two foods hardly consistent with subtlety in seasoning—rye bread, tolerant of few added tastes except poppy seed and caraway, and cabbage, the basis of one of the two national soups (one might almost say meals) of Russia, *shchi;* the other is borscht, based on beets, not very hospitable to delicate flavorings either.

As in Germany, onions, often eaten raw, are commoner than garlic. As in Germany, grated horseradish is a favorite condiment. As in Germany, many vegetables and fruits are pickled in vinegar, and as in Germany, when fruit is eaten fresh it often accompanies meat. The fruits are not always the same: Russia makes considerable use of quinces, persimmons, pomegranates, and *kliukvy,* which resembles, in looks and in taste, a small cranberry. As in Germany, mushroom fanciers comb the woods for wild fungi, which are often pickled or dried. Other foods which are gathered wild include various greens, onions, garlic, and nettles, to which the south adds mallow and sorrel. Only a few herbs are used, those which can be grown locally, like dill, parsley, and for sweet pastries, that native of the far north, angelica. The Ukraine is partial to sunflower seeds.

One has the impression that in the vast domain controlled directly or indirectly by the Soviet Union, flavor is concentrated on the fringes and becomes progressively fainter as you move into the interior, until on the steppes of Central Asia taste has only minimum interest for peoples who eat much as their nomadic ancestors did, with a diet dominated by yoghurt and *koumiss* (fermented mares' milk). However, a good deal of onion is consumed in the center; after all, this is thought to be the area where the onion originated.

One of the most unexpected flavors crossed the southern border from Moslem territory—rose petals in jam. Soviet Armenia has imported eating habits acquired farther south. Armenian kebabs are hotly spiced, their beef sausages redolent of strong pepper, allspice, cinnamon, and cumin, their dry salted beef flavored with cumin. Armenians also use pumpkin seeds, pine nuts, and the cracked wheat *(bulghur)* of the Middle East, and differ from Russians by eating a good deal of garlic. So do Georgians, who are also adventurous in their seasoning. They use a paste made from crushed walnuts as a basis for the region's two distinctive sauces, *satsivi* and *hazha.*

The dominant flavor of Polish cooking is dill, the country's most important herb. A favorite Polish condiment is a small sharp-tasting pickled purple plum flavored with cinnamon and cloves; the famous kielbasa sausage contains, at its mildest, caraway and garlic and is sometimes smoked over juniper wood.

The Baltic States in general are more receptive to garlic than Russia proper. Lithuania uses it in sausage, along with chopped parsley, black pepper, and nutmeg. Estonia's habit of serving lingonberries with stuffed cabbage is attributed to Swedish influence. Scandinavians have a predilection, probably inherited from their Viking ancestors, for flavors which are apt to strike non-Scandinavians as overpowering: *lutefisk,* cod cured in lye; *surströmming,* fermented sour Baltic herring, which when canned develops so much gas that the can bulges visibly and has to be opened with caution, like a champagne bottle; *syr,* milk which, after being kept for several months, develops a taste like exceptionally bitter vinegar and is indeed used as a vinegar substitute; *rakørret,* fermented trout which becomes so buttery that it is spread on bread and, according to an unsympathetic observer, "smells like raw petroleum and tastes like strong cheese."

These extreme examples of the sturdiness of Scandinavian taste buds are honored especially in Norway and Sweden. Danish flavoring is blander, Finnish is more woodsy. Allspice seems to be the favorite exotic flavorer of the Scandinavians; cinnamon, nutmeg, and cloves are apt to be saved for desserts (Scandinavians go in heavily for sweets, except the Finns). Denmark, however, despite the fact that its cooking is not spicy, uses the strong clove as well as allspice, white pepper, and anchovy to season its calves' liver paste. It is less extreme when it cooks cabbage with caraway seeds (which Norway saves for sauerkraut).

Dill is the favorite Scandinavian herb. *Gravlax,* raw salmon, is cured with it, aided by white pepper and salt (and sometimes sugar as well!), and is customarily served with a sweet-and-sour mustard-dill sauce. The Finns, who make a rite of eating crawfish, cook them with fresh dill, including the flowers. Dill is one of the seasoners at the disposition of herring fanciers, whose skill at seasoning is given full play in their innumerable fashions of preparing this fish with countless combinations of dill, red or white vinegar (Scandinavian white vinegar is gaspingly acid), carrots, red and yellow onions in rings or slices, parsley, chives, bay leaves, capers, allspice, ginger, mustard (powdered, or in the form of crushed seeds), horseradish, black and white pepper (chili pepper does not seem to appeal to Scandinavians), and once more, sugar.

Scandinavian seasoning is mildest when it comes from the woods—nuts, several sorts of wild mushrooms (particularly prized in Finland), and fruit, especially berries. Although other fruits are used as condiments, for instance when the Swedish stuff goose with apples and prunes, berries are dominant. Long exposure to the sun during the northern summer makes them exceptionally flavorful and performs the same service for some herbs—thyme, for instance, is more zestful in Scandinavia. The berries most commonly used as flavorers in Scandinavia include the lingonberry, something like the American cranberry, but only one quarter as big; the honeyberry (like a tiny raspberry), the fruit of the Arctic bramble; the rowan berry (fruit of the mountain ash); and the orange-yellow cloudberry.

Sweden's famous smörgåsbord is presented on long tables that customarily bear more than sixty dishes—herring in every guise, eggs, fish, vegetables, cold cuts, and hot dishes such as meatballs in gravy.

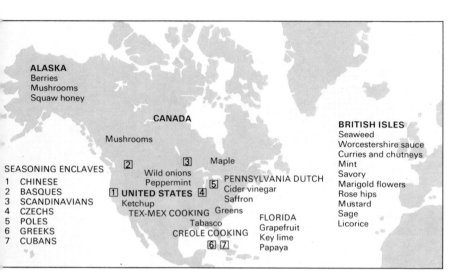

ALASKA
Berries
Mushrooms
Squaw honey

CANADA
Mushrooms

BRITISH ISLES
Seaweed
Worcestershire sauce
Curries and chutneys
Mint
Savory
Marigold flowers
Rose hips
Mustard
Sage
Licorice

SEASONING ENCLAVES
1 CHINESE
2 BASQUES
3 SCANDINAVIANS
4 CZECHS
5 POLES
6 GREEKS
7 CUBANS

Maple

Wild onions
Peppermint

① UNITED STATES ④

② ③

⑤ PENNSYLVANIA DUTCH
Cider vinegar
Saffron

Ketchup
TEX-MEX COOKING Greens

Tabasco
CREOLE COOKING

⑥ ⑦

FLORIDA
Grapefruit
Key lime
Papaya

ANGLO-SAXON SEASONERS

British Isles

Capers, Chives, Cinnamon,
Cloves, Fennel, Juniper,
Licorice, Marigold flowers,
Mint (esp. Peppermint), Mustard,
Parsley, Rose hips, Sage,
Salt (to excess), Savory,
Sugar (to excess),
Worcestershire sauce (and its
fellows), Vinegar

United States—Canada

Chilies (southwest), Chocolate,
Coconut, Greens (southeast),
Ketchup, Maple syrup,
Okra (south), Onions, Sage,
Sugar (to excess), Tabasco,
Vanilla

Americans and Britons are both descended, in the unsympathetic words of William Edward Mead (*The English Medieval Feast*), from "men and women who were coarse-feeders, whose palates were dulled by sharp sauces, by spiced wines, and by peppers, mustard and ginger and cubebs and cardamom and cinnamon with which the most innocent meats and fruits were concocted." There is indeed a curious anomaly about the cooking of English-speaking countries, where food often described by foreigners as drab and tasteless coexists with violent seasoners, while in between there is almost nothing. Anglo-Saxon seasoning lacks a middle class.

The favorite foods of the British Isles are not such as encourage subtle seasoning, or indeed any seasoning at all more imaginative than salt and pepper. The prevailing cereal, wheat, does not inspire it, as does the rice of the Orient, while the oats of Scotland and the potatoes of Ireland are even worse. What the English cook best are roasts and chops, which allow little scope for seasoning. Usually they are gratified only with Worcestershire sauce or one of its fellows, which contain, but to a certain extent re-

strain, such pungent ingredients as anchovy essence, sharp vinegar, soybean sauce, garlic, and strong spices, or are accompanied by mustard or horseradish. If the meat happens to be lamb or mutton, it is flanked by mint sauce (sometimes caper sauce is substituted). The peppery mint is one of England's favorite herbs, added for instance to garden peas, which tend to be cowed by it. Shropshire and Yorkshire even put mint into sweet buns.

The average Briton is devoted to the two overwhelming seasoners at the sweet and bitter extremes of the taste scale—sugar and salt, which tend to blot out others. Observe him in a restaurant: he salts his food automatically without tasting it to find out whether it needs salting. His sugar consumption is 111 pounds (50 kilos) per person per year, compared to 99 pounds (45 kilos) for the United States, though Americans make excessive use of sugar also. Only three countries eat more; two of them belong to the British sphere of gastronomic influence, Australia and Ireland; Eire is the world's number-one consumer of sugar.

In addition to mint, herbs popular in the British Isles include savory, with beans; fennel or parsley, with fish; chives, in salads; and sage, to stuff roast leg of veal or, with onions, any kind of poultry. Fresh sage juice accounts for the green streak in Sage Derby cheese. One can only approve of the cooks who, in parts of England characterized by moors or heaths, use their juniper berries, cloudberries, and whortleberries to flavor game; but it is sad to see the delicate whitebait seasoned not only with lemon juice, but stunned with a sprinkling of cayenne pepper.

A few other herbs benefit from the promotion given them by localities where they are traditionally grown. Peppermint comes from Hertfordshire, chamomile from Lincolnshire, lavender from Norfolk, and licorice from Pontefract, Yorkshire.

The British interest in spices, which had cooled after the Middle Ages (though there were some survivals, like the strongly flavored marigold flowers still found in stews in the Channel Islands), revived with the conquest of India; for a while sauces and stews were choked with coriander, turmeric, hot pepper, cumin, and cardamom. Then interest waned again, leaving as vestigial reminders curries, chutneys, and a few isolated dishes like the kedgeree eaten at breakfast. But these remain exotic borrowings which have never been integrated into British cooking and exert no influence on its basic nature. Spices subsist most commonly in pastry: Eccles and Banbury cakes (dried fruit and spices); the Bath bun (candied peel, caraway seeds, sometimes saffron); or barm brack, a raised bread served especially at Halloween (bits of fruit, nutmeg, cinnamon, cloves, and allspice). But the herb and spice content of meat pies, mincemeat, plum pudding, and the like has diminished. (However, the sweet biscuit-like parkin, of oatmeal and wheat flour, with a dosage of ginger and cinnamon which causes it to keep for weeks, improving as it ages, has not yet given up the ghost.)

Some hotly seasoned dishes remain from a more courageous past, with flavorings which strike us today as rather excessive: hot mustard in pickles; chilies in vinegar; potted shrimps with nutmeg, mace, and cayenne pepper; kipper paste with anchovy, cloves, mace, and cayenne pepper; dry spiced beef cured with salt, saltpeter, brown sugar, allspice, peppercorns, cloves, and juniper berries; or deviled beef bones with spicy sauce *and* Worcestershire sauce, mustard *and* curry powder, black pepper *and* cayenne pepper.

As for the future of the English cuisine, a contemporary French writer is hardly optimistic: "English cooking is becoming Americanized. It is falling from Charybdis into Scylla.

If this is true, Anglo-Saxon cooking is meeting itself coming back; for American cooking, including its seasoning, is based on English cooking. When the first English-speaking colonists arrived in North America, they picked up virtually nothing new from the Indians, except that Colonial housewives used maple sugar as often as salt for seasoning. (Today it has disappeared as a day-to-day spice, for maple sugar and maple syrup have become expensive luxuries.) They borrowed few flavorers from the Indians, but Negro slaves gave the South its "mess o' greens." Only a few favorite herbs were imported from England. Records of seventeenth-century gardens in Salem, Plymouth, and Charleston rarely list any except rosemary, coriander, and pennyroyal. Nevertheless these early Americans were fond of imported ginger: during the Revolution soldiers were issued regular rations of ginger, sugar, molasses, and rum—three of them condiments, or even all four, depending on what was done with the rum. After

The influx of immigrants to the United States in the nineteenth century brought with it many Old World techniques of farming and growing. This photograph, taken in a Wisconsin cornfield about 1895, shows a Scandinavian family proudly displaying the produce that they have obviously grown well.

One of America's contributions to the culinary arts of the world is the renowned hamburger. A fast-food staple, it is available everywhere in numerous guises. Arguably one of the greatest assets of the "Big Mac" variety is its special spicy sauce, the ingredients of which are a trade secret. Pictured above is a "floating" McDonald's that is permanently anchored on the Mississippi River near the city of St. Louis. The arch in the background is not one of the chain's famous "golden arches," but the famous Gateway Arch of the Jefferson National Expansion Memorial.

the war American cooking became spicier as American ships became faster. Their speed made Salem for half a century the world's leading port for spices, with a monopoly on Sumatra pepper, and a substantial interest in cinnamon, cassia, and cloves. The consequent stimulation of the taste buds no doubt contributed to increased demand for greater variety in herb gardens. One of their growers was Thomas Jefferson, who liked tansy pudding at breakfast, made from an herb which is now less often used. Mulligatawny soup, with its seasoning of turmeric, coriander, black pepper, and the western hemisphere's own cayenne pepper, was for a while a favorite American dish. Curries were relatively common, heavy doses of cloves went into sausage meat, and the American housewife made in her own kitchen a large variety of sauces—with mint, with capers, with "nasturtians," with celery, with white onions or brown, with mushrooms or with anchovy.

The immigrant Pennsylvania Dutch brought with them a taste for lusty seasoning: their apple butter was spicier than that of New England, they used cider vinegar in their cooking for tartness, cloves went into scrapple, coriander and sage were popular,

ham was smoked over hickory or sassafras wood, and by the accident that one of their families, the Schwenckfelders, had grown saffron in Germany, that plant was imported by them and planted on their land. The Pennsylvania Dutch taste for spiciness is still exemplified by their many relishes, of which "seven sweets and seven sours" are traditionally provided at important dinners.

The Shakers, of whom Charles Dickens wrote that they "are good farmers, and all their produce is eagerly purchased and highly esteemed," built up a business in herbs so important that they were at one time able to supply 350 different kinds of leaves, flowers, roots, barks, and seeds for culinary or medical purposes, while in their own cooking they made good use of chives, mint, chervil, rosemary, summer savory, borage, basil, sorrel, tarragon, and nutmeg. Their apple pies were flavored with rose water, their blue-flower omelets with chive blossoms. Before the Civil War, the United States had reached the highest point of seasoning in its history.

But the military demand for unspoilable foods in forms easily handled gave a mighty fillip to the development of canning and meat processing. In the vulgarization and commercialization of flavor which followed, Americans lost their former appreciation of seasoning. Spices and herbs in the form of packaged powders failed to inspire the imagination or educate the taste buds. The American housewife accepted cassia and left cinnamon to Europeans, who recognized the difference in quality and were willing to pay for it. She used powdered or liquid vanilla substitutes while genuine vanilla beans, native to the New World, were shipped to the Old. Seasoning was reduced to its commonest elements—chives, onions (a recent recourse to garlic seems to have been more of a fad than a tribute), parsley and watercress used more for orna-

124

ment than for taste, and sage in poultry stuffings. Native flavors—peppermint, wintergreen, beechnut, spruce—were abandoned to chewing gum. Subtle or assertive flavors had to be looked for in gastronomic enclaves of foreign inspiration—among the Chinese of the Pacific coast, the Spanish-Americans of Tex-Mex cooking, the Creoles of Louisiana, the Scandinavians and Poles near the Great Lakes. The French-Americans of New England contributed little, for the French who first settled Canada came mostly from Normandy, which uses little seasoning even in France. British Canadians, like Americans, followed in the footsteps of the mother country. (So did Australians, willy-nilly, for they found no useful flavorers on their continent, except the macadamia nut and eucalyptus juice, used by the aborigines before the white man came, but not now.)

In 1975, in preparation for a projected joint operation by American and Russian astronauts and cosmonauts, they tasted each other's space foods. The Americans found the Russian food too spicy, the Russians found the American food too sweet.

One of the first new foods Columbus and his men noticed when they landed in the West Indies was the spice they called *agi* (it is *ají* today in Peru). It would have been hard not to notice it, for it was (a) fiery and (b) ubiquitous. It still is. From the Caribbean islands through Mexico, Central America, and South America until one reaches the temperate climates of Argentina and Chile, it seems that no dish is without it. This is, of course, the chili, which provides the red pepper now used throughout the world. It is the most important contribution of the New World to seasoning.

The second in importance is probably vanilla. One might put cacao, which gives us chocolate, ahead of it, if it were not for the fact that vanilla is always and only a seasoner, while chocolate must most often

be considered primarily as a food or a drink; one of its chief uses as a flavorer comes precisely from its own area, in the chocolate *molé* sauces of Mexico, employed especially on poultry. Chocolate on chicken may sound barbarous, but in chocolate molé

NATIVE SEASONERS OF LATIN AMERICA

Allspice, Cashew nut, Chilies, Chocolate, Peanuts, Squash (seeds, flowers), Vanilla

IMPORTED SEASONERS OF LATIN AMERICA

Almonds, Anise seeds, Bay leaf, Cinnamon, Cloves, Coriander (leaves, seeds), Garlic, Ginger, Lime juice, Malegueta pepper, Onions, Oregano, Palm oil, Pepper, Pine nuts, Pomegranate seeds, Sesame seeds

Roger Williams (d. 1683) landing in the New World. The American Indians introduced Europeans to tobacco, but more pertinently for us, the Indians also gave the world one of its most important spices, red pepper, as well as allspice, vanilla, and chocolate.

Chili peppers everywhere are strung together and hung in the sun to dry.

The Latin American chili is so hot that some varieties literally blister the lips of those not used to them. The trade grades its countless kinds on a heat scale running from 1 to 120: the popular jalapeño, which numbs the mouths of northerners, is rated only at 15. The heating constituent in chilies, capsaicin, is so pungent that its taste can be detected in a solution of one part capsaicin to 100,000 parts of solvent.

sauce you do not taste the chocolate as such unless you make a deliberate effort to single out its flavor from the riot of competing savors in which it is submerged—several kinds of chilies, black pepper too, almonds, sesame seeds, anise seeds, coriander seeds, cinnamon, cloves, garlic, onion, and tomato.

Another American seasoner which has become a citizen of the world is allspice. Universal too is the peanut, American also, sometimes a food, sometimes a flavorer, and sometimes the source of a cooking oil. Less widespread is the cashew nut, which depends like an overgrown comma from the base of the cashew apple, but had better not be pulled out and eaten fresh, for its acrid juice is dangerously irritating, and has to be processed out of it.

A Latin American plant which has not spread from its native land is quinoa, whose leaves are eaten like spinach, but its seeds are used as a spice; both leaves and seeds contain essential nutritive elements lacking in the potato, which grows side by side with it in the high altitudes of the Andes and is the basic food of the Andean Indians; for them quinoa is consequently an indispensable complementary element. Another native condiment with only faint flavor is *farufa,* manioc meal, of which large shakers appear on Brazilian restaurant tables, like Parmesan cheese shakers in Italy. Its function is less to add taste to the moist dishes over which it is sprinkled than to soak up juices and sauces so that no drop will be lost.

Latin American squashes are believed originally to have had virtually no flesh, but to have been filled with large edible seeds; throughout Latin America squash seeds are still roasted and eaten like peanuts; or crushed into a greenish meal which flavors sauces; or pressed for a likewise green oil which can be used for seasoning or cooking; the flowers are eaten as well.

Not native to America are coconuts, which

probably took root first on the Peruvian coast after drifting across the Pacific, and now offer their meat for desserts and their milk or oil for flavoring and cooking. Coriander is one of the most used foreign herbs, chiefly in the form of its leaves, though the seeds are employed also; so are pomegranate seeds, while pine nuts are native and popular. As though chili pepper were not enough, tiny hot malegueta peppers have been introduced from Africa, and of course black pepper from Asia. Other commonly used seasoners are lime juice (on avocados), onions, garlic, cinnamon, ginger, bay leaves, and oregano.

Though the variety of spices used in Latin America is wide, the chili remains the king. On restaurant tables everywhere, very small, very hot ones are found whole, or larger ones chopped, in olive or dendé oil. Mexico provides one more example of the interdependence between basic cereals and seasoning. Of its twenty-nine states only one, Sonora, consistently prefers mild chilies to hot ones and even offers many dishes containing no chilies at all. Sonora is also the only Mexican state which, instead of maize, makes wheat its basic grain.

Chili, one of America's favorite standard dishes, most likely originated, not in Mexico, but among Caribbean Indians who used the red pods to spice up their food. Chiles are not "peppers," as is commonly supposed, but rather part of the pod-bearing genus *Capsicum,* which encompasses five species and more than 300 plant varieties. For making chili, fresh or dried chiles are vastly superior to commercially prepared chili powder, which is most often a blend of ground chiles, oregano, cumin, salt, and garlic.

AFRICA

Africa south of the Sahara, one is almost tempted to say, has no seasoners; or, contradictorily, that it has them all. Before whites penetrated the Dark Continent, Africans, we are told, seem to have paid little attention to taste; their basic food was often curds and whey wherever the tsetse fly had not eliminated milch animals. Then the colonial period began, with the colonizers importing their own seasoners: Arabs from the north; spice ships from the Orient leaving on the east coast samples of their wares; Europeans and Asiatics in the south; and on the western coast, slavers from the New World deposited its new foods. The basic African grain became maize (mealie); there had been only millet before, and not much of that. The peanut took Africa by storm. But the most important arrival was the red chili pepper, which quickly became, and remains, the dominant spice of the continent. Africa itself originated very few of the flavorers it eats today. Among spices, the most important, after red pepper, are turmeric (from tropical Asia) and cloves (from the Moluccas), black pepper (from India) and vanilla (from America). The most popular herb is mint (probably from southern Europe) and after it thyme (from southern Europe also).

Except in the North African coastal strip, only one African territory achieved (in pre-colonial times) government above the tribal level: Ethiopia. It is also the only one whose seasoning presents a characteristic consistent native flavoring, perhaps not unconnected with the fact that it is also the only one which has retained millet as the basic grain. Ethiopia possesses an all-purpose seasoner, which goes onto or into almost all cooked dishes: *berberé* sauce, a fiery-red paste whose most essential component seems to be identified by the fact that even outside the sauce it is also called *berberé*. But as it is *Capsicum abyssinicum* and Capsicum identifies it as a descendant of the

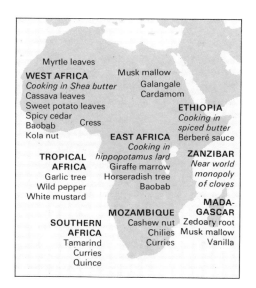

American chili, it cannot have been the original pepper of this age-old condiment. This was probably African or Guinea pepper, also called Ethiopian pepper and scientifically *Xylopia aethiopica*, although it seems to have originated farther south; or it could have been Ashanti or Benin pepper, also called Guinea cubebs, which is *Piper guineense*, and thus a true pepper. Either or both of these may, indeed, still be ingredients of *berberé* sauce, for Westerners have not yet identified all the native herbs and spices which may enter it, a task rendered difficult by the probability that the recipe varies almost with every family. Among its chief ingredients, which, though originally foreign, have become naturalized in Africa, are, besides red pepper, black pepper (in the form of whole peppercorns), salt, cumin, coriander seeds, crushed fenugreek seeds and dried fenugreek leaves, basil, cardamom pods and seeds, allspice, nutmeg, cinnamon (in sticks), cloves, ginger, onions, and garlic. Every Ethiopian kitchen contains a cooking fat known as *niter kebbeh*, butter into which has been worked such seasoners as turmeric, cinnamon, nutmeg, ginger, garlic, basil, cardamom, and bish-

The map shows:

Myrtle leaves

WEST AFRICA   Musk mallow
Cooking in Shea butter   Galangale
Cassava leaves   Cardamom
Sweet potato leaves
Spicy cedar   **ETHIOPIA**
Baobab   Cress   *Cooking in*
Kola nut   *spiced butter*
   EAST AFRICA   Berberé sauce
   Cooking in
TROPICAL   *hippopotamus lard*   **ZANZIBAR**
AFRICA   Giraffe marrow   *Near world*
Garlic tree   Horseradish tree   *monopoly*
Wild pepper   Baobab   *of cloves*
White mustard
   MADA-
   MOZAMBIQUE   **GASCAR**
SOUTHERN   Cashew nut   Zedoary root
AFRICA   Chilies   Musk mallow
Tamarind   Curries   Vanilla
Curries
Quince

SEASONERS USED THROUGHOUT AFRICA

Cloves, Dill, Mace, Mint, Nutmeg, Peanut, Pepper, Rosemary, Sage, Thyme, Turmeric, Vanilla
A curious fact: *all* the seasoners eaten throughout Africa are foreign to that continent. The few native spices and herbs are used locally, each in its own region. But it is possible that Africa possesses seasoners as yet unknown to Westerners.

A Kenyan woman prepares maize. First brought from America to feed Negroes waiting to be shipped into slavery, maize has become the mealie-mealie of Africa, its universal cereal.

op's weed (an herb which probably reached Ethiopia from Asia Minor).

East Africa, the territory east of the Great Rift Valley (Kenya, Uganda, and Tanzania), likes milder food, despite the circumstance that Zanzibar, now part of Tanzania, enjoys what is very nearly a world monopoly of cloves. Arabs from the north probably brought into this region such subtle dishes as chicken cooked in pomegranate juice, which then becomes part of the gravy, along with crushed fried walnuts.

The most popular seasoners are fenugreek and coriander, plus several shared with tropical regions: malegueta pepper, cinnamon, ginger, dill, and hoary or American basil, also called the tea bush, since it is much used there for making tea. Of secondary popularity are sage and rosemary, while East Africa shares with West Africa the calabash nutmeg, called in French the false nutmeg; there is a false nutmeg in English also, eaten throughout equatorial Africa, probably native to Angola. The balloon vine of East Africa, whose pods are eaten as a vegetable, becomes a spice when its seeds are used, so it is known by the alternative name of heart seed. A thoroughly native delicacy is the marrow from giraffe bones, cooked, when it can be had, in what is said to be one of Nature's finest lards—hippopotamus fat.

The spice miscalled wild or Cameroon cardamom is actually a variety of malegueta pepper. Indian mustard is probably indeed Indian as its name indicates, though it has been cultivated in central Africa for a long time. The horseradish tree, whose powdered root serves as a substitute for this seasoner, might well be native, for there is an African species, but in fact the one commonly eaten is probably the Indian variety. A seasoner native to West Africa is the plant called in English the spicy cedar and in French laurel, which gives an idea of its flavor; both seeds and flowers are widely used. A flavorer listed as "musk," between quotation marks, in the World Food Organization's roster of African aliments seems to be a spicy variety of the kola nut. It is a delayed action seasoner: a piece of it chewed before eating other foods makes them taste better. Palm nuts and palm oils are much used, the latter for deep frying, enriched by chili or nutmeg; when it is a case of cooking fish, crushed herbs, pepper, onions, and garlic are frequently combined with the palm oil.

Since West Africa is where the slavers arrived from America, this part of the continent has been particularly receptive to New World foods, but it uses them sometimes in fashions unknown in their land of origin—for instance both cassava leaves and sweet potato leaves serve as seasoners in cooking. The peanut is indispensable for sauces, and we must suspect Mexican influence behind a dish of plantains (vegetable bananas) embellished with hot chocolate sauce.

Elsewhere in tropical Africa, the former Congo is addicted to white mustard, while Mozambique grows, and uses, great quantities of two American seasoners, cashew nuts (to flavor chicken), which are recognized as foreign, and chilies, which are not. It is difficult to single out any dominant flavorings or national characteristics in South African cooking; its settlers have been too diverse—the Dutch at the end of the seventeenth century; the first non-African slaves from the East, the "Cape Malays," though there were as many Indonesians as Malays among them, who introduced the tamarind; the French Huguenots; in the nineteenth century, Indians, imported to work the sugarcane plantations, who brought along curries, mangoes, and papayas; there was even some German influence on the food. Meanwhile the cooks who put this mosaic of influence together were of course the indigenous Negroes.

GLOSSARY OF BOTANICAL TERMS

Achene : Hard, dry 1-seeded fruit.

Adnate : One organ united to another.

Alternate : Where leaves are arranged one after another.

Annual : A plant completing its life cycle within 12 months.

Axil : The upper angle formed by leaf and stem.

Axillary : Flowers borne at the axils of leaf and stem.

Bark : The outer rind of a tree's trunk or branch.

Berry : A fruit whose seeds are embedded in its own juice.

Biennial : A plant flowering or fruiting in the year following that in which the seed is sown.

Bifoliate : Double leaved; with 2 leaflets.

Bracteoles : Small bracts attached to the base of the pedicels.

Bracts : Small (modified) leaves differing from the others and present on the flower stalks.

Calyx : The green whorl of leaf-like organs situated below the corolla of a flower.

Capitate : Growing in heads, as in Compositae.

Capsule : A dry, many-seeded fruit vessel.

Carpel : Free or united divisions of the ovary.

Caulin : Leaves belonging to or produced from the stem.

Climber : A plant with long straggling shoots requiring support.

Cone : A scale-like fruit containing seeds.

Cordate : A heart-shaped leaf with 2 rounded lobes at the base.

Corolla : A whorl of floral leaves known as petals.

Corymb : Raceme of flowers or pedicels which decrease in length as they approach the top of the stem.

Cruciferae : An order whose flowers of 4 petals are arranged in the form of a cross.

Cyme : A terminal inflorescence beneath which are side branches bearing a terminal flower.

Deciduous : A tree, shrub or plant losing its leaves each year.

Decumbent : Stems of a plant which lie flat on the ground.

Decussate : With 4 leaves arranged cross-like.

Dentate : Leaves with triangular teeth at the margins.

Dioecious : Plants with differently sexed flowers on different plants with stamens on one; pistils on another.

Disk : Surface or central florets of a flower as in Compositae (Disc florets).

Division : Propagation by dividing a plant into pieces containing roots.

Entire : Leaves neither divided nor toothed at the margins.

Evergreen : A tree, shrub or plant retaining its leaves all the year.

Eye : The dormant bud of a plant.

Filament : The lower stem-like part of a stamen.

Fistular : The hollow stems of plants as in many umbellifers.

Florets : The small rayed petals of flowers as in Compositae.

Follicle : An inflated 1-celled carpel.

Genus : A group of related species.

Glabrous : A plant which is smooth, glossy — without surface hairs.

Glandular : A cellular secreting organ.

Glaucous : Leaves which are blue-green as in Rue.

Half-hardy : Plants needing protection in winter or spring.

Hirsute : Leaves covered in long silky hairs.

Imbricate : Arranged over each other, like the scales of a leaf bud.

Involucre : Whorled bracts at the base of a flower or flower head.

Keel : The pair of petals of Pea-like flowers.

Labiate : Lipped : the corolla or calyx divided into 2 unequal parts as in lavender, thyme.

Lanceolate : Lance-shaped leaves, tapering at each end.

Lateral : A shoot growing out sideways from the main stem.

Linear : Leaves which are long and narrow.

Nectary : Honey-secreting organs at the base of petals.

Node : A point or stem where a leaf is produced.

Obovate : Egg-shaped. Leaves with the broad end outwards.

Opposite : Leaves growing opposite to each other.

Palmate : Segments of a leaf spread out from a central point.

Panicle : Flowers borne in an elongated spray.

Pappus : The hairy appendage of a seed.

Peduncle : Stalk connecting leaves on flowers to stem.

Pellucid : Transparent. Dots or glands on leaves containing essential oil.

Peltate : A leaf with its point of attachment on the face.

Perennial : A plant which grows and blooms each year indefinitely.

Perfoliate : When a leaf encircles the stem.

Perianth : When calyx and corolla are indistinguishable.

Petiole : The stalk of a leaf where it joins the main stem.

Pinnate : Leaflets arranged in pairs.

Pollen : Dust or grains on the anther containing the male cells to fertilise the ovules.

Pratense : Growing in meadows.

Pubescent : Leaves or stems closely covered in hairs or down.

Raceme : Stalked flowers borne in a spike or cluster.

Radical : A tuft of leaves arising from the root.

Rhizome : A stem with a thickened base, growing horizontally, usually beneath the soil.

Rosette : Leaves radiating from a central underground stem, often overlapping to form a circle.

Sagittate : Leaves shaped like an arrow.

Segment : A petal of a flower, or parts of a leaf divided almost to the midrib.

Self-fertile : Flowers which fruit and set seed when fertilised by their own pollen.

Serrate : Leaves which are saw-edged or toothed.

Sessile : Leaves which are without stalks.

Simple : Leaves not divided or serrate.

Sinuate : Leaves with blunt lobes.

Solitary : Flowers borne singly, one to a stalk.

Spike : A raceme, except that the flowers are stalkless.

Spur : The extension of the lower part of a corolla.

Stamen : The male organ of a flower composed of filament and anther.

Stellate : Star-like, radiating from a central point as in Star anise.

Stigma : The cellular part at the top of a carpel or style to which pollen adheres.

Stipule : Leaf-like appendages at the base of the petioles.

Stolon : Runners growing out from a plant and rooting at the leaf nodes.

Style : Termination of a carpel bearing the stigma.

Taproot : The main root, descending far into the soil.

Tomentose : Leaves covered with entangled silky hairs.

Trefoil : A leaf composed of 3 leaflets.

Umbel : Stalked flowers arising from one point and radiating to the same level.

Whorl : Flowers of leaves arranged in a circle of 3 or more around a stem.

Wing : The lateral petals of a pea-like flower.

PICTURE CREDITS

Alfieri, Bernard, Horticultural Picture Library, Leatherhead: 35 (24), 41 (44), 45 (59)

Artus, *Hand Atlas*, Vol I + II + III: 10 far left, 29 (5), 32 (15), 33 (17), 36, (26 and 27), 37 (30), 38 (34), 40 (40), 42 (48 and 49), 44 (57), 45 (58 and 60), 47 (66), 48 (70b), 53 (85), 54 (90)

Atlas-Photo, Paris: 119 top (PH: Lauros)

Aurness, Craig, Los Angeles: 126 top

A–Z, Botanical Collection, Dorking: 27, 28 (2), 44, (32), 33 (19), 34 (20), 39 (37 bottom), 32 (55), 48 (69 and 70a), 51 (81), 53 (87), 68 (88), 69 (94a), 103 above right, center right, 103 above right

A–Z Collection, Dorking (PH: Brian Furner): 11 second from left, 12, 13 second from right and far right, 28 (3), 35 (22), 37 (32), 46 (61 and 64)

Bock Hieronymus, *Kreütterbuch*, Strassburg 1577: 13

British Library, London: (Beda's *Vita Sancti Cuthberti*, Add. Ms. 39943 f. 2r) 11 bottom

Bucher Verlag, Lucerne: 128

Buishand, Tjerk, Alkmaar: 51 (79)

Bullaty & Lomeo, New York: 50/77

Bührer, Lisbeth, Lucerne: 12 left

Coleman Collection, Uxbridge: 29 (5b), 56 (97), 57 (98)

Coray, Franz, Lucerne: 28 (1), 29 (4), 30 (7 and 9), 31 (12), 32 (14), 33 (18), 34 (21b), 35 (25), 38 (35), 39 (36 and 38), 40 (43), 54 (89), 57 (99)

Culinas PR AG, Lucerne: 78

Da Spaloti, Cherubino, *Fior de Virtu*, Venice 1490: 82

Döbler, Hansferdinand, *Kochkünste und Tafelfreuden*, Munich 1972: 83

Duna Ungarn Anzeiger, Fahrwangen: 119

Freeman, John, London: 85

Genders, Roy, Worthing: (PH: John Gledhill), 102 above center

Harding, Robert, Picture Library, London: 103 below right

Hauser, Prof. Dr. A Wädenswill: 75

Held, André, Ecublens: 6

Hortus Sanitatis, Strassburg c. 1497: 8

Imber, Walter, Laufen: 102 bottom

Köhler, *Medizinal-Pflanzenatlas*, Vol I + II + III, Gera-Untermhaus 1887: 13 second from left, 30 (8), 31 (11), 43 (51 and 52), 44 (54 and 56), 49 (72), 50 (76), 52 (82 and 84), 55 (92)

Lonicerus, Adamus, *Kreuterbuch*, Frankfurt 1679: 2

Losch, F., *Les Plantes Médicinales*, Biel: 41 (46), 42 (50), 47 (67), 49 (73), 56 (95)

Magnum, Paris:

Mansell Collection, London: 125

Metropolitan Museum of Art, New York (The Harrys Brisbane Dick Fund 1926): 89

Operakällaren, Restaurant, Stockholm: 121

Otto, Monika A., Lucerne: 100

Picturepoint, London: 9 (6)

Publisher's Archives: 9 far left, 42 (47), 57 (100), 59 (PH: James Perret), 77 (PH: James Perret).

Rauh, Prof. Dr. W., Institut für Systematische Botanik und Pflanzengeographie der Universität Heidelburg: 52 (83)

Rüedi, Ruth, Lucerne: 78, 79, 106.

Smith, Harry, Photographic Collection, Chelmsford: 9 second from right, 31 (10), 32 (13), 39 (37 above), 41 (45)

State Historical Society of Wisconsin: 123

Taddei, Fototecnica, Lugano: 116

Tate & Lyle Limited, London: 103

Topham, John, Picture Library, Edenbridge: 43 (41), 46 (75), 55 (94b), 102 above left

Treviso-Coll., G. Comisso: 84 above

Turner, William, *A New Herball*, Collen 1568: 1

Victoria & Albert Museum, London: 103 top

Von Schuberts, Prof. Dr. G. H., *Naturgeschichte des Pflanzenreichs: Lehrbuch der Pflanzengeschichte*, Esslingen 1887: 34 (21a), 35 (23), 36 (28 and 29), 37 (31), 38 (33), 39 (39), 40 (42), 43 (53), 46 (62 and 63), 47 (65), 48 (68), 49 (71 and 74), 50 (77), 50 (78 and 80), 53 (86), 54 (91), 55 (93), 56 (96)

Wymann, Werner, Bern: 85 below.

INDEX

Note: (r) indicates that the reference is to a recipe.

Italic page numbers indicate that the reference is part of a caption.

A

Africa, seasoners in, 111–113, 127–128
Allgood. *See* Good-King-Henry
Allium ascalonicum. See Shallot
Allium cepa. See Onion
Allium fistulosum. See Scallion
Allium porrum. See Leek
Allium sativum. See Garlic
Allium schoenoprasum. See Chive
Allium scorodoprasum. See Rocambole
Allspice *(Pimenta officinalis)*, 11, 14–15, 49, 60–61
Almond *(Prunus amygdalus)*, 14–15, 51, 60–61
see also Pistachio
Almond soup (r), 87
Aloysia citriodora. See Lemon verbena
Alpinia officinarum. See Galingale
American Cress. *See* Winter cress
Amomum melegueta. See Melegueta pepper
Anethum graveolens. See Dill
Angelica *(Angelica archangelica)*, 14–15, 31, 60–61
Angelica archangelica. See Angelica
Anglo-Saxon seasoners, 122–125
Anise *(Pimpinella anisum)*, 14–15, 49, 60–61
see also Star anise
Aniseed. *See* Anise
Aniseed tree. *See* Star anise
Anthriscus cerefolium. See Chervil
Apium graveolens. See Celery
Apples, with lemon or orange marmalade, sauteed (r), 98
Arachis hypogaea. See Peanut
Armoracia rusticana. See Horseradish
Artemisia dracunculus. See Tarragon
Artemisia vulgaris. See Mugwort
Artichoke
flan (r), 92
hearts in red wine (r), 97
Asafetida *(Ferula assafoetida)*, 14–15, 40, 60–61

B

Badian, *See* Star anise
Bali, seasoners in, 105–107
Balm *(Melissa officinalis)*, 14–15, 44, 60–61
see also Bergamot
Bamboo *(Bambusa vulgaris)*, 33, 60–61
shoots, culinary uses, 14–15
Bambusa vulgaris. See Bamboo
Barbarea vulgaris. See Winter cress
Barber, Richard, 118
Basil. *See* Sweet basil
Basil sauce
fresh (pesto) (r), 88
for lamb or chicken (r), 87
Bates, Caroline, 104
Bay *(Laurus nobilis)*, 14–15, 43, 60–61, 73
liver brochettes with (r), 94
Bearnaise sauce (r), 88
Bede, Venerable, 11
Bee balm. *See* Bergamot
Beef
marinade (r), 83
rib steaks in the style of Rome (r), 94
star anise, Mme Chu's (r), 94
Bennet. *See* Herb bennet
Bergamot *(Monarda didyma)*, 14–15, 45, 60–61
Bird pepper, *See* Chili
Bird's foot. *See* Fenugreek
Black caraway. *See* Burnet
Black elder. *See* Elder
Black mustard *(Brassica nigra)*, 34, 64–65
Black pepper *(Piper nigrum)*, 14–15, 50, 60–61
Blond, Georges and Germaine, 118
Blowball. *See* Dandelion
Borage *(Borago officinalis)*, 14–15, 34, 60–61
Borago officinalis. See Borage
Bouquet garni. *See* Herb bouquet
Brandy, herb or spice (r), 84
Brassica nigra. See Black mustard
Bread, Moroccan (r), 99
Breadcrumbs, seasoned, for fried foods, (r), 81
British Isles, seasoners in, 122–123
Broad bean salad, fool midammis (r), 112
Burma, seasoners in, 105
Burnet *(Pimpinella saxifraga)*, 14–15, 49, 60–61
see also Salad burnet
Burnet saxifrage. *See* Burnet
Butter
chive, for fish (r), 88
lemon herb (r), 80
maitre d'hotel (r), 81
white sauce, classic (r), 88

C

Cacao *(Theobroma cacao)*, 14–15, 55, 60–61
Cake, with walnuts, honey cinnamon (r), 99
Calendula officinalis. See Marigold
Cambodia, seasoners in, 105–107
Canada, seasoners in, 122, 123
Caper *(Capparis spinosa)*, 14–15, 35, 60–61
and olive relish (r), 88
Capparis spinosa. See Caper
Capsicum annuum. See Paprika
Capsicum frutescens. See Chili
Caraway *(Carum carvi)*, 11, 16–17, 36, 60–61
zucchini salad with (r), 90
see also Burnet
Cardamom *(Elettaria cardamomum)*, 16–17, 39, 60–61
Carrot salad (r), 89
and orange (r), 90
Carthamus tinctorius. See Safflower
Carum carvi. See Caraway
Cayenne pepper. *See* Chili
Celery *(Apium graveolens)*, 16–17, 32, 60–61
with coriander seed, pureed green (r), 96
Cheese, 80
Chenopodium bonus-henricus. See Good-King-Henry
Cherries with mace, sweet and sour (r), 98
Chervil *(Anthriscus cerefolium)*, 16–17, 31, 60–61
with eggs, scrambled (r), 93
Chicken
basil sauce for (r), 87
with forty cloves of garlic (r), 95
livers, on croutons (r), 95
with Moroccan spice mixture (r), 95
paella (r), 97
with sesame seeds, fried (r), 96
stew with chick peas, gingered (r), 96
Chick peas, gingered chicken stew with (r), 96
Chili *(Capsicum frutescens)*, 16–17, 35, 62–63, 105, 125–126, 127
con carne (r), 93
China, seasoners in, 108–109
Chinese parsley, 10
Chinese steamed fish (r), 92
Chive *(Allium schoenoprasum)*, 16–17, 30, 62–63
butter, for fish (r), 88
Chocolate. *See* Cacao
Ciboule. *See* Scallion
Cinnamomum zeylanicum. See Cinnamon
Cinnamon *(Cinnamomum zeylanicum)*, 10, 16–17, 36–37, 62–63
honey cake with walnuts and (r), 99
Citron *(Citrus medica)*, 16–17, 37, 62–63
Citrus medica. See Citron
Cive. *See* Chive
Clove *(Eugenia caryophyllata)*, 10, 16–17, 39, 62–63, 109
orange ice (r), 98
Clover. *See* Melilot
Cloveroot. *See* Herb bennet
Cobnut. *See* Hazel
Cochlearia officinalis. See Scurvy grass
Cocoa. *See* Cacao
Coffee, spice mixture for, 89
Cole. *See* Horseradish
Common myrtle. *See* Myrtle
Condiment, defined, 12
Cookies
filbert crisps (r) 98
pepper, Andre Daguin's (r), 98
Coriander, *(Coriandrum sativum)*, 10, 16–17, 37, 62–63, 113
pureed green celery with (r), 96
Coriandrum sativum. See Coriander
Corn poppy. *See* Poppy
Corylus avellana. See Hazel
Court-bouillon, for salmon (r), 92
Crab boil, for gumbo (r), 91
Creme anglaise (r), 84
Cress *(Lepidium sativum)*, 16–17, 43, 62–63
see also Nasturtium; Watercress; Winter cress
Crocus sativus. See Saffron
Cubeb *(Piper cubeba)*, 16–17, 50, 62–63
Cucumber salad (r), 89
Cumin *(Cuminum cyminum)*, 18–19, 38, 62–63, 113
Cuminum cyminum. See Cumin
Curcuma longa. See Turmeric
Curcuma zedoaria. See Zedoary
Curry, 104–105

D

Daguin, Andre, pepper cookies (r), 98
Dandelion *(Taraxacum officinale)*, 18–19, 55, 62–63
Desserts, 84
recipes, 98–99
Dill *(Anethum graveolens)*, 18–19, 31, 62–63, 121
Dill seed, culinary uses, 18–19
Dragon plant. *See* Tarragon
Dyer's saffron. *See* Safflower

E

Eggs, 80
in brioche with mustard tarragon sauce (r), 93
with chervil, scrambled (r), 93
Elder *(Sambucus nigra)*, 18–19, 53, 62–63
Elettaria cardamomum. See Cardamom
Eruca vesicaria subsp. sativa. See Rocket
Estragon. See Tarragon
Eugenia caryophyllata. See Clove

F

Far East, seasoners, 108–110
Fat hen. *See* Good-King-Henry
Felon herb. *See* Mugwort
Fennel *(Foeniculum vulgare)*, 9, 18–19, 40, 62–63, 109
Fenugreek *(Trigonella foenum-graecum)*, 18–19, 56, 62–63
Fern. *See* Sweet cicely
Ferula assafoetida. See Asafetida
Field poppy. *See* Poppy
Filbert. *See* Hazel
Filbert crisps (r), 98
Fine herbs (fines herbes), 74, 117
recipe, 78
Fish, 80
recipes, 86, 87, 88, 91, 92, 96
Flan, artichoke (r), 92

Austria

Austria, seasoners in, 118–119

Foeniculum vulgare. See Fennel

Food of the gods. *See* Asafetida

Food midammis broad bean salad (r), 112

France, seasoners in, 114, 117

French sorrel *(Rumex scutatus),* 52
see also Sorrel

G

Galanga. *See* Galingale

Galingale *(Alpinia officinarum),*18–19, 30, 62–63

Garden cress. *See* Cress

Garden thyme. *See* Thyme

Garlic *(Allium sativum),* 18–19, 29, 62–63, 75 104, 121

Geranium. *See* Scented-leaf geranium

Germany, seasoners in, 114, 117–118

Geum urbanum. See Herb bennet

Ginger *(Zingiber officinalis),* 11, 18–19, 57, 62–63, 102

Gingered chicken stew with chick peas (r), 96

Glycine max. See Soybean

Glycine soja. See Soybean

Glycyrrhiza glabra. See Licorice

Golden-buttons. *See* Tansy

Goober. *See* Peanut

Good-King-Henry *(Chenopodium bonus-henricus),* 18–19, 36, 62–63

Goosefoot. *See* Good-King-Henry

Grains of paradise. *See* Melegueta pepper

Grass. *See* Scurvy grass

Greek mixed salad (r), 90

Green almond. *See* Pistachio

Green celery with coriander seed, pureed (r), 96

Green pepper. *See* Paprika

Gremolata (r), 88

Groundnut. *See* Peanut

Gumbo, seafood, ham, and okra (r), 91

H

Halibut, with parsley sauce (r), 91

Ham, seafood, and okra gumbo (r), 91

Hazel *(Corylus avellana),* 18–19, 38, 64–65

Helianthus annuus. See Sunflower

Hemphill, Rosemary, 10

Herb(s)
 baste (r), 81
 brandy (r), 84
 defined, 8–10
 dried, 73, 76
 fresh, 74–75
 vinegar (r), 81–82

Herb bennet *(Geum urbanum),* 18–19, 40, 64–65

Herb bouquet *(bouquet garni),* 73
 recipes, 74

Herb-of-grace. *See* Rue

Honey cinnamon cake, with walnuts (r), 99

Hop *(Humulus lupulus),* 18–19, 41, 64–65

Horseradish *(Armoracia rusticana),* 12, 18–19, 32, 64–65

Humulus lupulus. See Hop

Hungary, seasoners in, 114, 119

Hyssop *(Hyssopus officinalis),* 18–19, 42, 64–65

Hyssopus officinalis. See Hyssop

I

Ice, clove orange (r), 98

Illicium verum. See Star anise

India, seasoners in, 104–105

Indian cress. *See* Nasturtium

Indonesia, seasoners in, 105–107

Italian roast squab with juniper berries (r), 96

Italy, seasoners in, 114–116

J

Japan, seasoners in, 108–110

Juglans regia. See Walnut

Juniper *(Juniperus communis),* 20–21, 42, 64–65
 Italian roast squab with (r), 96

Juniperus communis. See Juniper

K

King's clover. *See* Melilot

Knotted marjoram. *See* Sweet marjoram

Korea, seasoners in, 110

L

Lamb
 basil sauce for (r), 87
 marinade (r), 83

Moroccan spice mixture for stew (r), 95
 roast Arab style (r), 95
 steaks with olive sauce (r), 94
 stew with marjoram (r), 93
 tartlets, Middle Eastern (r), 94

Laos, seasoners in, 106–107

Latin-American seasoners, 125–126

Laurel. *See* Bay

Laurus nobilis. See Bay

Lavandula spica. See Lavender

Lavender *(Lavandula spica),* 20–21, 43, 64–65

Leek *(Allium porrum),* 20–21, 29, 64–65
 grated potato cake stuffed with (r), 96
 see also Rocambole

Lemon balm. *See* Balm

Lemon herb butter (r), 80

Lemon thyme, cultivation, 64–65

Lemon verbena *(Lippia citriodora),* 20–21, 44, 64–65

Lepidium sativum. See Cress

Levisticum officinale. See Lovage

Lexicon, plant, 26–57

Licorice *(Glycyrrhiza glabra),* 20–21, 41, 64–65, 109

Lippa citriodora. See Lemon verbena

Liver
 brochettes, with bay leaves (r), 94
 chicken, on croutons (r), 95

Lovage *(Levisticum officinale),* 20–21, 44, 64–65

M

Mace
 culinary uses, 20–21
 sweet and sour cherries, with (r), 98
 see also Nutmeg

Madeira nut. *See* Asafetida

Maitre d'hotel butter (r), 81

Malabar cardamom. *See* Cardamom

Malaysia, seasoners in, 105–107

Marigold *(Calendula officinalis),* 20–21, 35, 64–65

Marinade, 82–83
 cooked (r), 83
 uncooked (r), 83

Marjoram. *See* Oregano, Sweet marjoram

Marmalade, sauteed apples with (r), 98

Mead, Edward, 122

Meat, 80–81
 recipes, 83, 86, 87, 91, 93–95

Mediterranean fish soup (r), 86

Melegueta pepper *(Amomum melegueta),* 20–21, 30, 64–65

Melilot *(Melilotus officinalis),* 20–21, 44, 64–65

Melilotus officinalis. See Melilot

Melissa officinalis. See Balm

Mentha piperita. See Peppermint

Mercury. *See* Good-King-Henry

Mexican fish soup (r), 86

Middle East, seasoners in, 111–113

Middle Eastern lamb tartlets (r), 94

Mirasol. *See* Sunflower

Mme Chu's star anise beef (r), 94

Monarda didyma. See Bergamot

Monkey nut. *See* Peanut

Moroccan bread (r), 99

Moroccan spice mixture, for chicken (r), 95

Mugwort *(Artemisia vulgaris),* 20–21, 33, 64–65

Mustard
 culinary uses, 20–21
 sauce (r), 80
 tarragon sauce, for eggs in brioche (r), 93
 see also Black mustard; White mustard

Myristica fragrans. See Nutmeg

Myrrhis odorata. See Sweet cicely

Myrtle *(Myrtus communis)* 20–21, 46, 66–67

Myrtus communis. See Myrtle

N

Nasturtium *(Tropaeolum majus),* 20–21, 56, 66–67

Nasturtium officinale. See Watercress

Near East, seasoners in, 111–113

North Africa, seasoners in, 111–113

Nutmeg *(Myristica fragrans),* 20–21, 45, 66–67, 102

Nut pine *(Pinus edulis),* 50

O

Ocimum basilicum. See Sweet basil

Okra, seafood and ham

gumbo with (r), 91

Olea europaea. See Olive

Olive *(Olea europaea),* 20–21, 47, 66–67
 and caper relish (r), 88
 sauce, for lamb steaks (r), 94
 sauce, for spaghetti (r), 89

Onion *(Allium cepa),* 20–21, 28, 66–67
 sweet, 12

Orange
 and grated carrot salad (r), 90
 ice, clove (r), 98

Oregano *(Origanum vulgare),* 9, 20–21, 47, 66–67

Oriental meatball soup, (r), 86

Origanum majorana. See Sweet marjoram

Origanum vulgare. See Oregano

Oswego tea. *See* Bergamot

P

Paella (r), 97

Papaver rhoeas. See Poppy

Paprika *(Capsicum annuum)* 20–21, 35, 66–67, 70–71, 119

Parsley *(Petroselinum crispum),* 22–23, 48, 66–67, *73,* 75
 sauce, for halibut or pollock (r), 91

Parsnip. *See* Angelica

Peanut *(Arachis hypogaea),* 22–23, 32, 66–67

Pelagonium capitatum. See Scented-leaf geranium

Pepper
 cookies, Andre Daguin's (r), 98
 see also Black pepper; Chili; Melegueta pepper; Paprika

Peppermint *(Mentha piperita),* 22–23, 45, 66–67

Pesto (fresh basil sauce (r), 88

Petroselinum crispum. See Parsley

Philippines, seasoners in, 105–107

Phytolacca americana. See Poke

Pigeon berry. *See* Poke

Pimenta officinalis. See Allspice

Pimpinella anisum. See Anise

Pimpinella saxifraga. See Burnet

Pine, cultivation, 66–67

Pine nut, culinary uses, 22–23

Pinus edulis. See Nut pine

Pinyon. *See* Nut pine

Piper cubeba. See Cubeb

Piper nigrum. See Black pepper
Pistachio *(Pistacia vera),* 22–23, 51, 66–67
Pistacia vera. See Pistachio
Poke *(Phytolacca americana),* 22–23, 49, 66–67
Poke weed. *See* Poke
Pollock, with parsley sauce (r), 91
Poppy *(Papaver rhoeas),* 22–23, 48, 66–67
Porret. See Leek
Portugal, seasoners in, 114, 116–117
Portulaca oleracea. See Purslane
Potato cake stuffed with leeks, grated (r), 96
Poterium sanguisorba. See Salad burnet
Pot herbs, 74
Pot marigold. *See* Marigold
Pot marjoram, cultivation of 66–67
Potted salmon (r), 92
Poultry, 80–81
   recipes, 95–96
Prunus amygdalus. See Almond
Purslane *(Portulaca oleracea),* 22–23, 51, 66–67
   salad (r), 90

R

Red poppy. *See* Poppy
Relish, olive and caper (r), 88
Rib steaks in the style of Rome (r), 94
Rice, 102
   and seasoners, 102, 103, 105, 106
Rocambole *(Allium scorodoprasum),* 22–23, 30, 66–67
Rocket *(Eruca vesicaria subsp. sativa),* 22–23, 39, 66–67
Rosemary *(Rosmarinus officinalis),* 22–23, 27, 52, 68–69, 75, 102
Rosmarinus officinalis. See Rosemary
Rue *(Ruta graveolens),* 22–23, 52, 68–69
Rugula. See Rocket
Rumex acetosa. See Sorrel
Rumex scutatus. See French sorrel
Russian fish soup (r), 87
Ruta graveolens. See Rue

S

Safflower (Carthamus tinctorius), 22–23, 36, 68–69

Saffron *(Crocus sativus),* 11, 38, 68–69
   see also Safflower
Sage *(Salvia officinalis),* 22–23, 53, 68–69
Salad, 83
   herbs, 74
   recipes, 89–90, 112
Salad burnet *(Poterium sanguisorba),* 22–23, 51, 68–69
Salmon, potted (r), 92
Salvia officinalis. See Sage
Sambucus nigra. See Elder
Sand leek. *See* Rocambole
Satureja hortensis. See Summer savory
Satureja montana. See Winter savory
Sauce, recipes, 78–80, 87–89, 91, 93, 94
Sauce bearnaise (r), 88
Sausage, seafood le plaisir (r), 91
Savory. *See* Summer savory; Winter savory
Saxifrage. *See* Burnet
Scallion *(Allium fistulosum),* 22–23, 28, 68–69
Scallops, in papillote with watercress and tomatoes (r), 92
Scandinavian seasoners, 120–121
Scented-leaf geranium *(Pelargonium capitatum),* 24–25, 48, 68–69
Scurvy grass *(Cochlearia officinalis),* 24–25, 37, 68–69
Seafood
   gumbo with ham and okra (r), 91
   paella (r), 97
   sausage le plaisir (r), 91
Sea Scallops in papillote with watercress and tomatoes (r), 92
Seasoned salt (r), 75
Seasoners, 72–84
   Africa, 127–128
   Anglo-Saxon, 122–125
   Continental Europe, 114–119
   Far East, 108–110
   India, 104–105
   Latin-America, 125–126
   Near East and Middle East, 111–113
   Scandinavia, 120–121
   Southeast Asia, 105–107
   and staples, 102–103
Sedum. *See* Stonecrop
Sedum reflexum. See Stonecrop
Seasame *(Sesamum indicum),* 24–25, 54, 68–69
   fried chicken with (r), 96
Sesamum indicum. See Sesame

Shallot *(Allium ascalonicum),* 24–25, 28, 68–69
   vinegar (r), 82
Sinapis alba. See White mustard
Skoke. *See* Poke
Slavic seasoners, 120–121
Sorrel *(Rumex acetosa),* 24–25, 52, 68–69
Soup, 78
   recipes, 86–87
Southeast Asia, seasoners in, 105–107
Soybean *(Glycine max),* 24–25, 40, 68–69, 108, 109
Spaghetti, with olive sauce (r), 89
Spain, seasoners in, 114, 116
Spearmint, cultivation of, 68–69
Spice, 73, 76–77
   brandy (r), 84
   defined, 10–11
   mixture for coffee (r), 89
   Moroccan mixture for chicken (r), 95
   vinegars (r), 81–82
Spoonwort. *See* Scurvy grass
Squab with juniper berries, Italian roast (r), 96
Staples and seasoners, 102–103
Star anise *(Illicium verum),* 24–25, 42, 68–69, 109
Star anise beef, Mme Chu's (r), 94
Stew
   gingered chicken with chick peas (r), 96
   lamb with marjoram (r), 93
   Moroccan spice mixture for (r), 95
Stonecrop *(Sedum reflexum),* 24–25, 54, 68–69
Summer savory *(Satureja hortensis),* 22–23, 53, 68–69
Sunflower *(Helianthus annuus),* 24–25, 41, 70–71
Sweet basil *(Ocimum basilicum),* 24–25, 46–47, 70–71
   see also Basil sauce
Sweet bay. *See* Bay.
Sweet chervil. *See* Chervil
Sweet cicely *(Myrrhis odorata),* 24–25, 46, 70–71
Sweet clover. *See* Melilot
Sweet ferm. *See* Sweet cicely
Sweet herbs, 74
Sweet marjoram *(Origanum majorana),* 24–25, 47, 70–71
Sweet pepper, *102*
   see also Paprika

Sweet violet. *See* Violet
Sweetwood. *See* Licorice
Szechwan pepper, 108, *109*

T

Tabasco pepper. *See* Chili
Talewort *See* Borage
Tamarind *(Tamarindus indica),* 24–25, 54, 70–71
Tamarindus indica. See Tamarind
Tanecetum vulgare. See Tansy
Tansy *(Tanacetum vulgare),* 24–25, 54, 70–71
Taraxacum officinale. See Dandelion
Tarragon *(Artemisia dracunculus),* 24–25, 32–33, 70–71
   mustard sauce, for eggs in brioche (r), 93
Tartar sauce (r), 79
Thailand, seasoners in, 105–106
Theobroma cacao. See Cacao
Thyme *(Thymus vulgaris),* 24–25, 55, 70–71, *73*
Thymus vulgaris. See Thyme
Tomatoes
   stuffed (r), 97
   sea scallops with (r), 92
   and sweet green pepper salad, cooked (r), 89
Trigonella foenum-graecum. See Fenugreek
Tropaeolum majus. See Nasturtium
Truffle *(Tuber melanosporum),* 24–25, 56, 70–71
Tuber melanosporum. See Truffle
Tunisian mixed salad (r), 90
Turmeric *(Curcuma longa),* 24–25, 39, 70–71, 104–105, 107

U

United States, seasoners in 122, 123–125

V

Vanilla *(Vanilla planifolia),* 24–25, 57, 70–71
Vanilla planifolia. See Vanilla
Venison marinade (r), 83
Verbena. *See* Lemon verbena
Vietnam, seasoners in, 105–106
Vietnamese sour soup (r), 87
Vinegar, herb and spice (r), 81–82
Viola odorata. See Violet

Violet *(Viola odorata),* 24–25, 57, 70–71

W

Walnut *(Juglans regia),* 24–25, 42, 70–71
   honey cinnamon cake with (r), 99
Watercress *(Nasturtium officinale),* 24–25, 46, 70–71
   sea scallops in papillote with tomatoes and (r), 92
   see also Cress
Welsh onion. *See* Scallion
Wheat, 102
   and seasoners, 102, 103
White butter sauce, classic (r), 88
White mustard *(Sinapis alba),* 34, 64–65
Wild marjoram. *See* Oregano
Wild parsnip. *See* Angelica
Wild spinach. *See* Good-King-Henry
Willan, Ann, 102
Winter cress *(Barbarea vulgaris),* 24–25, 33, 70–71
   see also Cress
Winter rocket. *See* Winter cress
Winter savory *(Satureja montana),* 22–23, 53, 68–69
Wood avens. *See* Herb bennet

Z

Zedoary *(Curcuma zedoaria),* 39, 70–71
   see also Turmeric
Zingiber officinalis. See Ginger
Zucchini and caraway salad (r), 90